HUMAN RIGHTS
Acts, Statutes and Constitutional Provisions

HUMAN RIGHTS

Acts, Statutes and Constitutional Provisions

(Volume I)

D.N. Gupta
Chandrachur Singh

KALPAZ PUBLICATIONS
Delhi–110 052

HUMAN RIGHTS
Acts, Statutes and Constitutional Provisions
(Human Rights, Law)

Rs. 1800 (Set)

ISBN: 81-7835-098-X (Set)
ISBN: 81-7835-156-0 (Vol. I)

Published in 2003 in India by
Kalpaz Publications
C-30, Satyawati Nagar
Delhi–110 052

e-mail: kalpaz@hotmail.com

Lasertypesetting at: Varsha Graphics, Delhi
Printed at: Mehra Offset Printers, Delhi

Contents

Foreword 7

Preface 9

Acknowledgements 15

Introduction 17

1. United Nations and Human Rights 31

Charter of United Nations, 1945 31

Universal Declaration of Human Rights, 1948 62

Declaration by the Government of India, 1979 69

International Covenant on Civil and Political Rights, 1966 71

International Covenant on Economic, Social and Cultural Rights, 1966 92

2. Indian Constitution and Human Rights 105

Indian National Congress—Karachi Resolution, 1931 105

Constitution of India—Preamble 107

Fundamental Rights, 1950 108

Directive Principles of State Policy, 1950 120

3. The Protection of Human Rights Act, 1993 145

Constitution of National Human Rights Commission, 1993 145

National Human Rights Commission (Procedure) Regulations, 1994 156

Basic Standards Recommended by Amnesty International Relating to National Human Rights Commission, 1994 161

Formation of State Human Rights Commission, 1993 166

Protection of Civil Rights Act, 1955 175

The Protection of Civil Rights Rules, 1977 187

4.	**Scheduled Castes, Scheduled Tribes, Backward Classes, *Safai Karamcharis*, Minorities and Human Rights**	**189**
	The Scheduled Castes and The Scheduled Tribes (Prevention of Atrocities) Act, 1989	189
	The Scheduled Castes and The Scheduled Tribes (Prevention of Atrocities) Rule, 1995	200
	The National Commission for Backward Classes Act, 1993	230
	The National Commission for *Safai Karamcharis* Act, 1993	237
	The National Commission for Minorities Act, 1992	244
	Christian Marriage and Matrimonial Causes Bill, 1994	250
	Christian Adoption and Maintenance Bill, 1994	252
	Indian Succession Amendment Bill, 1994	253
5.	**Women, Children and Human Rights**	**255**
	The Dowry Prohibition Act, 1961	255
	The Commission of Sati (Prevention) Act, 1987	273
	The National Commission for Women Act, 1990	284
	The Child Labour (Prohibition and Regulation) Act, 1986	292
	The Child Labour (Prohibition and Regulation) Rules, 1988	308
	The Pre-natal Diagnostic Techniques (Regulation and Prevention of Misuse) Act, 1994	314

Foreword

The Second World War (1939 – 1945) shook up mankind all over the globe. It turned the whole world into a battle field. The new concept of total war was a real menace. Millions of people were killed and crippled. Generations of *homo sapiens,* yet to be born were seriously affected by the atom bomb.

Right-thinking leaders started working on total elimination of war and ensuring a war-free world. Lasting peace for mankind was the dream.

The United Nations replaced the League. A new instrumentality – the Security Council was vested with the duty of maintaining peace. The U.N. Charter in its preamble emphasised upon the need of greater understanding among the people and the rights of the people to be recognized. It provided that a commission be set-up to enlist the rights of everyone and the same should be implemented. The General Assembly of the United Nations adopted the report of the Commission and on the 10th December, 1948, the Universal Declaration was made. In the preamble, the Declaration recognized the inherent dignity and the equal and inalienable rights of all members of the human family and declared that disregard and contempt for human which have resulted in barbarous acts and outraged the conscience of mankind must end.

The Universal Declaration has set out the inalienable human rights and has called upon mankind to be aware of them, to recognize and respect them and ensure their acceptance and performance by generation of a strong culture of human rights.

The United Nations in its fifty four years of operation has highlighted the concept of one human family, recognition of the rights specified in the Declaration and has looked for the generation of a strong human rights culture which alone would ensure a pro-uniform human-rights conduct in the *homo sapiens* society.

These fifty-four years have been a crucial period in the life and history of human rights. The literature created during this period through teaching and reading would provide the base on which the edifice of human rights would be strengthened.

I am happy that this compilation seeks to make the literature available to the reader in two exquisite volumes. I welcome this attempt and congratulate the authors.

Ranganath Misra

14 August, 2002

Formerly Chief Justice of India

Preface

Keeping in view the relevance and importance of human rights in our everyday life, this two-volume compilation of documents on human rights is being published. Ever since the formation of the United Nations (1945) the concept of civil liberties and human rights has been both institutionalized and universalized. However, the situation is quite paradoxical. It is a fact that with the increasing expansion of the scope of human rights and its relevance to the living process, their violation also continues unabated. As Justice Ranganath Misra, former Chief Justice of India and the first Chairman of the National Human Rights Commission, once remarked :

> As of now, violation of human rights is widely rampant. Violation of human rights is in the homes, the streets, the public offices [and] educational institutions.

How can such a paradox be resolved? Spread of awareness about, and promotion and protection of human rights, respect for each other's rights and fulfillment of our obligations/duties towards the society and fellow beings, are the only possible solutions. As Justice Misra has suggested :

> Promotion and protection of human rights are the only way by which the society can be saved in an effective way. We are degenerating and degenerating very fast, and unless there is first stoppage of the degenerating process and then an attempt for elevation, thereafter, we might lose our status of being *homo sapiens* and a group above animal life.

Unless we are adequately armed with the knowledge of our rights and the existing remedies available against their violations, it is not really possible to move in the direction suggested by Justice Mr. Misra. As such the basic purpose of the present work is to acquaint scholars working on various aspects of human rights, human rights activists and Non-Government Organizations (NGOs) engaged in the task of spreading awareness about human rights and particularly the citizens who are directly affected by the violations of their rights, with the Statutory and Constitutional provisions enacted to guarantee such rights. Moreover, inadequacies of the present machinery that exists for the protection and promotion of human rights can be removed only with its proper knowledge and understanding. Therefore, it is hoped that this two-volume collection of documents on human rights will be useful to all those who are either concerned with or affected by their violations.

The present study has been divided into two volumes, each containing five chapters. In every chapter, documents concerning a specific human rights issue have been presented.

As the United Nations Charter (1945) and the Universal Declaration of Human Rights (1948) introduced the concept of human rights at global level, these two world famous documents form the opening of Chapter One. India was not only a signatory to the Charter but also accepted the Universal Declaration of Human Rights in 1948. And consonant with the acceptance of these United Nations Declarations, India also gave her consent to the two International Covenants that had been adopted by the General Assembly of the United Nations in its resolution 2200 (XXI) of 16 December, 1966 and came into force in 1976. The basic purpose of these Covenants was to supplement the Charter and the Universal Declaration of Human Rights. However, it is noteworthy that India accepted these Covenants with certain reservations which have been spelt out in the Government of India's Declaration of 1979. India's Declaration and the two International Covenants are also included in Chapter One.

As this compilation is mainly concerned with human rights in India, the rest of the nine chapters are devoted to various aspects of human rights in India.

Much before the United Nations Charter and the Declaration laid the foundations of human rights globally, the Karachi Resolution of the Indian National Congress on Fundamental Rights and on Economic Equality (1931) had popularized the concept of civil liberties and human rights in India. In fact, the Karachi Resolution formed the basis of the Fundamental Rights and the Directive Principles of State Policy which were enshrined in the Indian Constitution (1950). The Karachi Resolution, the Fundamental Rights and the Directive Principles of State Policy are the subject matter of Chapter Two. It may be noted that the difference between the Fundamental Rights and the Directive Principles is due to the fact that whereas the State could straightway guarantee political and civil liberties, it could only strive to secure economic and social justice. Therefore, Fundamental Rights are judicially enforceable, but the Directive Principles are not justiciable. Nevertheless, the Apex Court of the Country has, from time to time, asserted that none of the two is subordinate to the other and also that while making laws, the two should be read together rather than in competition to each other.

The Ordinance of 1993 that created the National Human Rights Commission and provided for the formation of Human Rights Commissions in States was another milestone in the development of human rights in India. For many years, it was felt that India did not require such an organization because of the presence of Fundamental Rights in the Indian Constitution and the elaborate judicial system that stood guarantee for the protection and promotion of civil liberties and human rights. But with the passage of time, it became impossible for the Government of India to resist the increasing internal and external pressures for the formation of the National Human Rights Commission.

National Human Rights Commission, despite its many limitations, has emerged as a prominent institution for safeguarding the rights of Indian citizens. It not only looks into human rights violations but also recommends action against such violations to the appropriate authorities. It is an autonomous body under the Chairmanship of a former Chief Justice of India. It submits its annual report to the Indian Parliament.

As far as the formation of Human Rights Commissions in States is concerned, the record has not been that encouraging. Even after the passage of the Act (1993), only twelve states have formed such Commissions. These include Assam, Chhattisgarh, Himachal Pradesh, Jammu and Kashmir, Kerala, Madhya Pradesh, Manipur, Maharashtra, Punjab, Rajasthan, Tamil Nadu and West Bengal.

In Chapter Three the Ordinance and the subsequent Act (1993) for the formation of Human Rights Commission in India and such Commissions in Indian States have been included. Since the Ordinance is quite comprehensive, it does not require any elaboration.

The next two Chapters, i.e., Four and Five deal with the human rights of the weaker sections of India. Undoubtedly, Scheduled

Castes, Scheduled Tribes, Other Backward Classes (OBCs), *Safai Karamcharis,* Women and Children are certainly important segments of the weaker sections of India. These, in themselves, make over 70% of the Indian population. If their rights are not adequately safeguarded, the concept of human rights will have no meaning in the Indian context.

The specific constitutional provisions to safeguard the interests of the Scheduled Castes relate to the abolition of untouchability and the prohibition on its practice in any form (Article 17); prohibition of *begar* or forced labour (Article 23); consideration of the claims of the Scheduled Castes and Scheduled Tribes in appointments to services and posts in connection with the affairs of the Union or a state (Article 335); and reservations of seats in proportion to their numbers in the Lok Sabha (Article 330) and in the Vidhan Sabha (Article 332). Over a period of time, however, it was discovered that mere constitutional provisions will not improve the lot of these important segments of Indian society. Therefore, since independence and the promulgation of the Indian Constitution in 1950, successive governments have taken several steps to uplift the weaker sections. The Untouchability Act, 1955, Protection of Civil Rights Act, 1976, Bonded Labour System (Abolition) Act, 1976 and the Child Labour Prohibition and Regulation Act,1976, have been some of the steps taken to improve the position of the SCs/STs. Institutional structures for the upliftment of the SCs/STs, OBCs, *Safai Karamcharis* and Minorities in the form of the National Commissions for SCs/STs, OBCs, *Safai Karamcharis* and Minorities have been created. These Commissions are included in Chapter Four.

Indian society, like any other society, is also divided on the basis of gender. While sexual differences are biologically determined, gender differences are culturally constructed. It is a paradox that while Indian Women enjoyed an equal status with man during the early Vedic period, in contemporary India, they are discriminated against. They do not get the same access to healthcare, education and economic opportunities as men do. Violence against women in the form of rape, molestation, eve-teasing, sati and dowry deaths is quite common. Even though the Indian Constitution guarantees equal rights to women, the Indian Parliament has taken many further steps to enhance the status of women in India by enacting a number of laws including that which has constituted the National

Commission for Women. These Acts and Regulations are detailed in Chapter Five.

One of the most pressing social problems confronting Indian society is that of the working child. In Indian context, child labour is aptly described as 'children without childhood'. Children are employed both in formal and informal sectors of our economy. According to the 1991 census, child labour formed 1.34 per cent of the total population and 3.59 per cent of the total workforce. In spite of many provisions in the Indian Constitution regarding the upliftment of Indian Children (Articles 24, 39 (e), 39 (f) and 45), the Government of India announced the National Child Labour Policy only in 1987. In Chapter Five steps that the Government of India has taken to improve the lot of this 'tongueless' and 'speechless' segment of society have been included.

D.N. Gupta
Chandrachur Singh

Acknowledgements

We are indeed indebted to Justice Mr. Ranganath Misra, former Chief Justice of India and the first Chairman of National Human Rights Commission of India. Justice Misra not only initiated us into the human rights movement in India, but has also given us his paternal love and affection which has sustained us in the movement. He has been kind enough to have written the foreword to the present work. Words are inadequate to express our gratitude to honourable *Judge Saheb.*

We would never have ventured into the exciting arena of human rights but for the constant encouragement and support we have received from Prof. Bipan Chandra. Prof. Chandra has always been a source of inspiration to us. He has been gracious enough to give us permission to make liberal use of his writings on India's struggle for independence.

We are grateful to Shri P.C. Verma, former Principal, Hindu College, Delhi University, for supporting us through thick and thin.

We have benefitted immeasurably from the valuable discussions with Prof. Suhash Chakravarty which have sharpened our understanding of a complex, yet dynamic subject. We are indeed thankful to him.

We are grateful to Prof. Subrata Mukherjee for his continual help and encouragement. We also appreciate Shri Ratan Lal's co-operation and help.

We also acknowledge our sincere thanks to Mr. Rakesh Kumar Sharma and Ms. Rajesh Sharma for typesetting.

Uday, Shivani, Hena and Suchitra Gupta have given us their love and support. However, we do not think it necessary to thank them.

Last, but not the least, we express our gratitude to the editorial and production team of Kalpaz Publications, specially Shri Amit and Shalini Garg for associating us with this work and for doing a splendid and painstaking job in bringing out these volumes.

Delhi

D.N. Gupta
Chandrachur Singh

Introduction

The issue of human rights is of immense importance, as they are the corner-stone of civilisation, the alpha and omega of humanity's mission for a better life. The struggle for human rights is a part of the quest for collective happiness. It is believed that a civil society is only actualised by the fulfillment of rights. Modern society's prosperity and state are interlinked. But the state has the tendency of monopolizing power, thereby increasing the possibilities of coercion obstructing freedom of the individual.

Modern endeavour for human rights is an attempt to reconcile the opposite pulls of power of the state and the urge for social freedom which would result in human progress and prosperity. Even though the concept of human rights has got a new thrust in the contemporary times, its roots can be traced back to 1215 when the Magna Carta curtailed the power of the King John of England. After the King violated a number of ancient laws and customs, his subjects forced him to sign the Magna Carta, or Great Charter, which enumerates what later come to be known as human rights. Among them were the rights of church to be free from governmental interference, the right of all free citizens to own and inherit property and to be free from excessive tax. It established the right of widows who owned property to choose not to remarry and established principles of due process and equality before the law. It also contained provisions forbidding bribery and official misconduct.

I

The political and religious traditions in other parts of the world also proclaimed what have come to be called human rights, by calling on rulers to rule justly and compassionately and delineating limits on their power over the lives, property and activities of their citizens. The Hindu concept of Dharma explicitly maintains that all expressions are inter-related and bound in a visible unity; that no violence shall be done to a person by another except with the due process of law, which at all times must be free from anger and hatred; and that the political and legal governance of human relationship shall have as their chief aim enhancement of the individual and the progress of the people. It is from these that the principles of law and government must be derived, and it is in them that they shall have their ultimate validation.

In the eighteenth and the nineteenth centuries several philosophers in Europe proposed the concept of 'natural rights', i.e. belonging to a person by nature and because he/she was a human being, not by virtue of his/her citizenship in a particular country or membership in a particular religious or ethnic group. Though this conception was rejected by some philosophers such as Bentham, still it found its advocates in Thomas Paine and J.S. Mill. The late eighteenth century revolutions namely American War of Independence and the French Revolution drew heavily on this concept. In 1776 most of British colonies in North America proclaimed their independence from the British Empire in a document which still stirs feelings and debate. The World famous American Declaration of Independence maintained:

> We hold these truths to be self evident: That all men are created equal; that they are endowed by their Creator with certain unalienable rights; that among these are life, Liberty and the pursuit of happiness . . .;

In 1789 the people of France overthrew their monarchy and established the First French Republic. Out of the revolution came to the Declaration of Rights of Man.

Although the term natural right eventually fell into disfavour, the concept of universal rights took root. Philosophers such as Thomas Paine, John Stuart Mill and Henry David Thoreau expanded the concept. It is said that Thoreau was the first philosopher to use the word "Human Right" in his treatise, 'Civil Disobedience'. The work which was to influence people such as Leo Tolstoy, Mahatma Gandhi and Martin Luther King; Gandhi and King in particular, developed their ideas on non-violent resistance to unethical governmental actions.

II

The middle and the late 19th century saw a number of issues take centre stage, which later in 20th century are issues of human rights. They included i.e. slavery, serfdom, brutal working conditions, starvation, wages, child labour etc. In the United States a bloody war over slavery came close to destroying a country founded on the conception of equality. For the last part of 19th century and first decades of 20th century, human rights activism remained largely tied to political and religious groups and beliefs. Revolutionaries pointed to the atrocities of governments as proof of their ideology, which stressed violent action. The state on the other hand also resorted to violence and stern approach towards dissent. However, even then many specific civil rights and human rights movements managed to condition social change. Labour unions brought about laws granting workers the right to strike, establishing minimum working conditions, forbidding or regulating child labour, establishing forty hours a week working hours in USA. The women's rights movement succeeded in gaining for many women the right to vote. National liberation movements in many countries succeeded in driving out colonial powers. One of the most influential mass action was the Indian National Movement which, under the stewardship of Mahatma Gandhi, based itself on human dignity. As a matter of fact, the Indian Constitution which guarantees fundamental freedom and stresses on human dignity, draws inspiration from it.

III

However, the year 1914-18 saw immense brutalities. War crimes, violence and deaths devastated the World and human essence was lost. Immediately after the war, attempts were made to restore peace and establish universal principles acceptable to all, so that humanity could be saved.

The League of Nations (1918) was entrusted with the responsibility to administer certain provisions of the First World War; while peace treaties protected the rights of racial, religious and linguistic refugees and minorities. Thus, the League of Nations institutionalised two principles of humanism. Beyond this, the League had little involvement with human rights, and its Covenant did not mention them. The desire for peace was short-lived, and then came the Second World War—the most horrifying so far in human memory. A greater need for peace and human dignity was felt and this led to a search for an effective international alternative to guarantee peace and security. Protracted deliberations and mutual negotiations led to the inception of United Nations Organisation in 1945. The objectives of the United Nations Organisation clearly point out that it was an effort towards guaranteeing human rights. There were four major objectives:

1. To save the succeeding generations from the scourge of war.
2. To reaffirm faith in fundamental human rights, in the work and dignity of human persons and equal rights of men, women and nations large and small.
3. To establish conditions under which justice and respect for the obligations arising from treaties and other sources of international law can be maintained.
4. To promote social progress and better standards of life in larger freedom.

These objectives envisaged a better and peaceful life to the people of the world through living together in peace, tolerance and harmony with one another. The UN Charter thereby provided the foundation for a global approach to human rights.

IV

The UN lost no time in dealing with Human Rights. The third General Assembly (1948) adopted a Universal Declaration of Human Rights submitted by the UN Commission on human rights chaired by Eleanor Roosevelt. Several articles cover a wide range of basic human rights and fundamental freedoms. Article 29 imposes duties and restrictions upon those enjoying rights and freedoms. This was a proper recognition that individual duty and responsibilities go hand in hand with personal rights and privileges. The declaration runs:

> . . . a common standard of achievement for all peoples and all nations, to the end that every individual and every organ of society, keeping this declaration constantly in mind, shall strive by teaching and education to promote respect for these rights and freedoms and by progressive measures, national and International to secure their universal and effective recognition and observance, both among the peoples of member states themselves and among the peoples of territories under their jurisdiction.

Each year, the 10th December, is observed internationally

as Human Rights Day. The Universal Declaration included civil, economic, social and cultural freedom, justice and equality. It is a quest for a larger and broader base for social values. It is yet only a beginning because there is a great hiatus between word and deed. The march of human rights, however continued. In 1966 two Covenants were adopted to add meaning and volume to 1948 Declaration of Universal Human Rights. These came into force in 1976. The UN has been continuing its other efforts.

United Nations Treaties Concerning Human Rights

Treaties	*Year of Force*
Convention on prevention and punishment of the crime of Genocide	1951
Convention for the suppression of Traffic in persons and of the Exploitation of the prostitution of others	1951
Protocol Amending slavery convention	1953
Convention relating to status of Refugees	1954
Convention on Political Rights of Women	1954
Slavery convention of 25 September 1926 as Amended	1955
Supplementary convention on the abolition of slavery, the slave Trade, Institution and Practice, similar to slavery	1957
Convention on Nationality of married women	1958
Convention relating to status of stateless persons	1960
Convention on International Right of correction	1962
Convention on consent of marriage, minimum age for marriage, and Registration of marriage	1964
Convention on elimination of all forms of racial discrimination	1969
Convention on non-applicability of statutory limitation to War crimes and crimes against Humanity	1970
Convention on Reduction of statelessness	1975
International covenant on Economic, Social and Cultural rights	1976
International covenant on civil and political rights	1976
Optional protocol on complaints from individuals	1976

V

As the UN Charter (1945) and its Universal Declaration of Human Rights 1948 both universalised and institutionalised the concept of Human Rights, it has been argued that the sections of the Indian Constitution on Fundamental Rights and the Directive Principles of State Policy emulated the United Nations Declaration of Human Rights. Apart from the fact that the drafting of the Indian Constitution 1947-1948 coincided with the UN Declaration (1948), the remarkable similarities between the two documents have also been cited in favour of this theory. Also the fact that colonial India was an original signatory to the Charter and Independent India adopted the UN declaration in 1948, itself. However, the theory that the two Chapters on Fundamental Rights and the Directive Principles of State Policy in the Indian Constitution reflected the pitch of the UN Declaration seems to be an over-simplified view because of the fact that it was the anti-imperialist movement of Indian people that made it possible for them to recover their lost rights and dignity. The Indian liberation movement, apart from attaining political Independence, stood for the establishment of a democratic and liberal society that encompassed the essence of civil liberty. Therefore, in order to appreciate the adoption of the UN Declaration by India and the provisions for Fundamental Rights and Directive Principles of State Policy in the Indian Constitution, one has to comprehend and assess the nature, policy and programme and achievements of India's struggle for independence.

VI

It was due to the establishment and consolidation of the British imperialist rule during the period from 1757 to 1857 that the Indian people lost most of their human rights and dignity. The assault of the alien rulers on the basic human rights and dignity, though began with the establishment and consolidation of its strangle hold over India, it was only with the emergence of anti-imperialist sentiments and movement that it became increasingly threatening. For example, in order to counter the rising political consciousness in India, section 124A was incorporated in the Indian Penal Code 1870. According to section 124A 'Whomsoever attempts to excite feelings of dissatisfaction, to the Government established by law in British

India,' was to be punished by transportation for life or for any term or with imprisonment upto three years. The Vernacular Act (1878) provided for the confiscation of the printing press, paper and other materials of a newspaper if the Government believed that it was publishing 'seditious' materials and had flouted an official warning.

It was this kind of an authoritarian, undemocratic, and arbitrary regime that the Indian people were confronted with. Committed as they were to the rights and civil liberties of our people, politically conscious Indians led the struggle for the establishment of a rational social order based on civil liberties, human rights and dignity. This national struggle was a part of the political struggle against the subjugation of India and for the attainment of independence. Therefore, it was a long drawn out battle. Instead of implementing liberal ideas, the colonial rulers took the position that democracy was not suited to India. Hot and humid climate of India, the historical traditions of the Indian people, the nature of their religious and social structure, particularly the caste system and authoritarian and tyrannical nature of their pre-British political system were some of the arguments that were advanced against the introduction of democratic institutions in India. If this was the nature of colonial mindset, how could they think of introducing freedoms of speech, association and the press?

The struggle for the establishment of civil liberties and human rights and dignity began with the struggle for the freedom of the press. In the absence of mass meetings and other means of reaching the people like a powerful political party, the leaders of our liberation movement realised that the press could play an instrumental role in arousing, training and mobilizing nationalist public opinion in India. That was the reason why a large number of newspapers like the *Hindu, Swadeshmitran, Kesari, Maratha, Bengalee, Amrit Bazar Patrika, Sudharak, Indian Mirror, Voice of India* and *Hindustani* were started by the nationalist leaders—G. Subramaniya Iyer, B.G. Tilak, Surendranath Banerjee, Sisir Kumar and Motilal Ghosh, G.K. Gokhale, N.N. Sen, Dadabhai Naoroji and G.P. Verma. *Tribune* and *Akhbar-I-Aam* in Punjab, *Indu Prakash, Dhyan Prakash, Kal* and *The Gujrati* in Western India, *Som Prakash, Banganivasi* and *Sadharni* in Bengal also played significant role of opposition to the Government. The important role that the Vernacular Press played in opposing the authoritarianism of the colonial regime can be gauged from Lord Dufferin's following observation:

> Day after day, hundreds of sharp-witted Babus pour forth their indignation against their oppressors in a very pungent and effective diatribe. In this way there can be no doubt there is generated in the minds of those who read these papers a sincere conviction that we are all of us the enemies of mankind in general and of India in particular.

VII

Even though Raja Ram Mohan Roy started the struggle for the freedom of the press and Surendranath Banerjee was the first national leader who was sent to jail in 1883, for performing his duty as a journalist, it was Tilak who really launched the movement for a free press. A great champion of civil liberties and human dignity, Tilak often remarked that 'liberty of the press and liberty of speech (and association) gave birth to a nation and nourish it'. When in 1897 Lokmanya was arrested under Section 124 A of the Indian Penal Code on the charge of spreading dissatisfaction and hatred against the Government and sent to rigorous imprisonment for eighteen months and some of his friends tried to pressurise him to apologize, Tilak's reply was:

> My position (as a leader) amongst the people entirely depends on my character . . . Their (Governments') object is to humiliate the Poona leaders, and I think in me they will not find kutcha (weak) reed . . . Then you must remember that beyond a certain stage we are all servants of the people. You will be betraying and disappointing them if you show a lamentable want of courage at a critical time.

With the emergence of the Swadeshi and Boycott Movement in Bengal in 1905, there started a new wave of official repression in India. Hundreds of political workers were imprisoned for making so called seditious speeches, many newspapers were either closed down or their editors imprisoned and Tilak was again arrested in 1908 and sent to prison for six years. Just a few days before his arrest, a friendly police officer warned him of the impending arrest and suggested him to take precautionary steps, Tilak's reply to the friendly advice was:

> The Government has converted the entire nation into a prison and we are all prisoners. Going to prison only means that from a big cell one is confined to a smaller one.

And when there were demonstrations, closures of markets, strikes of textile mills workers and railway workshops and resistance to the police and the army broke the strike leaving sixteen workers dead, it simply meant that it was a protest against the Government attack on the civil liberties and human dignity.

VIII

Therefore, it is not at all surprising that the first all India mass movement was organised on the issue of civil liberties in 1918-1919. In January 1919 the Government of India presented two bills to the Imperial Legislative Council. These Bills are known as Rowlatt Bills. The second of the two Bills was designed to invest the Government of India with the discretionary power to keep a person in prison without trial in a court of law. But despite the unanimous opposition of the Indian members of the Council, the new legislation was rushed through the legislature with indecent haste. Having failed in the Council to stop the passage of the Bills, the nationalist leaders particularly Gandhi took up the challenge and organised the first all India Rowlatt Satyagraha because the Rowlatt Bills, as Professor Ravindra Kumar has opined, reflected a deep rooted distrust of the common man. These acts demonstrated the British Governments' reluctance to part with its arbitrary powers, and, invalidated the impact of the reforms (Montagu-Chelmsford Act 1919) which were meant to hold out the prospect of self-determination to the peoples of India.

IX

It is an axiomatic truth that Gandhiji made most outstanding contribution to the establishment of rights, dignity and self-respect of the Indian people. From the days of his struggle in South Africa where he fought against the denial of basic human rights and racial discrimination for nearly twenty years, till the end of his life, he waged a struggle against all sorts of existing social inequalities and denial of civil liberties. That was the reason why he was pained at General Dyer's action at Jallianwala Bagh leaving 379 innocent and peaceful marchers dead, but more so at the proceedings in the House of Lords that ultimately exonerated General Dyer and endorsed his inhuman action.

Gandhiji was of the firm view that the two basic human rights, i.e., rights of free speech and association, must be available to the Indians. One could not talk about other rights if these were not available to the people. Emphasizing the significance of these rights in human life, he wrote in January 1922:

> We must first make good the rights of free speech and free association before we can make any further progress towards our goal. We must defend these elementary rights with our lives. Liberty of speech means that it is unassailed even when the speech hurts, liberty of the Press can be said to be truly respected when the Press can comment in the severest terms upon and even misrepresent matters. Freedom of association is truly respected when assemblies of people can discuss even revolutionary projects.

Irrespective of their political and ideological differences, nationalist leaders of different orientations defended each others' civil liberties and human dignity. For example, Shaheed Bhagat Singh and his comrades being tried in Lahore Conspiracy case and the Communists and others in the Meerut conspiracy case, were defended by Motilal Nehru, M.C. Chagla and C.B. Gupta, who, otherwise did not endorse their political line. Similarly, the Public Safety Bill and the Trade Disputes Bill, aimed at suppressing the industrial workers, the left wing and the communists were opposed not only by Motilal Nehru but also by Madan Mohan Malaviya and M.R. Jayakar.

X

Alongwith Gandhiji, Nehru was a great adherent and champion of civil liberties and human rights. His assertion that: "If Civil Liberties are suppressed, a nation loses all its vitality and becomes impotent for anything substantial', was the basis of his position on human rights and dignity. That was the reason why he took initiative in forming the Indian Civil Liberties Union. In 1936, Nehru wrote a letter to 160 prominent intellectuals of the country explaining the need for an all-India organisation for the protection of civil liberties and human rights of the Indian people. His efforts led to the formation of the Indian Civil Liberties Union in August 1936 at Bombay with Rabindranath Tagore as the President, Sarojini Naidu as the Chairperson and Head of its National Council and K.B. Menon as General Secretary.

The Civil Liberties Union was formed on non party, non sectarian lines to collect and publish data and to mobilise public opinion against all enroachment on civil liberties. The Civil Liberties Union investigated cases of political imprisonment and harassment, police brutalities, bans and restrictions on citizens' rights imposed not only by the British but also by the rulers of the princely states and published and lodged complaints on the basis of its investigations.

Nehru was also of the opinion that press could play an instrumental role in popularising the concepts of civil liberties and human rights. Therefore, commenting on the desirability of the freedom of the press, he observed in 1940;

> The freedom of the press does not consist in our permitting such things as we like to appear. Even a tyrant is agreeable to this type of freedom. Civil liberties and freedom of the press consist in our permitting what we do not like, in our putting up with criticism of ourselves.

Even though struggle for civil liberties and human rights was made a part of India's liberation struggle, Nehru attached importance as an end in itself. For example, Nehru took up the case of Rani Gaidinliu, the young Naga girl, sponsored in the Indian Liberties Union and also placed it before the British Civil Liberties Union in London. Professor S. Gopal has described Nehru's position on civil liberties as follows:

> The struggle for civil liberties is obviously part and parcel of any national movement but Nehru attached importance to it even in itself and was insistent that civil liberties to the utmost extent possible should be promoted even in such a blatantly colonial society as India was

before 1947. Take for example, the case of Rani Gaidinliu, the young Naga girl who later became the leader of the Nagas. In the early thirties, she was arrested and placed in prison for many years without trial on a charge which was only remotely connected with politics. But Nehru took it up when he heard about it, sponsored a case in the Indian Civil Liberties Union, also placed it before the British Civil Liberties Uniôn in London, wrote to people to whom he normally would not have bothered to write to, like Lady Astor and Eleanor Rathbone. He also wrote to the British Press so that finally everybody was so stirred up in England that the British Government had to take action, hold a trial and release her. The case of Rani Gaidinliu has been a cause celebre and has integrated the Nagas with the rest of India.

XI

As Nehru was committed to the cause of civil liberties and human rights and dignity of the Indian people, he had sponsored the Karachi Resolution on fundamental rights in 1931. The Karachi Resolution (1931) on the Fundamental Rights, was the climax of the commitment of the nationalist leaders to the basic human rights of our countrymen. The Karachi Resolution is a landmark in the history of Indian liberation movement not only because it included important fundamental rights but also because of the safeguards it guaranteed to the rights of the minorities. While fighting against the mightiest of imperialisms for political independence, restoration of human rights and dignity and for the establishment of a new value system, the nationalist leaders were confronted with a serious issue, the problem of minorities rights. Their rights had to be protected—a cause that was inherent in the pluralistic nature of the Indian society. That was the reason why the rights of the minorities were protected in the Karachi Resolution. Emphasis on free profession and practice of religion, subject to public order and morality, protection of the culture, language and scripts of the minorities and religious neutrality on the part of the state, were some of the guarantees for the minority rights.

XII

From the beginning, the nationalist leaders were also conscious of the multi-lingual, multi-caste, multi-community and multi-religious nature of the Indian society alongwith the existence of many ethnic groups. The unity in diversity or diversity in unity could not be ignored if a joint all-India front had to be organised against British imperialism. Taking a serious note of these complexities, as early as 1888, the Indian National Congress passed the following resolution:

> That no subject shall be passed for discussion by the subject committee, or allowed to be discussed at any Congress by the president thereof, to the introduction of which the Hindu or Mohammadan Delegates as a body object unanimously or nearly unanimously.

The Lucknow Pact (1916) that put up the Congress-League Joint Charter of Demands was again a nationalist policy to protect the minority rights. The Lucknow Pact was certainly motivated by a sincere desire to allay minority fears about majority domination. And when the Pact was criticised in certain quarters on the ground that too much had been conceded to the Muslims by accepting separate Electorates, Tilak defended the Pact and said:

> When we have to fight against a third party—it is very important that we stand on this platform United, United in race, United in religion, United as regards all different shades of political creed.

Thus, as Professor Bipan Chandra pointed out:

> It was the national movement and not the bureaucratic, authoritarian colonial state that indigenised, popularised and rooted parliamentary democracy and civil liberties in India. The grass-roots level nationalist workers carried the national movement to the remotest of villages. In the speeches that they made, simultaneously with the idea of nationalism, they talked about democracy and civil liberties.

Over the years, the nationalist movement successfully created an alternative political culture based on respect for dissent, freedom of expression, the majority principle and the right of minority opinions to exist and grow.

XII

In short, by the time India attained independence in 1947, the Indian peoples' anti-imperialist struggle had already laid the foundations of a socio-cultural and politico-economic system based on the philosophy of civil liberties and human dignity. Therefore, it is not surprising that the framers of the Indian Constitution included chapters on the Fundamental Rights and the Directive Principles of State Policy. Adoption of the United Nations Charter and the Universal Declaration of Human Rights by India was not a sudden decision. It was indeed rooted in the principle that was inherent in the Indian peoples' struggle against the British imperialism. That explains why India has been also a willing party to the two Covenants that the United Nations General Assembly adopted in 1966 and which came into force in 1976.

D.N. Gupta
Chandrachur Singh

1

United Nations and Human Rights

CHARTER OF THE UNITED NATIONS, 1945

WE THE PEOPLES OF THE UNITED NATIONS, DETERMINED

to save succeeding generations from the scourge of war, which twice in our lifetime has brought untold sorrow to mankind, and

to reaffirm faith in fundamental human rights, in the dignity and worth of the human person, in the equal rights of men and women and of nations large and small, and

to establish conditions under which justice and respect for the obligations arising from treaties and other sources of international law can be maintained, and

to promote social progress and better standards of life in larger freedom.

AND FOR THESE ENDS

to practice tolerance and live together in peace with one another as good neighbours, and

to unite our strength to maintain international peace and security, and

to ensure, by the acceptance of principles and the institution of methods, that armed force shall not be used, save in the common interest, and

to employ international machinery for the promotion of the economic and social advancement of all peoples.

HAVE RESOLVED TO COMBINE OUR EFFORTS TO ACCOMPLISH THESE AIMS

Accordingly, our respective Governments, through representatives assembled in the city of San Francisco, who have exhibited their full powers found to be in good and due form, have agreed to the present Charter of the United Nations and do hereby establish an international organization to be known as the United Nations.

Purposes and Principles

Article 1

The Purposes of the United Nations are:

1. To maintain international peace and security, and to that end: to take effective collective measures for the prevention and removal of threats to the peace, and for the suppression of acts of aggression or other breaches of the peace, and to bring about by. peaceful means, and in conformity with the principles of justice and international law, adjustment or settlement of international disputes or situations which might lead to a breach of the peace;

2. To develop friendly relations among nations based on respect for the principles of equal rights and self-determination of peoples, and to take other appropriate measures to strengthen universal peace;

3. To achieve international co-operation in solving international problems of an economic, social, cultural, or humanitarian character, and in promoting and encouraging respect for human rights and for fundamental freedoms for all without distinction as to race, sex, language, or religion; and

4. To be a centre for harmonizing the actions of nations in the attainment of these common ends.

Article 2

The Organization and its members, in pursuit of the purposes stated in Article 1, shall act in accordance with the following Principles:

1. The organization is based on the principle of the sovereign equality of all its Members.

2. All members, in order to ensure to all of them the rights and benefits resulting from membership, shall fulfil in good faith the obligations assumed by them in accordance with the present Charter.

3. All members shall settle their international disputes by peaceful means in such a manner that international peace and security, and justice, are not endangered.

4. All members shall refrain in their international relations from the threat or use of force against the territorial integrity or political independence of any state, or in any other manner inconsistent with the Purposes of the United Nations.

5. All members shall give the United Nations every assistance in any action it takes in accordance with the present Charter, and shall refrain from giving assistance to any state against which the United Nations is taking preventive or enforcement action.

6. The organization shall ensure that states which are not members of the United Nations act in accordance with these Principles so far as may be necessary for the maintenance of peace and security.

7. Nothing contained in the present Charter shall authorize the United Nations to intervene in matters which are essentially within the domestic jurisdiction of any state or shall require the members to submit such matters to settlement under the present Charter, but this principle shall not prejudice the application of enforcement measures under Charter VII.

Membership

Article 3

The original members of the United Nations shall be the states which, having participated in the United Nations Conference on International Organization at San Francisco, or having previously signed the Declaration by United Nations on 1 January 1942, sign the present Charter and ratify it in accordance with Article 110.

Article 4

1. Membership in the United Nations is open to all other peace-loving states which accept the obligations contained in the present Charter and, in the judgment of the Organization, are able and willing to carry out these obligations.

2. The admission of any such state to membership in the United Nations will be effected by a decision of the General Assembly upon the recommendation of the Security Council.

Article 5

A member of the United Nations against which preventive or enforcement action has been taken by the Security Council may be suspended from the exercise of the rights and privileges of membership by the General Assembly upon the recommendation of the Security Council. The exercise of these rights and privileges may be restored by the Security Council.

Article 6

A member of the United Nations which has persistently violated the Principles contained in the present Charter may be expelled from the Organization by the General Assembly upon the recommendation of the Security Council.

ORGANS

Article 7

1. These are established as the principal organs of the United Nations: a General Assembly, a Security Council, an Economic and Social Council, a Trusteeship Council, an International Court of Justice, and a Secretariat.
2. Such subsidiary organs as may be found necessary may be established in accordance with the present Charter.

Article 8

The United Nations shall place no restrictions on the eligibility of men and women to participate in any capacity and under conditions of equality in its principal and subsidiary organs.

THE GENERAL ASSEMBLY

Composition

Article 9

1. The General Assembly shall consist of all the members of the United Nations.
2. Each member shall have not more than five representatives in the General Assembly.

Functions and Powers

Article 10

The General Assembly may discuss any questions or any matters within the scope of the present Charter or relating to the powers and functions of any organs provided for in the present Charter, and, except as provided in Article 12, may make recommendations to the members of the United Nations or to the Security Council or to both on any such questions or matters.

Article 11

1. The General Assembly may consider the general principles of co-operation in the maintenance of international peace and security, including the principles governing disarmament and the regulation of armaments, and may make recommendations with regard to such principles to the members or to the Security Council or to both.

2. The General Assembly may discuss any question relating to the maintenance of international peace and security brought before it by any member of the United Nations, or by the Security Council, or by a state which is not a member of the United Nations in accordance with Article 35, paragraph 2, and, except as provided in Article 12, may make recommendations with regard to any such questions to the state or states concerned or to the Security Council or to both. Any such question on which action is necessary shall be referred to the Security Council by the General Assembly either before or after discussion.

3. The General Assembly may call the attention of the Security Council to situations which are likely to endanger international peace and security.

4. The powers of the General Assembly set forth in this Article shall not limit the general scope of Article 10.

Article 12

1. While the Security Council is exercising in respect of any dispute or situation the functions assigned to it in the present Charter, the General Assembly shall not make any recommendation with regard to that dispute or situation unless the Security Council so requests.

2. The Secretary-General, with the consent of the Security Council, shall notify the General Assembly at each session of any matters relative to the maintenance of international peace and security which are being dealt with by the Security Council and shall similarly notify the General Assembly, or the members of the United Nations if the General Assembly is not in session, immediately the Security Council ceases to deal with such matters.

Article 13

1. The General Assembly shall initiate studies and make recommendations for the purpose of:

(a) promoting international co-operation in the political field and encouraging the progressive development of international law and its codification;
(b) promoting international co-operation in the economic, social, cultural, educational, and health fields, and assisting in the realization of human rights and fundamental freedoms for all without distinction as to race, sex, language or religion.

2. The further responsibilities, functions and powers of the General Assembly with respect to matters mentioned in paragraph 1 (b) above are set forth in Chapters IX and X.

Article 14

Subject to the provisions of Article 12, the General Assembly may recommend measures for the peaceful adjustment of any situation, regardless of origin, which it deems likely to impair the general welfare or friendly relations among nations, including situations resulting from the violation of the provisions of the present Charter setting forth the Purposes and Principles of the United Nations.

Article 15

1. The General Assembly shall receive and consider annual and special reports from the Security Council; these reports shall include an account of the measures that the Security Council has decided upon or taken to maintain international peace and security.

2. The General Assembly shall receive and consider reports from the other organs of the United Nations.

Article 16

The General Assembly shall perform such functions with respect to the international trusteeship system as are assigned to it under Chapters XII and XIII, including the approval of the trusteeship agreements for areas not designated as strategic.

Article 17

1. The General Assembly shall consider and approve the budget of the Organization.

2. The expenses of the Organization shall be borne by the members as apportioned by the General Assembly.

3. The General Assembly shall consider and approve any financial and budgetary arrangements with specialized agencies referred to in Article 57 and shall examine the administrative budgets of such specialized agencies with a view to making recommendations to the agencies concerned.

Voting

Article 18

1. Each member of the General Assembly shall have one vote.

2. Decisions of the General Assembly on important questions shall be made by a two-thirds majority of the members present and voting. These questions shall include: recommendations with respect to the maintenance of international peace and security, the election of the non-permanent members of the Security Council, the election of the members of the Economic and Social Council, the election of members of the Trusteeship Council in accordance with paragraph 1(c) of Article 86, the admission of new members to the United Nations, the suspension of the rights and privileges of membership, the expulsion of members, questions relating to the operation of the trusteeship system, and budgetary questions.

3. Decisions on other questions, including the determination of additional categories of questions to be decided by a two-thirds majority, shall be made by a majority of the members present and voting.

Article 19

A member of the United Nations which is in arrears in the payment of its financial contributions to the Organization shall have no vote in the General Assembly if the amount of its arrears equals or exceeds the amount of the contributions due from it for the preceding two full years. The General Assembly may, nevertheless, permit such a member to vote if it is satisfied that the failure to pay is due to conditions beyond the control of the member.

Procedure

Article 20

The General Assembly shall meet in regular annual sessions and in such special sessions as occasion may require. Special sessions shall be convoked by the Secretary-General at the request of the Security Council or of a majority of the members of the United Nations.

Article 21

The General Assembly shall adopt its own rules of procedure. It shall elect its President for each session.

Article 22

The General Assembly may establish such subsidiary organs as it deems necessary for the performance of its functions.

THE SECURITY COUNCIL

Composition

Article 23

1. The Security Council shall consist of fifteen members of the United Nations. The Republic of China, France, the Union of Soviet Socialist Republics, the United Kingdom of Great Britain and Northern Ireland, and the United States of America shall be permanent members of the Security Council. The General Assembly shall elect ten other members of the United Nations to be non-permanent members of the Security Council, due regard being specially paid, in the first instance to the contribution of members of the United Nations to the maintenance of international peace and security and to the other purposes of the Organization, and also to equitable geographical distribution.

2. The non-permanent members of the Security Council shall be elected for a term of two years. In the first election of the non-permanent members after the increase of the membership of the Security Council from eleven to fifteen, two of the four additional members shall be chosen for a term of one year. A retiring member shall not be eligible for immediate re-election.

3. Each member of the Security Council shall have one representative.

Functions and Powers

Article 24

1. In order to ensure prompt and effective action by the United Nations, its members confer on the Security Council primary responsibility for the maintenance of international peace and security, and agree that in carrying out its duties under this responsibility the Security Council acts on their behalf.

2. In discharging these duties the Security Council shall act in accordance with the Purposes and Principles of the United Nations. The specific powers granted to the Security Council for the discharge of these duties are laid down in Chapters VI, VII, VIII and XII.

3. The Security Council shall submit annual and, when necessary, special reports to the General Assembly for its consideration.

Article 25

The members of the United Nations agree to accept and carry out the decisions of the Security Council in accordance with the present Charter.

Article 26

In order to promote the establishment and maintenance of international peace and security with the least diversion for armaments of the world's human and economic resources, the Security Council shall be responsible for formulating, with the assistance of the Military Staff Committee referred to in Article 47, plans to be submitted to the Members of the United Nations for the establishment of a system for the regulation of armaments.

Voting

Article 27

1. Each member of the Security Council shall have one vote.

2. Decisions of the Security Council on procedural matters shall be made by an affirmative vote of nine members.

3. Decisions of the Security Council on all other matters shall be made by an affirmative vote of nine members including the concurring votes of the permanent members; provided that, in

decisions under Chapter VI, and under Paragraph 3 of Article 52, a party to a dispute shall abstain from voting.

Procedure

Article 28

1. The Security Council shall be so organized as to be able to function continuously. Each member of the Security Council shall for this purpose be represented at all times at the seat of the Organization.

2. The Security Council shall hold periodical meetings at which each of its members may, if it so desires, be represented by a member of the government or by some other specially designated representative.

3. The Security Council may hold meetings at such places other than the seat of the Organization as in its judgment will best facilitate its work.

Article 29

The Security Council may establish such subsidiary organs as it deems necessary for the performance of its functions.

Article 30

The Security Council shall adopt its own rules of procedure, including the method of selecting its President.

Article 31

Any member of the United Nations which is not a member of the Security Council may participate, without vote, in the discussion of any question brought before the Security Council whenever the latter considers that the interests of that Member are specially affected.

Article 32

Any member of the United Nations which is not a member of the Security Council or any state which is not a member of the United Nations, if it is a party to a dispute under consideration by the Security Council, shall be invited to participate, without vote, in the discussion relating to the dispute. The Security Council shall lay down such conditions as it deems just for the participation of a state which is not a member of the United Nations.

PACIFIC SETTLEMENT OF DISPUTES

Article 33

1. The parties to any dispute, the continuance of which is likely to endanger the maintenance of international peace and security, shall, first of all, seek a solution by negotiation, enquiry, mediation, conciliation, arbitration, judicial settlement, resort to regional agencies or arrangements, or other peaceful means of their own choice.

2. The Security Council shall, when it deems necessary, call upon the parties to settle their dispute by such means.

Article 34

The Security Council may investigate any dispute, or any situation which might lead to international friction or give rise to a dispute, in order to determine whether the continuance of the dispute or situation is likely to endanger the maintenance of international peace and security.

Article 35

1. Any member of the United Nations may bring any dispute, or any situation of the nature referred to in Article 34, to the attention of the Security Council or of the General Assembly.

2. A state which is not a Member of the United Nations may bring to the attention of the Security Council or of the General Assembly any dispute to which it is a party if it accepts in advance, for the purposes of the dispute, the obligations of pacific settlement provided in the present Charter.

3. The proceedings of the General Assembly in respect of matters brought to its attention under this Article will be subject to the provisions of Articles 11 and 12.

Article 36

1. The Security Council may, at any stage of a dispute of the nature referred to in Article 33 or of a situation of like nature, recommend appropriate procedures or methods of adjustment.

2. The Security Council should take into consideration any procedures for the settlement of the dispute which have already been adopted by the parties.

3. In making recommendations under this Article the Security Council should also take into consideration that legal disputes should as a general rule be referred by the parties to the International Court of Justice in accordance with the provisions of the Statute of the Court.

Article 37

1. Should the parties to a dispute of the nature referred to in Article 33 fail to settle it by the means indicated in that Article, they shall refer it to the Security Council.

2. If the Security Council deems that the continuance of the dispute is in fact likely to endanger the maintenance of international peace and security, it shall decide whether to take action under Article 36 or to recommend such terms of settlement as it may consider appropriate.

Article 38

Without prejudice to the provisions of Articles 33 to 37, the Security Council may, if all the parties to any dispute so request, make recommendations to the parties with a view to a pacific settlement of the dispute.

ACTION WITH RESPECT TO THREATS OF THE PEACE, BREACHES OF THE PEACE, AND ACTS OF AGGRESSION

Article 39

The Security Council shall determine the existence of any threat to the peace, breach of the peace, or act of aggression and shall make recommendations, or decide what measures shall be taken in accordance with Articles 41 and 42, to maintain or restore international peace and security.

Article 40

In order to prevent an aggravation of the situation, the Security Council may, before making the recommendations or deciding upon the measures provided for in Article 39, call upon the parties concerned to comply with such provisional measures as it deems necessary or desirable. Such provisional measures shall be without prejudice to the rights, claims, or position of the parties concerned. The Security Council shall duly take account of failure to comply with such provisional measures.

Article 41

The Security Council may decide what measures not involving the use of armed forces are to be employed to give effect to its decisions, and it may call upon the members of the United Nations to apply such measures. These may include complete or partial interruption of economic relations and of Rail, Sea, Air, Postal, Telegraphic, Radio, and other means of communication, and the severance of diplomatic relations.

Article 42

Should the Security Council consider that measures provided for in Article 41 would be inadequate or have proved to be inadequate, it may take such action by Air, Sea, or Land forces as may be necessary to maintain or restore international peace or security. Such action may include demonstrations, blockade, and other operations by Air, Sea, or Land forces of Members of the United Nations.

Article 43

1. All Memoers of the United Nations, in order to contribute to the maintenance of international peace and security, undertake to make available to the Security Council, on its call and in accordance with a special agreement or agreements, Armed forces, assistance, and facilities, including rights of passage, necessary for the purpose of maintaining international peace and security.

2. Such agreement or agreements shall govern the numbers and types of forces, their degree of readiness and general location, and the nature of the facilities and assistance to be provided.

3. The agreement or agreements shall be negotiated as soon as possible at the initiative of the Security Council. They shall be concluded between the Security Council and Members or between the Security Council and groups of Members and shall be subject to ratification by the signatory states in accordance with their respective constitutional processes.

Article 44

When the Security Council has decided to use force it shall, before calling upon a Member not represented on it to provide armed forces in fulfilment of the obligations assumed under Article 43, invite that member, if the member so desires, to participate in the decisions of the Security Council concerning the employment of contingents of that Members's Armed forces.

Article 45

In order to enable the United Nations to take urgent military measures, Members shall hold immediately available national Airforce contingents for combined international enforcement action. The strength and degree of readiness of these contingents and plans for their combined action shall be determined, within the limits laid down in the special agreement or agreements referred to in Article 43, by the Security Council with the assistance of the Military Staff Committee.

Article 46

Plans for the application of Armed force shall be made by the Security Council with the assistance of the Military Staff Committee.

Article 47

1. There shall be established a Military Staff Committee to advise and assist the Security Council on all questions relating to the Security Council's military requirements for the maintenance of international peace and security, the employment and command of forces placed at its disposal, the regulation of armaments, and possible disarmament.

2. The Military Staff Committee shall consist of the Chiefs of Staff of the permanent members of the Security Council or their representatives. Any Member of the United Nations not permanently represented on the Committee shall be invited by the Committee to be associated with it when the efficient discharge of the Committee's responsibilities requires the participation of that member in its work.

3. The Military Staff Committee shall be responsible under the Security Council for the strategic direction of any armed forces placed at the disposal of the Security Council. Questions relating to the command of such forces shall be worked out subsequently.

4. The Military Staff Committee, with the authorization of the Security Council and after consultation with appropriate regional agencies, may establish regional sub-committees.

Article 48

1. The action required to carry out the decisions of the Security Council for the maintenance of international peace and security shall be taken by all the Members of the United Nations or by some of them, the Security Council may determine.

2. Such decisions shall be carried out by the Members of the United Nations directly and through their action in the appropriate international agencies of which they are members.

Article 49

The Members of the United Nations shall join in affording mutual assistance in carrying out the measures decided upon by the Security Council.

Article 50

If preventive or enforcement measures against any state are taken by the Security Council, any other state, whether a Member of the United Nations or not, which finds itself confronted with special economic problems arising from the carrying out of those measures shall have the right to consult the Security Council with regard to a solution of those problems.

Article 51

Nothing in the present Charter shall impair the inherent right of individual or collective self-defence if an armed attack occurs against a Member of the United Nations, until the Security Council has taken measures necessary to maintain international peace and security. Measures taken by Members in the exercise of this right of self-defence shall be immediately reported to the Security Council and shall not in any way affect the authority and responsibility of the Security Council under the present Charter to take at any time such action as it deems necessary in order to maintain or restore international peace and security.

REGIONAL ARRANGEMENTS

Article 52

1. Nothing in the present Charter precludes the existence of regional arrangements or agencies for dealing with such matters

relating to the maintenance of international peace and security as are appropriate for regional action, provided that such arrangements or agencies and their activities are consistent with the purpose and Principles of the United Nations.

2. The Members of the United Nations entering into such arrangements or constituting such agencies shall make every effort to achieve pacific settlement of local disputes through such regional arrangements or by such regional agencies before referring them to the Security Council.

3. The Security Council shall encourage the development of pacific settlement of local disputes through such regional arrangements or by such regional agencies either on the initiative of the states concerned or by reference from the Security Council.

4. The Article in no way impairs the application of Articles 34 and 35.

Article 53

1. The Security Council shall, where appropriate, utilize such regional arrangements or agencies for enforcement action under its authority. But no enforcement action shall be taken under regional arrangements or by regional agencies without the authorization of the Security Council, with the exception of measures against any enemy state, as defined in paragraph 2 of this Article, provided for pursuant to Article 107 or in regional arrangements directed against renewal of aggressive policy on the part of any such state, until such time as the organization may, on request of the Governments concerned, be charged with the responsibility for preventing further aggression by such a state.

2. The term enemy state as used in Paragraph 1 of this Article applies to any state which during the Second World War has been an enemy of any signatory of the present Charter.

Article 54

The Security Council shall at all times be kept fully informed of activities undertaken or in contemplation under regional arrangements or by regional agencies for the maintenance of international peace and security.

INTERNATIONAL, ECONOMIC AND SOCIAL CO-OPERATION

Article 55

With a view to the creation of conditions of stability and well-being which are necessary for peaceful and friendly relations among nations based on respect for the principle of equal rights and self-determination of peoples, the United Nations shall promote:

(a) higher standards of living, full employment, and conditions of economic and social progress and development;

(b) solutions of international economic, social, health, and related problems; and international cultural and educational co-operation; and

(c) universal respect for, and observance of, human rights and fundamental freedoms for all without distinction as to race, sex, language, or religion.

Article 56

All Members pledge themselves to take joint and separate action in co-operation with the Organization for the achievement of the purposes set forth in Article 55.

Article 57

1. The various specialized agencies, established by inter-governmental agreement and having wide international responsibilities, as defined in their basic instruments, in economic, social, cultural, educational, health, and related fields, shall be brought into relationship with the United Nations in accordance with the provisions of Article 63.

2. Such agencies thus brought into relationship with the United Nations are hereinafter referred to as specialized agencies.

Article 58

The Organization shall make recommendations for the co-ordination of the policies and activities of the specialized agencies.

Article 59

The Organization shall, where appropriate, initiate negotiations among the states concerned for the creation of any new specialized agencies required for the accomplishment of the purpose set forth in Article 55.

Article 60

Responsibility for the discharge of the functions of the Organization set forth in this Chapter shall be vested in the General Assembly and, under the authority of the General Assembly, in the Economic and Social Council, which shall have for this purpose the powers set forth in Chapter X.

THE ECONOMIC AND SOCIAL COUNCIL

Composition

Article 61

1. The Economic and Social Council shall consist of fifty-four Members of the United Nations elected by the General Assembly.

2. Subject to the provisions of paragraph 3, eighteen members of the Economic and Social Council shall be elected each year for a term of three years. A retiring member shall be eligible for immediate re-election.

3. At the first election after the increase in the membership of the Economic and Social Council from twenty-seven to fifty-four members, in addition to the members elected in place of the nine members whose term of office expires at the end of that year, twenty-seven additional members shall be elected. Of these twenty-seven additional members, the term of office of nine members so elected shall expire at the end of one year, and of nine other members at the end of two years, in accordance with arrangements made by the General Assembly.

4. Each member of the Economic and Social Council shall have one representative.

Functions and Powers

Article 62

1. The Economic and Social Council may make or initiate studies and reports with respect to international economic, social, cultural, educational, health and related matters and may make recommendations with respect to any such matters to the General

Assembly, to the Members of the United Nations, and to the specialized agencies concerned.

2. It may make recommendations for the purpose of promoting respect for, and observance of, human rights and fundamental freedoms for all.

3. It may prepare draft conventions for submission to the General Assembly, with respect to matters falling within its competence.

4. It may call, in accordance with the rules prescribed by the United Nations, international conferences on matters falling within its competence.

Article 63

1. The Economic and Social Council may enter into agreements with any of the agencies referred to in Article 57, defining the terms on which the agency concerned shall be brought into relationship with the United Nations. Such agreements shall be subject to approval by the General Assembly.

2. It may co-ordinate the activities of the specialized agencies through consultation with and recommendations to such agencies and through recommendations to the General Assembly and to the Members of the United Nations.

Article 64

1. The Economic and Social Council may take appropriate steps to obtain regular reports from the specialized agencies. It may make arrangements with the Members of the United Nations and with the specialized agencies to obtain reports on the steps taken to give effect to its own recommendations and to recommendations on matters falling within its competence made by the General Assembly.

2. It may communicate its observations on these reports to the General Assembly.

Article 65

The Economic and Social Council may furnish information to the Security Council and shall assist the Security Council upon its request.

Article 66

1. The Economic and Social Council shall perform such functions as fall within its competence in connection with the carrying out of the recommendations of the General Assembly.

2. It may, with the approval of the General Assembly, perform services at the request of Members of the United Nations and at the request of specialized agencies.

3. It shall perform such other functions as are specified elsewhere in the present Charter or as may be assigned to it by the General Assembly.

Voting

Article 67

1. Each Member of the Economic and Social Council shall have one vote.

2. Decisions of the Economic and Social Council shall be made by a majority of the members present and voting.

Procedure

Article 68

The Economic and Social Council shall set up commission in economic and social fields and for the promotion of human rights, and such other commissions as may be required for the performance of its functions.

Article 69

The Economic and Social Council shall invite any Member of the United Nations to participate, without vote, in its deliberations on any matter of particular concern to that Member.

Article 70

The Economic and Social Council may make arrangements for representatives of the specialized agencies to participate, without vote, in its deliberations and in those of the commissions established by it, and for its representatives to participate in the deliberations of the specialized agencies.

Article 71

The Economic and Social Council may make suitable arrangements for consultation with non-governmental organizations which are concerned with matters within its competence. Such arrangements may be made with international organization and, where appropriate, with national organizations after consultation with the Member of the United Nations concerned.

Article 72

1. The Economic and Social Council shall adopt its own rules of procedure, including the method of selecting its President.

2. The Economic and Social Council shall meet as required in accordance with its rules, which shall include provision for the convening of meetings on the request of a majority of its members.

DECLARATION REGARDING NON-SELF-GOVERNING TERRITORIES

Article 73

Members of the United Nations which have or assume responsibilities for the administration of territories whose peoples have not yet attained a full measure of self-government recognize the principle that the interests of the inhabitants of these territories are paramount, and accept as a sacred trust the obligation to promote to the utmost, within the system of international peace and security established by the present Charter, the well-being of the inhabitants of these territories, and, to this end:

(a) to ensure, with due respect for the culture of the peoples concerned, their political, social, and educational advancement, their just treatment, and their protection against abuses;

(b) to develop self-government, to take due account of the political aspirations of the peoples, and to assist them in the progressive development of their free political institutions, according to the particular circumstances of each territory and its peoples and their varying stages of advancement;

(c) to further international peace and security;

(d) to promote constructive measures of development, to encourage research, and to co-operate with one another and, when and where appropriate, with specialized international bodies with a view to the practical achievement of the social, economic, and scientific purposes set forth in this Article; and

(e) to transmit regularly to the Secretary-General for information purposes, subject to such limitation as security and constitutional considerations may require, statistical and other information of a technical nature relating to economic, social, and educational conditions in the territories for which they are respectively responsible other than those territories to which Chapters XII and XIII apply.

Article 74

Members of the United Nations also agree that their policy in respect of the territories to which this Chapter applies, no less than in respect of their metropolitan areas, must be based on the general principle of good-neighbourliness, due account being taken of the interests and well-being of the rest of world, in social, economic, and commercial matters.

INTERNATIONAL TRUSTEESHIP SYSTEM

Article 75

The United Nations shall establish under its authority an international trusteeship system for the administration and supervision of such territories as may be placed thereunder by subsequent individual agreements. These territories are hereinafter referred to as trust territories.

Article 76

The basic objectives of the trusteeship system, in accordance with the Purposes of the United Nations laid down in Article 1 of the present Charter, shall be:

(a) to further international peace and security;

(b) to promote the political, economic, social, and educational advancement of the inhabitants of the trust territories, and their progressive development towards self-government or independence as may be appropriate to the particular circumstances of each territory and its peoples and the freely expressed wishes of the peoples concerned, and as may be provided by the terms of each trusteeship agreement;

(c) to encourage respect for human rights and for fundamental freedoms for all without distinction as to race, sex, language, or religion, and to encourage recognition of the interdependence of the peoples of the world; and

(d) to ensure equal treatment in social, economic, and commercial matters for all Members of the United Nations and their nationals, and also equal treatment for the latter in the administration of justice, without prejudice to the attainment of the foregoing objectives and subject to the provisions of Article 80.

Article 77

1. The trusteeship system shall apply to such territories in the following categories as may be placed thereunder by means of trusteeship agreements:

(a) territories now held under mandate;
(b) territories which may be detached from enemy states as a result of the Second World War; and
(c) territories voluntarily placed under the system by states responsible for their administration.

2. It will be a matter for subsequent agreement as to which territories in the foregoing categories will be brought under the trusteeship system and upon what terms.

Article 78

The trusteeship system shall not apply to territories which have become Members of the United Nations, relationship among which shall be based on respect for the principle of sovereign equality.

Article 79

The terms of trusteeship for each territory to be placed under the trusteeship system, including my alteration or amendment, shall be agreed upon by the states directly concerned, including the mandatory powers in the case of territories held under mandate by a Member of the United Nations, and shall be approved as provided for in Articles 83 and 85.

Article 80

1. Except as may be agreed upon in individual trusteeship agreements, made under articles 77, 79, and 81, placing each territory under the trusteeship system, and until such agreements have been concluded, nothing in this Chapter shall be construed in or of itself

to alter in any manner the rights whatsoever of any states or any peoples or the terms of existing international instruments to which Members of the United Nations may respectively be parties.

2. Paragraph 1 of this Article shall not be interpreted as giving grounds for delay or postponement of the negotiation and conclusion of agreements for placing mandated and other territories under the trusteeship system as provided for in Article 77.

Article 81

The trusteeship agreement shall in each case include the terms under which the trust territory will be administered and designate the authority which will exercise the administration of the trust territory. Such authority, hereinafter called the administering authority, may be one or more states or the Organization itself.

Article 82

There may be designated, in any trusteeship agreement, a strategic area or areas which may include part or all of the trust territory to which the agreement applies, without prejudice to any special agreement or agreements made under Article 43.

Article 83

1. All functions of the United Nations relating to strategic areas, including the approval of the terms of the trusteeship agreements and of their alteration or amendment, shall be exercised by the Security Council.

2. The basic objectives set forth in Article 76 shall be applicable to the people of each strategic area.

3. The Security Council shall, subject to the provisions of the trusteeship agreements and without prejudice to security considerations, avail itself of the assistance of the Trusteeship Council to perform those functions of the United Nations under the trusteeship system relating to political, economic, social, and educational matters in the strategic areas.

Article 84

It shall be the duty of the administering authority to ensure that the trust territory shall play its part in the maintenance of international peace and security. To this end the administering authority may make use of volunteer forces, facilities, and assistance from the trust territory in carrying out the obligations towards the Security Council undertaken in this regard by the administering authority, as well as for local defence and the maintenance of law and order within the trust territory.

Article 85

1. The functions of the United Nations with regard to trusteeship agreements for all areas not designated as strategic, including the approval of the terms of the trusteeship agreements and of their alteration or amendment, shall be exercised by the General Assembly.

2. The Trusteeship Council, operating under the authority of the General Assembly, shall assist the General Assembly in carrying out these functions.

THE TRUSTEESHIP COUNCIL

Composition

Article 86

1. The Trusteeship Council shall consist of the following Members of the United Nations:

(a) those Members administering trust territories;

(b) such of those Members mentioned by name in Article 23 as are not administering trust territories; and

(c) as many other Members elected for three-year terms by the General Assembly as may be necessary to ensure that the total number of members of the Trusteeship Council is equally divided between these Members of the United Nations which administer trust territories and those which do not.

2. Each member of the Trusteeship Council shall designate one specially qualified person to represent it therein.

Functions and Powers

Article 87

The General Assembly and, under its authority, the Trusteeship Council, in carrying out their functions, may:

(a) consider reports submitted by the administering authority;

(b) accept petitions and examine them in consultation with the administering authority;
(c) provide for periodic visits to the respective trust territories at times agreed upon with the administering authority; and
(d) take these and other actions in conformity with the terms of the trusteeship agreements.

Article 88

The Trusteeship Council shall formulate a questionnaire on the political, economic, social and educational advancement of the inhabitants of each trust territory, and the administering authority for each trust territory within the competence of the General Assembly shall make an annual report to the General Assembly upon the basis of such questionnaire.

Voting

Article 89

1. Each member of the Trusteeship Council shall have one vote.

2. Decisions of the Trusteeship Council shall be made by a majority of the members present and voting.

Procedure

Article 90

1. The Trusteeship Council shall adopt its own rules of procedure, including the method of selecting its President.

2. The Trusteeship Council shall meet as required in accordance with its rules, which shall include provisions for the convening of meetings on the request of a majority of its members.

Article 91

The Trusteeship Council shall, when appropriate, avail itself of the assistance of the Economic and Social Council and of the specialized agencies in regard to matters with which they are respectively concerned.

THE INTERNATIONAL COURT OF JUSTICE

Article 92

The International Court of Justice shall be the principal judicial organ of the United Nations. It shall function in accordance with the annexed Statute, which is based upon the Statute of the Permanent Court of International Justice and forms an integral part of the present Charter.

Article 93

1. All Members of the United Nations are *ipso facto* parties to the Statute of the International Court of Justice.

2. A state which is not a member of the United Nations may become a party to the Statute of the International Court of Justice on conditions to be determined in each case by the General Assembly upon the recommendation of the Security Council.

Article 94

1. Each member of the United Nations undertakes to comply with the decision of the International Court of Justice in any case to which it is a party.

2. If any party to a case fails to perform the obligations incumbent upon it under a judgment rendered by the Court, the other party may have recourse to the Security Council, which may, if it deems necessary, make recommendations or decide upon measures to be taken to give effect to the judgment.

Article 95

Nothing in the present Charter shall prevent Members of the United Nations from entrusting the solution of their difference to other tribunals by virtue of agreements already in existence or which may be concluded in the future.

Article 96

1. The General Assembly or the Security Council may request the International Court of Justice to give an advisory opinion on any legal question.

2. Other organs of the United Nations and specialized agencies, which may at any time be so authorized by the General Assembly, may also request advisory opinions of the Court on legal questions arising within the scope of their activities.

THE SECRETARIAT

Article 97

The Secretariat shall comprise a Secretary-General and such staff as the Organization may require. The Secretary-General shall be appointed by the General Assembly upon the recommendation of the Security Council. He shall be the chief administrative officer of the Organization.

Article 98

The Secretary-General shall act in that capacity in meetings of the General Assembly, of the Security Council, of the Economic and Social Council and of the Trusteeship Council, and shall perform such other functions as are entrusted to him by these organs. The Secretary-General shall make an annual report to the General Assembly on the work of the Organization.

Article 99

The Secretary-General may bring to the attention of the Security Council any matter which in his opinion may threaten the maintenance of international peace and security.

Article 100

1. In the performance of their duties the Security-General and the staff shall not seek or receive instructions from any government or from any other authority external to the Organization. They shall refrain from any action which might reflect on their position as international officials responsible only to the Organization.

2. Each Member of the United Nations undertakes to respect the exclusively international character of the responsibilities of the Secretary-General and the staff and not to seek to influence them in the discharge of their responsibilities.

Article 101

1. The staff shall be appointed by the Secretary-General under regulations established by the General Assembly.

2. Appropriate staff shall be permanently assigned to the Economic and Social Council, the Trusteeship Council, and, as required, to other organs of the United Nations. These staffs shall form a part of the Secretariat.

3. The paramount consideration in the employment of the staff and in the determination of the conditions of service shall be the necessity of securing the highest standards of efficiency,

competence, and integrity. Due regard shall be paid to the importance of recruiting the staff on as wide a geographical basis as possible.

MISCELLANEOUS PROVISIONS

Article 102

1. Every treaty and every international agreement entered into by any Member of the United Nations after the present Charter comes into force shall as soon as possible be registered with the Secretariat and published by it.

2. No party to any such treaty or international agreement which has not been registered in accordance with the provisions of paragraph 1 of this Article may invoke that treaty or agreement before any organ of the United Nations.

Article 103

In the event of a conflict between the obligations of the Members of the United Nations under the present Charter and their obligations under any other international agreement, their obligations under the present Charter shall prevail.

Article 104

The Organization shall enjoy in the territory of each of its Members such legal capacity as may be necessary for the exercise of its functions and the fulfilment of its purposes.

Article 105

1. The Organization shall enjoy in the territory of each of its Members such privileges and immunities as are necessary for the fulfilment of its purposes.

2. Representatives of the Members of the United Nations and officials of the Organization shall similarly enjoy such privileges and immunities as are necessary for the independent exercise of their functions in connection with the Organization.

3. The General Assembly may make recommendations with a view to determining the details of the application of paragraphs 1 and 2 of the Article or may propose conventions to the Members of the United Nations for this purpose.

TRANSITIONAL SECURITY ARRANGEMENTS

Article 106

Pending the coming into force of such special agreements referred to in Article 43 as in the opinion of the Security Council enable it to begin the exercise of its responsibilities under Article 42, the parties to the Four-Nation Declaration, signed at Moscow, 30 October 1943, and France, shall, in accordance with the provisions of paragraph 5 of that Declaration, consult with one another and as occasion requires with other Members of the United Nations with a view to such joint action on behalf of the Organization as may be necessary for the purpose of maintaining international peace and security.

Article 107

Nothing in the present Charter shall invalidate or preclude action, in relation to any state which during the Second World War has been an enemy of any signatory to the present Charter, taken or authorized as a result of that war by the Governments having responsibility for such action.

AMENDMENTS

Article 108

Amendments to the present Charter shall come into force for all Members of the United Nations when they have been adopted by a vote of two thirds of the members of the General Assembly and ratified in accordance with their respective constitutional processes by two thirds of the Members of the United Nations, including all the permanent members of the Security Council.

Article 109

1. A General Conference of the Members of the United Nations for the purpose of reviewing the present Charter may be held at a date and place to be fixed by a two-thirds vote of the members of the General Assembly and by a vote of any nine members of the Security Council. Each Member of the United Nations shall have one vote in the conference.

2. Any alteration of the present Charter recommended by a two-thirds vote of the conference shall take effect when ratified in accordance with their respective constitutional processes by two

thirds of the Members of the United Nations including all the permanent members of the Security Council.

3. If such a conference has not been held before the tenth annual session of the General Assembly following the coming into force of the present Charter, the proposal to call such a conference shall be placed on the agenda of that session of the General Assembly, and the conference shall be held if so decided by a majority vote of the members of the General Assembly and by a vote of any members of the Security Council.

RATIFICATION AND SIGNATURE

Article 110

1. The present Charter shall be ratified by the signatory states in accordance with their respective constitutional processes.

2. The ratifications shall be deposited with the Government of the United States of America, which shall notify all the signatory states of each deposit as well as the Secretary-General of the Organization when he has been appointed.

3. The present Charter shall come into force upon the deposit of ratifications by the Republic of China, France, the Union of Soviet Socialist Republics, the United Kingdom of Great Britain and Northern Ireland, and the United States of America, and by a majority of the other signatory states. A protocol of the ratifications deposited shall thereupon be drawn up by the Government of the United States of America which shall communicate copies thereof to all the signatory states.

4. The states signatory to the present Charter which ratify it after it has come into force will become original Members of the United Nations on the date of the deposit of their respective ratifications.

Article 111

The present Charter, of which the Chinese, French, Russian, English, and Spanish texts are equally authentic, shall remain deposited in the archives of the Government of the United States of America. Duly certified copies thereof shall be transmitted by that Government to the Governments of the other signatory states.

IN FAITH WHEREOF the representatives of the Governments of the United Nations have signed the present Charter.

Done at the city of San Francisco the twenty-sixth day of June, one thousand nine hundred and forty-five.

UNIVERSAL DECLARATION OF HUMAN RIGHTS, 1948

Adopted and proclaimed by General Assembly resolution 217 A (III) of 10 December 1948

Preamble

Whereas recognition of the inherent dignity and of the equal and inalienable rights of all members of the human family is the foundation of freedom, justice and peace in the world.

Whereas disregard and contempt for human rights have resulted in barbarous acts which have outraged the conscience of mankind, and the advent of a world in which human beings shall enjoy freedom of speech and belief and freedom from fear and want has been proclaimed as the highest aspiration of the common people,

Whereas it is essential, if man is not to be compelled to have recourse, as a last resort, to rebellion against tyranny and oppression, that human rights should be protected by the rule of law,

Whereas it is essential to promote the development of friendly relations between nations,

Whereas the peoples of the United Nations have in the Charter reaffirmed their faith in fundamental human rights, in the dignity and worth of the human person and in the equal rights of men and women and have determined to promote social progress and better standards of life in larger freedom,

Whereas Member states have pledged themselves to achieve, in co-operation with the United Nations, the promotion of universal respect for and observance of human rights and fundamental freedoms.

Whereas a common understanding of these rights and freedoms is of the greatest importance for the full realisation of this pledge,

Now, therefore

The General Assembly,

Proclaims this Universal Declaration of Human Rights as a common standard of achievement for all peoples and all nations, to the end that every individual and every organ of society, keeping this Declaration constantly in mind, shall strive by teaching and education to promote respect for these rights and freedoms and by progressive measures, national and international, to secure their universal and effective recognition and observance, both among the peoples of Member States themselves and among the peoples of territories under their jurisdiction.

Article 1

All human beings are born free and equal in dignity and rights. They are endowed with reason and conscience and should act towards one another in a spirit of brotherhood.

Article 2

Everyone is entitled to all the rights and freedoms set forth in this Declaration, without distinction of any kind, such as race, colour, sex, language, religion, political or other opinion, national or social origin, property, birth or other status.

Furthermore, no distinction shall be made on the basis of the political jurisdiction or international status of the country or territory to which a person belongs, whether it be independent, trust, non-self-governing or under any other limitation of sovereignty.

Article 3

Everyone has the right to life, liberty and security of person.

Article 4

No one shall be held in slavery or servitude; slavery and the slave trade shall be prohibited in all their forms.

Article 5

No one shall be subjected to torture or to cruel, inhuman or degrading treatment or punishment.

Article 6

Everyone has the right to recognition everywhere as a person before the law.

Article 7

All are equal before the law and are entitled without any discrimination to equal protection of the law. All are entitled to equal protection against any discrimination in violation of this Declaration and against any incitement to such discrimination.

Article 8

Everyone has the right to an effective remedy by the competent national tribunals for acts violating the fundamental rights granted him by the constitution or by law.

Article 9

No one shall be subjected to arbitrary arrest, detention or exile.

Article 10

Everyone is entitled in full equality to a fair and public hearing by an independent and impartial tribunal, in the determination of his rights and obligations and of any criminal charge against him.

Article 11

1. Every one charged with a penal offence has the right to be presumed innocent until proved guilty according to law in a public trial at which he has had all the guarantees necessary for his defence.

2. No one shall be held guilty of any penal offence on account of any act or omission which did not constitute a penal offence, under national or international law, at the time when it was committed. Nor shall a heavier penalty be imposed than the one that was applicable at the time the penal offence was committed.

Article 12

No one shall be subjected to arbitrary interference with his privacy, family, home or correspondence, nor to attacks upon his honour and reputation. Everyone has the right to the protection of the law against such interference or attacks.

Article 13

1. Everyone has the right to freedom of movement and residence within the borders of each state.

2. Everyone has the right to leave any country, including his own, and to return to his country.

Article 14

1. Everyone has the right to seek and to enjoy in other countries asylum from persecution.

2. This right may not be invoked in the case of prosecutions genuinely arising from non-political crimes or from acts contrary to the purposes and principles of the United Nations.

Article 15

1. Everyone has the right to a nationality.

2. No one shall be arbitrarily deprived of his nationality nor denied the right to change his nationality.

Article 16

1. Men and women of full age, without any limitation due to race, nationality or religion, have the right to marry and to found a family. They are entitled to equal rights as to marriage, during marriage and at its dissolution.

2. Marriage shall be entered only with the free and full consent of the intending spouses.

3. The family is the natural and fundamental group unit of society and entitled to protection by society and the state.

Article 17

1. Everyone has the right to own property alone as well as in association with others.

2. No one shall he arbitrarily deprived of his property.

Article 18

Everyone has the right to freedom of thought, conscience and religion; this right includes freedom to change his religion or belief, and freedom, either alone or in community with others and in public or private, to manifest his religion or belief in teaching, practice, worship and observance.

Article 19

Everyone has the right to freedom of opinion and expression; this right includes freedom to hold opinions without interference and to seek, receive and impart information and ideas through any media and regardless of frontiers.

Article 20

1. Everyone has the right to freedom of peaceful assembly and association.

2. No one may be compelled to belong to an association.

Article 21

1. Everyone has the right to take part in the government of his country, directly or through freely chosen representatives.

2. Everyone has the right to equal access to public service in his country.

3. The will of the people shall be the basis of the authority of government; this will shall be expressed in periodic and genuine elections which shall be by universal and equal suffrage and shall be held by secret vote or by equivalent free voting procedures.

Article 22

Everyone, as a member of society, has the right to social security and is entitled to realisation, through national effort and international co-operation and in accordance with the organisation and resources of each State, of the economic, social and cultural rights indispensable for his dignity and the free development of his personality.

Article 23

1. Everyone has the right to work, to free choice of employment, to just and favourable conditions of work and to protection against unemployment.

2. Everyone, without any discrimination, has the right to equal pay for equal work.

3. Everyone who works has the right to just and favourable remuneration ensuring for himself and his family an existence worthy of human dignity, and supplemented, if necessary, by other means of social protection.

4. Everyone has the right to form and to join trade unions for the protection of his interests.

Article 24

Everyone has the right to rest and leisure, including reasonable limitation of working hours and periodic holidays with pay.

Article 25

1. Everyone has the right to a standard of living adequate for the health and well-being of himself and of his family, including food, clothing, housing and medical care and necessary social services, and the right to security in the event of unemployment, sickness, disability, widowhood, old age or other lack of livelihood in circumstances beyond his control.

2. Motherhood and childhood are entitled to special care and assistance. All children, whether born in or out of wedlock, shall enjoy the same social protection.

Article 26

1. Everyone has the right to education. Education shall be free, at least in the elementary and fundamental stages. Elementary education shall be compulsory. Technical and professional education shall be made generally available and higher education shall be equally accessible to all on the basis of merit.

2. Education shall be entitled to the full development of the human personality and to the strengthening of respect for human rights and fundamental freedoms. It shall promote understanding, tolerance and friendship among all nations, racial or religious groups, and shall further the activities of the United Nations for the maintenance of peace.

3. Parents have a prior right to choose the kind of education that shall be given to their children.

Article 27

1. Everyone has the right freely to participate in the cultural life of the community, to enjoy the arts and to share in scientific advancement and its benefits.

2. Everyone has the right to the protection of the moral and material interests resulting from any scientific, literary or artistic production of which he is the author.

Article 28

Everyone is entitled to social and international order in which the rights and freedoms set forth in this Declaration can be fully realised.

Article 29

1. Everyone is entitled to the community in which alone the free and full development of his personality is possible.

2. In the exercise of his rights and freedoms, everyone shall be subject only to such limitations as are determined by law solely for the purpose of securing due recognition and respect for the rights and freedoms of others and the general welfare in a democratic society.

3. These rights and freedoms may in no case be exercised contrary to the purposes and principles of the United Nations.

Article 30

Nothing in this Declaration may be interpreted as implying for any State, group or person any right to engage in any activity or to perform any act aimed at the destruction of the rights and freedoms set forth herein.

DECLARATION BY THE GOVERNMENT OF INDIA, 1979

WHEREAS the International Covenant on Economic, Social and Cultural Rights and the International Covenant on Civil and Political Rights were adopted by the General Assembly of the United Nations in Resolution 2200 (XXI) of 16 December 1966, which Covenants are reproduced in the Annexure to this Document;

AND WHEREAS it is fit and expedient to accede to the aforesaid covenants subject to the following Declarations:

Declarations

I. With reference to Article I of the International Covenant on Economic, Social and Cultural Rights and Article I of the International Covenant on Civil and Political Rights, the Government of the Republic of India declares that the words "the right of self-determination" appearing in those articles apply only to the peoples under foreign dominations and that these words do not apply to sovereign independent States or to a Section of a people or nation—which is the essence of national integrity.

II. With reference to Article 9 of the International Covenant on Civil and Political Rights, the Government of the Republic of India takes the position that the provisions of the article shall be so applied as to be in consonance with the provisions of clauses (3) to (7) of Article 22 of the Constitution of India. Further under the Indian Legal System, there is no enforceable right to compensation for persons claiming to be victims of unlawful arrest or detention against the State.

III. With respect to Article 13 of the International Covenant on Civil and Political Rights, the Government of the Republic of India reserves its right to apply its law relating to foreigners.

IV. With respect to Articles 4 and 8 of the International Covenant on Economic, Social and Cultural Rights, and Articles 12, 19(3), 21 and 22 of the International Covenant on Civil and Political Rights, the Government of the Republic of India declares that the provisions of the said articles shall be so applied as to be in conformity with the provisions of Article 19 of the Constitution of India.

V. With reference to Article 7(c) of the International Covenant on Economic, Social and Cultural Rights, the Government of the Republic of India declares that the provisions of the said Article shall be so applied as to be in conformity with the provisions of

Article 16(4) of the Constitution of India.

NOW, THEREFORE, BE IT KNOWN that the Government of the Republic of India, having seen and considered the said Covenants, do hereby accede to the same, subject to the aforementioned Declarations.

IN TESTIMONY WHEREOF I, NEELAM SANJIVA REDDY, PRESIDENT OF INDIA, have signed these Presents and affixed hereunto my Seal at New Delhi this the sixth day of Chaitra of the Saka year one thousand nine hundred and one corresponding to the twenty-seventh day of March of the year one thousand nine hundred and seventy-nine A. D. in the Thirtieth year of the Republic of India.

Sd/-

(Neelam Sanjiva Reddy)
President of India

Deposited with the U. N. on
10.4.79

INTERNATIONAL COVENANT ON CIVIL AND POLITICAL RIGHTS, 1966

Adopted and opened for signature, ratification and accession by General Assembly resolution 2200 A (XXI) of 16 December 1966

Entry into Force: 23 March 1976, in accordance with Article 49

Preamble

The State Parties to the present Covenant,

Considering that, in accordance with the principles proclaimed in the Charter of the United Nations, recognition of the inherent dignity and of the equal and inalienable rights of all members of the family is the foundation of freedom, justice and peace in the world,

Recognising that these rights derive from the inherent dignity of the human person,

Recognising that, in accordance with the Universal Declaration of Human Rights, the idea of free human beings enjoying civil and political freedom and freedom from fear and want can only be achieved if conditions are created whereby everyone may enjoy his civil and political rights, as well as his economic, social and cultural rights.

Considering the obligation of States under the Charter of the United Nations to promote universal respect for, and observance of, human rights and freedoms,

Realising that the individual, having duties to other individuals and to the community to which he belongs, is under a responsibility to strive for the promotion and observance of the rights recognised in the present Covenant.

Agree upon the following articles:

Article 1

1. All peoples, have the right of self-determination. By virtue of that right they freely determine their political status and freely pursue their economic, social and cultural development.

2. All peoples may, for their own ends, freely dispose of their natural wealth and resources without prejudice to any obligations arising out of international economic co-operation, based upon the

principle of mutual benefit, and international law. In no case may a people be deprived of its own means of subsistence.

3. The States Parties to the present Covenant, including those having responsibility for the administration of Non-Self-Governing and Trust Territories, shall promote the realisation of the right of self-determination, and shall respect that right, in conformity with the provisions of the Charter of the United Nations.

Article 2

1. Each State Party to the present Covenant undertakes to respect and to ensure to all individuals within its territory and subject to its jurisdiction the rights recognised in the present Covenant, without distinction of any kind, such as race, colour, sex, language, religion, political or other opinion, national or social origin, property, birth or other status.

2. Where not already provided for by existing legislative or other measures, each State Party to the present Covenant undertakes to take necessary steps, in accordance with its constitutional processes and with the provisions of the present Covenant, to adopt such legislative or other measures as may be necessary to give the rights recognised in the present Covenant.

3. Each State party to the present Covenant undertakes:

(a) To ensure that any person whose rights or freedoms as herein recognised are violated shall have an effective remedy, notwithstanding that the violation has been committed by person acting in an official capacity;

(b) To ensure that any person claiming such a remedy shall have his right thereto determined by competent judicial, administrative or legislative authorities, or by any other competent authority provided for by the legal system of the State, and to develop the possibilities of judicial remedy;

(c) To ensure that the competent authorities shall enforce such remedies when granted.

Article 3

The States Parties to the present Covenant undertake to ensure the equal right of men and women to the enjoyment of all civil and political rights set forth in the present Covenant.

Article 4

1. In time of public emergency which threatens the life of the nation and the existence of which is officially proclaimed, the States Parties to the present Covenant may take measures derogating from their obligations under the present Covenant to the extent strictly required by the exigencies of the situation, provided that such measures are not inconsistent with their other obligations under international law and do not involve discrimination solely on the ground of race, colour, sex, language, religion or social origin.

2. No derogation from articles 6, 7, 8 (paragraphs 1 and 2), 11, 15, 16 and 18 may be made under this provision.

3. Any State Party to the present Covenant availing itself of the right of derogation shall immediately inform the other States Parties to the present Covenant, through the intermediary of the Secretary-General of the United Nations, of the provisions from which it has derogated and of the reasons by which it was actuated. A further communication shall be made, through the same intermediary, on the date on which it terminates such derogation.

Article 5

1. Nothing in the present Covenant may be interpreted as implying for any State, group or person any right to engage in any activity or perform any act aimed at the destruction of any of the rights and freedoms recognised herein or at their limitation to a greater extent than is provided for in the present Covenant.

2. There shall be no restriction upon derogation from any of the fundamental human rights recognised or existing in any State Party to the present Covenant pursuant to law, conventions, regulations or custom on the pretext that the present Covenant does not recognise such rights or that it reognises them to a lesser extent.

Article 6

1. Every human being has the inherent right to life. This right shall be protected by law. No one shall be arbitrarily deprived of his life.

2. In countries which have not abolished the death penalty, sentence of death may be imposed only for the most serious crimes in accordance with the law in force at the time of the commission of the crime and not contrary to the provisions of the present Covenant

and to the Convention on the Prevention and Punishment of Crime of Genocide. This penalty can only be carried out to a final judgement rendered by a competent court.

3. When deprivation of life constitutes the crime of genocide, it is understood that nothing in this article shall authorise any State Party to the present Covenant to derogate in any way from any obligation assumed under the provisions of the Convention on the Prevention and Punishment of the Crime of Genocide.

4. Anyone sentenced to death shall have the right to seek pardon or commutation of the sentence. Amnesty, pardon or commutation of the sentence of death may be granted in all cases.

5. Sentence of death shall not be imposed for crimes committed by persons below eighteen years of age and shall not be carried out on pregnant women.

6. Nothing in this article shall be invoked to delay or to prevent the abolition of capital punishment by any State Party to the present Covenant.

Article 7

No one shall be subjected to torture or to cruel, inhuman or degrading treatment or punishment. In particular, no one shall be subject without his free consent to medical or scientific experimentation.

Article 8

1. No one shall be held in slavery; slavery and the slave-trade in all their forms shall be prohibited.

2. No one shall be held in servitude.

3. (a) No one shall be required to perform forced or compulsory labour;

(b) Paragraph 3 (a) shall not be held to preclude, in countries where imprisonment with hard labour may be imposed as a punishment for a crime, the performance of hard labour in pursuance of a sentence to such punishment by a competent court;

(c) For the purpose of this paragraph the term "forced or compulsory labour" shall not include:

(i) Any work or service, not referred to in subparagraph (b), normally required of a person who is under detention in consequence of a lawful order of a court, or of a person during conditional release from such detention;

(ii) Any service of a military character and, in countries where conscientious objection is recognised, any national service required by law of conscientious objectors;

(iii) Any service exaced in cases of emergency or calamity threatening the life or well-being of the community;

(iv) Any work or service which forms part of normal civil obligations.

Article 9

1. Everyone has the right to liberty and security of person. No one shall be subjected to arbitrary arrest or detention. No one shall be deprived of his liberty except on such grounds and in accordance with such procedure as are established by law.

2. Anyone who is arrested shall be informed, at the time of arrest, of the reasons for his arrest and shall be promptly informed of any charges against him.

3. Anyone arrested or detained on a criminal charge shall be brought promptly before a judge or other officer authorised by law to exercise judicial power and shall be entitled to trial within a reasonable time or to release. It shall not be the general rule that persons awaiting trial shall be detained in custody, but release may be subject to guarantees to appear for trial, at any other stage of the judicial proceedings, and, should occasion arise, for execution of the judgement.

4. Anyone who is deprived of his liberty by arrest or detention shall be entitled to take proceedings before a court, in order that court may decide without delay on the lawfulness of his detention and order his release if the detention is not lawful.

5. Anyone who has been the victim of unlawful arrest or detention shall have an enforceable right to compensation.

Article 10

1. All persons deprived of their liberty shall be treated with humanity and with respect for the inherent dignity of the human person.

2. (a) Accused persons shall, save in exceptional circumstances, be segregated from convicted persons and shall be subject to separate treatment appropriate to their status as unconvicted persons;

(b) Accused juvenile persons shall be separated from adults and brought as speedily as possible for adjudication.

3. The penitentiary system shall comprise treatment of prisoners the essential aim of which shall be their reformation and social rehabilitation. Juvenile offenders shall be segregated from adults and be accorded treatment appropriate to their age and legal status.

Article 11

No one shall be imprisoned merely on the ground of inability to fulfil a contractual obligation.

Article 12

1. Everyone lawfully within the territory of a state shall, within that territory, have the right to liberty of movement and freedom to choose his residence.

2. Everyone shall be free to leave any country, including his own.

3. The above-mentioned rights shall not be subject to any restrictions except those which are provided by law, are necessary to protect national security, public order *(ordre public)*, public health or morals or the rights and freedoms of others, and are consistent with the other rights recognised in the present Covenant.

4. No one shall be arbitrary deprived of the right to enter his own country.

Article 13

An alien lawfully in the territory of a State Party to the present Covenant may be expelled therefrom only in pursuance of a decision reached in accordance with law and shall, except where compelling reasons of national security otherwise require, be allowed to submit the reasons against his expulsion and to have his case reviewed by, and be represented for the purpose before, the competent authority or a person or persons especially designated by the competent authority.

Article 14

1. All persons shall be equal before the courts and tribunals. In the determination of any criminal charge against him, or of his rights and obligations in a suit at law, everyone shall be entitled to a fair and public hearing by a competent, independent and impartial tribunal established by law. The press and the public may be excluded from all or part of a trial for reasons of morals, public order

(*ordre public*) or national security in a democratic society, or when the interest of the private lives of the parties so requires, or to the extent strictly necessary in the opinion of the court in special circumstances where publicity would prejudice the interests of justice; but any judgement rendered in a criminal case or in a suit at law shall be made public except where the interest of juvenile persons otherwise requires or the proceedings concern matrimonial disputes or the guardianship of children.

2. Everyone charged with a criminal offence shall have the right to be presumed innocent until proved guilty according to law.

3. In the determination of any criminal charge against him, everyone shall be entitled to the following minimum guarantees, in full equality:

(a) To be informed promptly and in detail in a language which he understands of the nature and cause of the charge against him;
(b) To have adequate time and facilities for the preparation of his defence and to communicate with counsel of his own choosing;
(c) To be tried without undue delay;
(d) To be tried in presence, and to defend himself in person or through legal assistance of his own choosing; to be informed, if he does not have legal assistance, of this right; and to have legal assistance assigned to him, in any case where the interests to justice so require, and without payment by him in any such case if he does not have sufficient means to pay for it;
(e) To examine, or have examined, the witnesses against him and to obtain the attendance and examination of witnesses on his behalf under the same conditions as witnesses against him;
(f) To have the free assistance of an interpreter if he cannot understand or speak the language used in court;
(g) Not to be compelled to testify against himself or to confess guilt.

4. In the case of juvenile persons, the procedure shall be such as will take account of their age and the desirability of promoting their rehabilitation.

5. Everyone convicted of a crime shall have the right to his conviction and sentence being reviewed by a higher tribunal according to law.

6. When a person has by a final decision been convicted of a criminal offence and when subsequently his conviction has been reversed or he has been pardoned on the ground that a new or newly discovered fact shows conclusively that there has been a miscarriage of justice, the person who has suffered punishment as a result of such conviction shall be compensated according to law, unless it is proved that the non-disclosure of the unknown fact in time is wholly or partly attributable to him.

7. No one shall be liable to be tried or punished again for an offence for which he has already been finally convicted or acquitted in accordance with the law and penal procedure of each country.

Article 15

1. No one shall be held guilty of any criminal offence on account of any act or ommission which did not constitute a criminal offence, under national or international law, at the time when it was committed. Nor shall a heavier penalty be imposed than the one that was applicable at the time when the criminal offence was committed. If, subsequent to the commission of the offence, provision is made by law for the imposition of the lighter penalty, the offender shall benefit thereby.

2. Nothing in this article shall prejudice the trial and punishment of any person for any act or omission which, at the time when it was committed, was criminal according to the general principles of law recognised by the community of nations.

Article 16

Everyone shall have the right to recognition everywhere as a person before the law.

Article 17

1. No one shall be subjected to arbitrary or unlawful interference with his privacy, family, home or correspondence, nor to unlawful attacks on his honour and reputation.

2. Everyone has the right to the protection of the law against such interference or attacks.

Article 18

1. Everyone shall have the right to freedom of thought, conscience and religion. This right shall include freedom to have or

to adopt a religion or belief of his choice, and freedom, either individually or in community with others and in public or private, to manifest his religion or belief in worship, observance, practice and teaching.

2. No one shall be subject to coercion which would impair his freedom to have or to adopt a religion or belief of his choice.

3. Freedom to manifest one's religion or beliefs may be subject only to such limitations as are prescribed by law and are necessary to protect public safety, order, health, or morals or the fundamental rights and freedoms of others.

4. The State Parties to the present Covenant undertake to have respect for the liberty of parents and, when applicable, legal guardians to ensure the religious and moral education of their children in conformity with their own convictions.

Article 19

1. Everyone shall have the right to hold opinions without interference.

2. Everyone shall have the right to freedom of expression; this right shall include freedom to seek, receive and impart information and ideas of all kinds, regardless of frontiers, either orally, in writing or in print, in the form of art, or through any other media of his choice.

3. The exercise of the rights provided for in Paragraph 2 of this article carries with it special duties and responsibilites. It may therefore be subject to certain restrictions, but these shall only be such as are provided by law and are necessary:

(a) For respect of the rights or reputations of others;

(b) For the protection of national security or of public order (*ordre public*), or of public health or morals.

Article 20

1. Any propaganda for war shall be prohibited by law.

2. Any advocacy of national, racial or religious hatred that constitutes incitement to discrimination, hostility or violence shall be prohibited by law.

Article 21

The right of peaceful assembly shall be recognised. No restrictions may be placed on the exercise of this right other than those imposed in conformity with the law and which are necessary in a democratic society in the interests of national security or public safety, public order *(ordre public)*, the protection of public health or morals or the protection of the rights and freedoms of others.

Article 22

1. Everyone shall have the right to freedom of association with others, including the right to form and join trade unions for the protection of his interests.

2. No restrictions may be placed on the exercise of this right other than those which are prescribed by law and which are necessary in a democratic society in the interests of national security or public safety, public order *(ordre public)*, the protection of public health or morals or the protection of the rights and freedoms of others. This article shall not prevent the imposition of lawful restrictions on members of the armed forces and of the police in their exercise of this right.

3. Nothing in this article shall authorise States Parties to the International Labour Organisation Convention of 1948 concerning Freedom of Association and Protection of the Right to Organise to take legislative measures which would prejudice, or to apply the law in such a manner as to prejudice, the guarantees provided for in that Convention.

Article 23

1. The family is the natural and fundamental group unit of society and is entitled to protection by society and the state.

2. The right of men and women of marriageable age to marry and to found a family shall be recognised.

3. No marriage shall be entered into without the free and full consent of the intending spouses.

4. States Parties to the present Covenant shall take appropriate steps to ensure equality of rights and responsibilities of spouses as to marriage, during marriage and at its dissolution. In the case of dissolution, provision shall be made for the necessary protection of any children.

Article 24

1. Every child shall have, without any discrimination as to race, colour, sex, language, religion, national or social origin,

property or birth, the right to such measures of protection as are required by his status as a minor, on the part of his family, society and the State.

2. Every child shall be registered immediately after birth and shall have a name.

3. Every child has the right to acquire a nationality.

Article 25

Every citizen shall have the right and the opportunity, without any of the distinctions mentioned in Article 2 and without unreasonable restrictions:

(a) To take part in the conduct of public affairs, directly or through freely chosen representatives;
(b) To vote and to be elected as genuine periodic elections which shall be by universal equal suffrage and shall be held by secret ballot, guaranteeing the free expression of the will of the electors;
(c) To have access, on general terms of equality, to public service in his country.

Article 26

All persons are equal before the law and are entitled without any discrimination to the equal protection of the law. In this respect, the law shall prohibit any discrimination and guarantee to all persons equal and effective protection against discrimination on any ground such as race, colour, sex, language, religion, political or other opinion, national or social origin, property, birth or other status.

Article 27

In those States in which ethnic, religious or linguistic minorities exist, persons belonging to such minorities shall not be denied the right, in community with the other members of their group, to enjoy their own culture, to profess and practise their own religion, or to use their own language.

Article 28

1. There shall be established a Human Rights Committee (hereafter referred to in the present Covenant as the Committee). It shall consist of eighteen members and shall carry out the functions hereinafter provided.

2. The Committee shall be composed of nationals of the States Parties to the present Covenant who shall be persons of high moral character and recognised competence in the field of human rights, consideration being given to the usefulness of the participation of some persons having legal experience.

3. The members of the Committee shall be elected and shall serve in their personal capacity.

Article 29

1. The members of the Committee shall be elected by secret ballot from a list of persons possessing the qualifications prescribed in article 28 and nominated for the purpose by the State Parties to the present Covenant.

2. Each State Party to the present Covenant may nominate not more than two persons. These persons shall be nationals of the nominating State.

3. A person shall be eligible for renomination.

Article 30

1. The initial election shall be held no later than six months after the date of entry into force of the present Covenant.

2. At least four months before the date of each election to the Committee, other than an election to fill a vacancy declared in accordance with article 34, the Secretary-General of the United Nations shall address a written invitation to the States Parties to the present Covenant to submit their nominations for membership of the Committee within three months.

3. The Secretary-General of the United Nations shall prepare a list in alphabetical order of all the persons thus nominated, with an indication of the States Parties which have nominated them, and shall submit it to the States Parties to the present Covenant no later than one month before the date of each election.

4. Election of the members of the Committee shall be held at a meeting of the States Parties to the present Covenant convened by the Secretary-General of the United Nations at the Headquarters of the United Nations. At that meeting, for which two thirds of the States Parties to the present Covenant shall constitute a quorum, the persons elected to the Committee shall be those nominees who obtain the largest number of votes and an absolute majority of the votes of the representatives of States Parties present and voting.

Article 31

1. The Committee may not include more than one national of the same State.

2. In the election of the Committee, consideration shall be given to equitable geographical distribution of membership and to the representation oif the different forms of civilisation and of the principal legal systems.

Article 32

1. The members of the Committee shall be elected for a term of four years. They shall be eligible for re-election if renominated. However, the terms of nine of the members elected at the first election shall expire at the end of two years; immediately after the first election, the names of these nine members shall be chosen by lot by the Chairman of the meeting referred to in Article 30, Paragraph 4.

2. Elections at the expiry of office shall be held in accordance with the preceding articles of this part of the present Covenant.

Article 33

1. If, in the unanimous opinion of the other members, a member of the Committee has ceased to carry out his functions for any cause other than absence of a temporary character, the Chairman of the Committee shall notify the Secretary. General of the United Nations, who shall then declare the seat of that member to be vacant.

2. In the event of the death or the resignation of a member of the Committee, the Chairman shall immediately notify the Secretary-General of the United Nations, who shall declare the seat vacant from the date of death or the date on which the resignation takes effect.

Article 34

1. When a vacancy is declared in accordance with Article 33 and if the term of office of the member to be replaced does not expire within six months of the declaration of the vacancy, the Secretary-General of the United Nations shall notify each of the State Parties to the present Covenant, which may within two months submit nominations in accordance with Article 29 for the purpose of filling the vacancy.

2. The Secretary-General of the United Nations shall prepare a

list in alphabetical order of the persons thus nominated and shall submit it to the States Parties to the present Covenant. The election to fill the vacancy shall then take place in accordance with the relevant provisions of this part of the present Covenant.

3. A member of the Committee elected to fill a vacancy declared in accordance with Article 33 shall hold office for the remainder of the term of the member who vacated the seat on the Committee under the provisions of that article.

Article 35

The members of the Committee shall, with the approval of the General Assembly of the United Nations, receive emoluments from United Nations resources on such terms and conditions as the General Assembly may decide having regard to the importance of the Committee's responsibilities.

Article 36

The Secretary-General of the United Nations shall provide the necessary staff and facilities for the effective performance of the functions of the Committee under the present Covenant.

Article 37

1. The Secretary-General of the United Nations shall convene the initial meeting of the Committee at the Headquarters of the United Nations.

2. After its initial meeting, the Committee shall meet at such times as shall be provided in its rules of procedure.

3. The committee shall normally meet at the Headquarters of the United Nations or at the United Nations Office at Geneva.

Article 38

Every member of the Committee shall, before taking up his duties, make a solemn declaration in open committee that he will perform his functions impartially and conscientiously.

Article 39

1. The Committee shall elect its officers for a term of two years. They may be re-elected.

2. The Committee shall establish its own rules of procedure, but these rules shall provide, *inter alia*, that:

(a) Twelve members shall constitute a quorum;
(b) Decisions of the Committee shall be made by a majority vote of the members present.

Article 40

1. The States Parties to the present Covenant undertake to submit reports on the measures they have adopted which give effect to the rights recognised herein and on the progress made in the enjoyment of those rights:

(a) Within one year of the entry into force of the present Covenant for the States Parties concerned;
(b) Thereafter whenever the Committee so requests.

2. All reports shall be submitted to the Secretary-General of the United Nations, who shall transmit them to the Committee for consideration. Reports shall indicate the factors and difficulties, if any, affecting the implementation of the present Covenant.

3. The Secretary-General of the United Nations may, after consultation with the Committee, transmit to the specialised agencies concerned copies of such parts of the reports as may fall within their field of competence.

4. The Committee shall study the reports submitted by the State Parties to the present Covenant. It shall transmit its reports, and such general comments as it may consider appropriate, to the States Parties. The Committee may also transmit to the Economic and Social Council these comments alongwith the copies of the reports it has received from States Parties to the present Covenant.

5. The States Parties to the present Covenant may submit to the Committee observations on any comments that may be made in accordance with Paragraph 4 of this Article.

Article 41

1. A State Party to the present Covenant may at any time declare under this Article that it recognises the competence of the Committee to receive and consider communications to the effect that a State Party claims that another State Party is not fulfilling its obligations under the present Covenant. Communications under this Article may be received and considered only if submitted by a State Party which has made a declaration recognising in regard to itself the competence of the Committee. No communication shall be received

by the Committee if it concerns a State Party which has not made such a declaration. Communications received under this Article shall be dealt with in accordance with the following procedure:

(a) If a State Party to the present Convenant considers that another State Party is not giving effect to the provisions of the present Covenant, it may, by written communication, bring the matter to the attention of that State Party. Within three months after the receipt of the communication the receiving State shall afford the State which sent the communication an explanation, or any other statement in writing clarifying the matter which should include, to the extent possible and pertinent, reference to domestic procedures and remedies taken, pending, or available in the matter;

(b) If the matter is not adjusted to the satisfaction of both States Parties concerned within six months after the receipt by the receiving State of the initial communication, either State shall have the right to refer the matter to the Committee, by notice given to the Committee and to the other State;

(c) The Committee shall deal with a matter referred to it only after it has ascertained that all available domestic remedies have been invoked and exhausted in the matter, in conformity with the generally recognised principles of international law. This shall not be the rule where the application of the remedies is unreasonably prolonged;

(d) The Committee shall hold closed meetings when examining communications under this article.

(e) Subject to the provisions of subparagraph (c), the Committee shall make available its good offices to the States Parties concerned with a view to a friendly solution of the matter on the basis of respect for human rights and fundamental freedoms as recognised in the present Covenant;

(f) In any matter referred to it, the Committee may call upon the States Parties concerned, referred to in subparagraph (b), to supply any relevant information;

(g) The States Parties concerned, referred to in subparagraph (b), shall have the right to be represented when the matter is being considered in the Committee and to make submissions orally and/or in writing;

(h) The Committee shall, within twelve months after the date of receipt of notice under subparagraph (b), submit a report:

(i) If a solution within the terms of subparagraph (e) is reached, the Committee shall confine its report to a brief statement of facts and of the solution reached;

(ii) If a solution within the terms of subparagraph (e) is not reached, the Committee shall confine its report to a brief statement of the facts; the written submissions and record of the oral submissions made by the States Parties concerned shall be attached to the report.

In every matter, the report shall be communicated to the State Parties concerned.

2. The provisions of this article shall come into force when ten State Parties to the present Covenant have made declarations under paragraph 1 of this article. Such declarations shall be deposited by the States Parties with the Secretary-General of the United Nations, who shall transmit copies thereof to the other States Parties. A declaration may be withdrawn at any time by notification to the Secretary-General. Such a withdrawal shall not prejudice the consideration of any matter which is the subject of a communication already transmitted under this article; no further communication by any State Party shall be received after the notification of withdrawal of the declaration has been received by the Secretary General, unless the State Party concerned has made a new declaration.

Article 42

1. (a) If a matter referred to the Committee in accordance with Article 41 is not resolved to the satisfaction of the States Parties concerned, the Committee may, with he prior consent of the States Parties concerned, appoint an *ad hoc* Conciliation Commission (hereinafter referred to as the Commission). The good offices of the Commission shall be made available to the States Parties concerned with a view to an amicable solution of the matter on the basis of respect for the present Covenant;

(b) The Commission shall consist of five persons acceptable to the States Parties concerned. If the States Parties concerned fail to reach agreement within three months on all or part of the composition of the Commission, the members of the Commission concerning whom no agreement has been reached shall be elected by secret ballot by a two-thirds majority vote of the Committee from among its members.

2. The members of the Commission shall serve in their personal

capacity. They shall not be nationals of the States Parties concerned, or of a State not Party to the present Covenant, or of a State Party which has not made a declaration under Article 41.

3. The Commission shall elect its own Chairman and adopt its own rules of procedure.

4. The meetings of the Commission shall normally be held at the Headquarters of the United Nations or at the United Nations Office at Geneva. However, they may be held at such other convenient places as the Commission may determine in consultation with the Secretary-General of the United Nations and the States Parties concerned.

5. The secretariat provided in accordance with Article 36 shall also service the commissions appointed under this article.

6. The information received and collected by the Committee shall be made available to the Commission and the Commission may call upon the States Parties concerned to supply any other relevant information.

7. When the Commission has fully considered the matter, but in any event not later than twelve months after having been seized of the matter, it shall submit to the Chairman of the Committee a report for communication to the State Parties concerned.

(a) If the Commission is unable to complete its consideration of the matter within twelve months, it shall confine its report to a brief statement of the status of its consideration of the matter;

(b) If an amicable solution to the matter on the basis of respect for human rights as recognised in the present Covenant is reached, the Commssion shall confine its report to a brief statement of the facts and of the solution reached;

(c) If a solution within the terms of subparagraph (b) is not reached, the Commission report shall embody its findings on all questions of fact relevant to the issues between the States Parties concerned, and its views on the possibilities of an amicable solution of the matter. This report shall also contain the written submissions and a record of the oral submissions made by the States Parties concerned.

(d) If the Commission's report is submitted under subparagraph (c), the States Parties concerned shall, within three months of the receipt of the report, notify the Chairman of the Committee whether or not they accept the contents of the report of the Commission.

8. The provisions of this article are without prejudice to the responsibilities of the Committee under Article 41.

9. The States Parties concerned shall share equally all the expenses of the members of the Commission in accordance with estimates to be provided by the Secretary-General of the United Nations.

10. The Secretary-General of the United Nations shall be empowered to pay the expenses of the members of the Commission, if necessary, before reimbursement by the States Parties concerned, in accordance with paragraph 9 of this article.

Article 43

The members of the Committee, and of the *ad hoc* conciliation commissions which may be appointed under Article 42, shall be entitled to the facilities, privileges, and immunities of experts on mission for the United Nations as laid down in the relevant sections of the Convention on the Privileges and Immunities of the United Nations.

Article 44

The provisions of the implementation of the present Covenant shall apply without prejudice to the procedures prescribed in the field of human rights by or under the constituent instruments and the conventions of the United Nations and of the specialized agencies and shall not prevent the States Parties to the present Covenant from having recourse to other procedures for settling a dispute in accordance with general or special international agreements in force between them.

Article 45

The Committee shall submit to the General Assembly of the United Nations, through the Economic and Social Council, an annual report on its activities.

Article 46

Nothing in the present Covenant shall be interpreted as impairing the provisions of the Charter of the United Nations and of the Constitutions of the specialised agencies which define the respective responsibilities of the various organs of the United Nations and of the specialized agencies in regard to the matters dealt with in the present Covenant.

Article 47

Nothing in the present Covenant shall be interpreted as impairing the inherent right of all peoples to enjoy and utilise full and freely their natural wealth and resources.

Article 48

1. The present Covenant is open for signature by any State Member of the United Nations or member of any of its specialised agencies, by any State Party to the Statute of the International Court of Justice, and by any other State which has been invited by the General Assembly of the United Nations to become a Party to the present Covenant.

2. The present Covenant is subject to ratification. Instruments of ratification shall be deposited with the Secretary-General of the United Nations.

3. The present Covenant shall be open to accession by any State referred to in paragraph 1 of this article.

4. Accession shall be effected by the deposit of an instrument of accession with the Secretary-General of the United Nations.

5. The Secretary-General of the United Nations shall inform all States which have signed this Covenant or acceded to it of the deposit of each instrument of ratification or accession.

Article 49

1. The present Covenant shall enter into force three months after the date of the deposit with the Secretary-General of the United Nations of the thirty-fifth instrument of ratification or instrument of accession.

2. For each State ratifying the present Covenant or acceding to it after the deposit of the thirty-fifth instrument of ratification or instrument of accession, the present Covenant shall enter into force three months after the date of the deposit of its own instrument of ratification or instrument of accession.

Article 50

The provisions of the present Covenant shall extend to all parts of federal States without any limitations or exceptions.

Article 51

1. Any State Party to the present Covenant may propose an amendment and file it with the Secretary-General of the United Nations. The Secretary-General of the United Nations shall thereupon communicate any proposed amendments to the States Parties to the present Covenant with a request that they notify him whether they favour a conference of States Parties for the purpose of considering and voting upon the proposals. In the event that at least one third of the States Parties favours such a conference, the Secretary-General shall convene the conference under the auspices of the United Nations. Any amendment adopted by a majority of the States Parties present and voting at the conference shall be submitted to the General Assembly of the United Nations for approval.

2. Amendments shall come into force when they have been approved by the General Assembly of the United Nations and accepted by a two-thirds majority of the States Parties to the present Covenant in accordance with their respective constitutional processes.

3. When amendments come into force, they shall be binding on those States Parties which have accepted them, other States Parties still being bound by the provisions of the present Covenant and any earlier amendment which they have accepted.

Article 52

Irrespective of the notifications made under article 48, paragraph 5, the Secretary-General of the United Nations shall inform all States referred to in paragraph 1 of the same article of the following particulars:

(a) Signatures, ratifications and accessions under Article 48;
(b) The date of the entry into force of the present Covenant under Article 49 and the date of the entry into force of any amendments under Article 51.

Article 53

1. The present Covenant, of which the Chinese, English, French, Russian and Spanish texts are equally authentic, shall be deposited in the archives of the United Nations.

2. The Secretary-General of the United Nations shall transmit certified copies of the present Covenant to all States referred to in Article 48.

INTERNATIONAL COVENANT ON ECONOMIC, SOCIAL AND CULTURAL RIGHTS, 1966

Adopted and opened for signature, ratification and accession by General Assembly resolution 2200 A (XXI) of 16 December 1966

Entry into Force: 3 January 1976, in Accordance with Article 27

Preamble

THE STATES PARTIES TO THE PRESENT COVENANT,

Considering that, in accordance with the principles proclaimed in the Charter of the United Nations, recognition of the inherent dignity and of the equal and inalienable rights of all members of the human family is the foundation of freedom, justice and peace in the world,

Recognizing that these rights derive from the inherent dignity of the human person,

Recognizing that, in accordance with the Universal Declaration of Human Rights, the ideal of free human beings enjoying freedom from fear and want can only be achieved if conditions are created whereby everyone may enjoy his economic, social and cultural rights, as well as his civil and political rights,

Considering the obligation of State under the Charter of the United Nations to promote universal respect for, and observance of, human rights and freedoms,

Realising that the individual, having duties to other individuals and to the community to which he belongs is under a responsibility to strive for the promotion and observance of the rights recognised in the present Covenant,

Agree upon the following articles:

Article 1

1. All peoples have the right of self-determination. By virtue of that right they freely determine their political status and freely pursue their economic, social and cultural development.

2. All peoples may, for their own ends, freely dispose of their natural wealth and resources without prejudice to any obligations arising out of international economic cooperation, based upon the principle of mutual benefit, and international law. In no case may a people be deprived of its own means of subsistence.

3. The States Parties to the present Covenant, including those having responsibility for the administration of Non-Self-Governing and Trust Territories, shall promote the realisation of the right of self-determination, and shall respect that right, in conformity with the provisions of the Charter of the United Nations.

Article 2

1. Each State Party to the present Covenant undertakes to take steps, individually and through international assistance and cooperation, especially economic and technical, to the maximum of its available resources, with a view to achieving progressively the full realisation of the rights recognised in the present Covenant by all appropriate means, including particularly the adoption of legislative measures.

2. The State Parties to the Covenant undertake to guarantee that the rights enunciated in the present Covenant will be exercised without discrimination of any kind as to race, colour, sex, language, religion, political or other opinion, national or social origin, property, birth or other status.

3. Developing countries, with due regard to human rights and their national economy, may determine to what extent they would guarantee the economic rights recognised in the present Covenant, to non-nationals.

Article 3

The State Parties to the present Covenant undertake to ensure the equal right of men and women to the enjoyment of all economic, social and cultural rights set forth in the present Covenant.

Article 4

The States Parties to the present Covenant recognise that, in the enjoyment of those rights provided by the State in conformity with the present Covenant, the State may subject such rights only to such limitations as are determined by law only in so far as this may be compatible with the nature of these rights and solely for the purpose of promoting the general welfare in a democratic society.

Article 5

1. Nothing in the present Covenant may be interpreted as

implying for any State, group or person any right to engage in any activity or to perform any act aimed at the destruction of any of the rights or freedoms recognised herein, or at their limitation to a greater extent than is provided for in the present Covenant.

2. No restriction upon or derogation from any of the fundamental human rights recognised or existing in any country in virtue of law, conventions, regulations or custom shall be admitted on the pretext that the present Covenant does not recognise such rights or that it recognises them to a lesser extent.

Article 6

1. The State Parties to the present Covenant recognise the right to work, which include the right of everyone to the opportunity to gain his living by work which he freely chooses or accepts, and will take appropriate steps to safeguard this right.

2. The steps to be taken by a State Party to the present Covenant to achieve the full realisation of this right shall include technical and vocational guidance and training programmes, policies and techniques to achieve steady economic, social and cultural development and full and productive employment under conditions safeguarding fundamental political and economic freedoms to the individual.

Article 7

The State Parties to the present Covenant recognise the right of everyone to the enjoyment of just and favourable conditions of work which ensure, in particular:

(a) Remuneration which provides all workers, as a minimum, with:

  (i) Fair wages and equal remuneration for work of equal value without distinction of any kind, in particular women being guaranteed conditions of work not inferior to those enjoyed by men, with equal pay for equal work;

  (ii) A decent living for themselves and their families in accordance with the provisions of the present Covenant;

(b) Safe and healthy working conditions;

(c) Equal opportunity for everyone to be promoted in his employment to an appropriate level, subject to no consideration other than those of seniority and competence;

(d) Rest, leisure and reasonable limitation of working hours and periodic holidays with pay, as well as remuneration for public holidays.

Article 8

1. The States Parties to the present Covenant undertake to ensure:

(a) The right of everyone to form trade unions and join the trade union of his choice, subject only to the rules of the organisation concerned, for the promotion and protection of his economic and social interests. No restrictions may be placed on the exercise of this right other than those prescribed by law and which are necessary in a democratic society in the interests of national security or public order or for the protection of the rights and freedoms of others;

(b) The right of trade unions to establish national federations or confederations and the right of the latter to form or join international trade union organisations;

(c) The right of trade unions to function freely subject to no limitations other than those prescribed by law and which are necessary in democratic society in the interests of national security or public order or for the protection of the rights and freedoms of others;

(d) The right to strike, provided that it is exercised in conformity with the laws of the particular country.

2. This article shall not prevent the imposition of lawful restrictions on the exercise of these rights by members of the armed forces or of the police or of the administration of the State.

3. Nothing in this article shall authorise State Parties to the International Labour Organisation Convention of 1948 concerning Freedom of Association and Protection of the Right to Organise to take legislative measures which would prejudice, or apply the law in such a manner as would prejudice, the guarantees provided for in that Convention.

Article 9

The State Parties to the present Covenant recognise the right of everyone to social security, including social insurance.

Article 10

The State Parties to the present Covenant recognise that :

1. The widest possible protection and assistance should be accorded to the family, which is the natural and fundamental group unit of society, particularly for its establishment and while it is responsible for the care and education of dependent children. Marriage must be entered into with the free consent of the intending spouses.

2. Special protection should be accorded to mothers during a reasonable period before and after childbirth. During such period working mothers should be accorded paid leave or leave with adequate social security benefits.

3. Speical measures of protection and assistance should be taken on behalf of all children and young persons without any discrimination for persons of parentage or other conditions. Children and young persons should be protected from economic and social exploitation. Their employment in work harmful to their morals or health or dangerous to life or likely to hamper their normal development should be punishable by law. States should also set age limits below which the paid employment of child labour should be prohibited and punishable by law.

Article 11

1. The States Parties to the present Covenant recognise the right of everyone to an adequate standard of living for himself and his family, including adequate food, clothing and housing, and to the continuous improvement of living conditions. The States Parties will take appropriate steps to ensure the realisation of this right, recognising to this effect the essential importance of international cooperation based on free consent.

2. The State Parties to the present Covenant, recognising the fundamental right of everyone to be free from hunger, shall take, individually and through international cooperation the measures, including specific programmes, which are needed:

(a) To improve methods of production, conservation and distribution of food by making full use of technical and scientific knowledge, by disseminating knowledge of the principles of nutrition and by developing or reforming agrarian systems in such a way as to achieve the most efficient development and utilisation of natural resources;

(b) Taking into account the problems of both food-importing and food-exporting countries, to ensure an equitable distribution of world food supplies in relation to need.

Article 12

1. The State Parties to the present Covenant recognise the right of everyone to the enjoymemt of the highest attainable standard of physical and mental health.

2. The steps to be taken by the State Parties to the present Covenant to achieve the full realisation of this right shall include those necessary for:

(a) The provision for the reduction of the stillbirth rate and of infant mortality and for the healthy development of the child;

(b) The improvement of all aspects of environmental and industrial hygiene;

(c) The prevention, treatment and control of epidemic, endemic, occupational and other diseases;

(d) The creation of conditions which would assure ot all medical service and medical attention in the event of sickness.

Article 13

1. The State Parties to the present Covenant recognise the right of everyone to education. They agree that education shall be directed to the full development of the human personality and the sense of its dignity, and shall strengthen the respect for human rights and fundamental freedoms. They further agree that education shall enable all persons to participate effectively in a free society, promote understanding, tolerance and friendship among all nations and all racial, ethnic or religious groups, and further the acitivities of the United Nations for the maintenance of peace.

2. The States Parties to the present Covenant recognise that, with a view to achieving the full realisation of this right:

(a) Primary education shall be compulsory and available free to all;

(b) Secondary education in its different forms, including technical and vocational secondary education, shall be made generally available and accessible to all by every appropriate means, and in particular by the progressive introduction of free education;

(c) Higher education shall be made equally accessible to all, on the basis of capacity, by every appropriate means, and in particular by the progressive introduction of free education;

(d) Fundamental education shall be encouraged or intensified as far as possible for those persons who have not received or completed the whole period of their primary education;

(e) The development of a system of schools at all levels shall be actively pursued, an adequate fellowship system shall be established, and the material conditions of teaching staff shall be continuously improved.

3. The State Parties to the present Covenant undertake to have respect for the liberty of parents and, when applicable, legal guardians to choose for their children schools, other than those established by the public authorities, which conform to such minimum educational standards as may be laid down or approved by the State and to ensure the religious and moral education of their children in conformity with their own convictions.

4. No part of this article shall be construed so as to interfere with the liberty of individuals and bodies to establish and direct educational institutions, subject always to the observance of the principles set forth in paragraph 1 of this article and to the requirement that the education given in such institutions shall conform to such minimum standards as may be laid down by the State.

Article 14

Each State Party to the present Covenant which, at the time of becoming a Party, has not been able to secure in its metropolitan territory or other territories under its jurisdiction compulsory primary education, free of charge, undertakes, within two years, to work out and adopt a detailed plan of action for the progressive implementation, within a reasonable number of years, to be fixed in the plan, of the principle of compulsory education free of charge for all.

Article 15

The States Parties to the present Covenant recognise the right of everyone:

(a) To take part in cultural life;
(b) To enjoy the benefits of scientific progress and its applications;
(c) To benefit from the protection of the moral and material interests resulting from any scientific, literary or artistic production of which he is the author.

2. The steps to be taken by the State Parties to the present Covenant to achieve the full realisation of this right shall include those necessary for the conservation, the development and the diffusion of science and culture.

3. The States Parties to the present Covenant undertake to respect the freedom indispensable for scientific research and creative activity.

4. The States Parties to the present Covenant recognise the benefits to be derived from the encouragement and development of international contacts and co-operation in the scientific and cultural fields.

Article 16

1. The States Parties to the present Covenant undertake to submit in conformity with this part of the Covenant reports on the measures which they have adopted and the progress made in achieving the observance of rights recognised herein.

2. (a) All reports shall be submitted to the Secretary-General of the United Nations, who shall transmit copies to the Economic and Social Council for consideration in accordance with the provisions of the present Covenant;

(b) The Secretary-General of the United Nations shall also transmit to the specialised agencies copies of the reports, or any relevant parts therefrom, from States Parties to the present Covenant which are also members of these specialised agencies insofar as these reports, or parts therefrom, relate to any matters which fall within the responsibilities of the said agencies in accordance with their constitutional instruments.

Article 17

1. The States Parties to the present Covenant shall furnish their reports in stages, in accordance with a programme to be established by the Economic and Social Council within one year of the entry into force of present Covenant after consultation with the State Parties and the specialised agencies concerned.

2. Reports may indicate factors and difficulties affecting the degree of fulfilment of obligations under the present Covenant.

3. Where relevant information has previously been furnished to the United Nations or to any specialised agency by any State Party to the present Covenant, it will not be necessary to reproduce that information, but a precise reference to the information so furnished will suffice.

Article 18

Pursuant to its responsibilities under the Charter of the United Nations in the field of human rights and fundamental freedoms, the Economic and Social Council may make arrangements with the specialised agencies in respect of their reporting to it on the progress made in achieving the observance of the provisions of the present Covenant falling within the scope of their activities. These reports may include particulars of decisions and recommendations on such implementation adopted by their competent organs.

Article 19

The Economic and Social Council may transmit to the Commission on Human Rights for study and general recommendation or, as appropriate, for information the reports concerning human rights submitted by States in accordance with articles 16 and 17, and those concerning human rights submitted by the specialised agencies in accordance with Article 18.

Article 20

The States Parties to the present Covenant and the specialised agencies concerned may submit comments on the Economic and Social Council on any general recommendation under Article 19 or reference to such general recommendation in any report of the Commission on Human Rights or any documentation referred to therein.

Article 21

1. The Economic and Social Council may submit from time to time to the General Assembly reports with recommendations of a general nature and a summary of the information received from the States Parties to the present Covenant and the specialised agencies on the measures taken and the progress made in achieving general observance of the rights recognised in the present Covenant.

Article 22

The Economic and Social Council may bring to the attention of other organs of the United Nations, their subsidiary organs and specialised agencies concerned with furnishing technical assistance any matters arising out of the reports referred to in this part of the present Covenant which may assist such bodies in deciding, each within its field of competence, on the advisability of international measures likely to contribute to the effective progressive implementation of the present Covenant.

Article 23

The States Parties to the present Covenant agree that international action for the achievement of the rights recognised in the present Covenant includes such methods as the conclusion of conventions, the adoption of recommendations, the furnishing of technical assistance and the holding of regional meetings and technical meetings for the purpose of consultation and study organised in conjunction with the Governments concerned.

Article 24

Nothing in the present Covenant shall be interpreted as impairing the provisions of the Charter of the United Nations and of the constitutions of the specialised agencies which define the respective responsibilities of the various organs of the United Nations and of the specialised agencies in regard to the matters dealt within the present Covenant.

Article 25

Nothing in the present Covenant shall be interpreted as impairing the inherent right of all peoples to enjoy and utilise fully and freely their natural wealth and resources.

Article 26

1. The present Covenant is open for signature by any State Member of the United Nations or member of any of its specialised agencies, by any State Party to the Statute of the International Court of Justice and by any other State which has been invited by the General Assembly of the United Nations to become a party to the present Covenant.

2. The present Covenant is subject to ratification. Instruments of ratification shall be deposited with the Secretary-General of the United Nations.

3. The present Covenant shall be open to accession by any State referred to in paragraph 1 of this article.

4. Accession shall be effected by the deposit of an instrument of accession with the Secretary-General of the United Nations.

5. The Secretary-General of the United Nations shall inform all States which have signed the present Covenant or acceded to it of the deposit of each instrument of ratification or accession.

Article 27

1. The present Covenant shall enter into force three months after the date of the deposit with the Secretary-General of the United Nations of the thirty-fifth instrument of ratification or instrument of accession.

2. For each State ratifying the present Covenant or acceding to it after the deposit of the thirty-fifth instrument of ratification or instrument of accession, the present Covenant shall enter into force three months after the date of the deposit of its own instrument of ratification or instrument of accession.

Article 28

The provisions of the present Covenant shall extend to all parts of federal States without any limitations or exceptions.

Article 29

1. Any State Party to the present Covenant may propose an amendment and file it with the Secretary-General of the United Nations. The Secretary-General shall thereupon communicate any proposed amendments to the State Parties to the present Convenant

with a request that they notify him whether they favour a conference of States Parties for the purpose of considering and voting upon the proposals. In the event that at least one-third of the State Parties favour such a conference, the Secretary-General shall convene the conference under the auspices of the United Nations. Any amendment adopted by a majority of the State Parties present and voting at the conference shall be submitted to the General Assembly of the United Nations for approval.

2. Amendments shall come into force what they have been approved by the General Assembly of the United Nations and accepted by a two-thirds majority of the States Parties to the present Covenant in accordance with their respective constitutional processes.

3. When amendments come into force they shall be binding on those States Parties which have accepted them, other States Parties still being bound by the provisions of the present Covenant and any earlier amendment which they have accepted.

Article 30

Irrespective of the notification made under Article 26, Paragraph 5, the Secretary-General of the United Nations shall inform all States referred to in Paragraph 1 of the same article of the following particulars:

(a) Signatures, ratifications and accessions under Article 26;

(b) The date of the entry into force of the present Covenant under article 27 and the date of the entry into force of any amendments under Article 29.

Article 31

1. The present Covenant, of which the Chinese, English, French, Russian and Spanish texts are equally authentic, shall be deposited in the archives of the United Nations.

2. The Secretary-General of the United Nations shall transmit certified copies of the present Covenant to all States referred to in Article 26.

2

Indian Constitution and Human Rights

INDIAN NATIONAL CONGRESS—KARACHI RESOLUTION, 1931

In order to end the exploitation of the masses, political freedom must include real economic freedom of the starving millions. The Congress, therefore, declares that any constitution which may be agreed to on its behalf should provide, or enable the Swaraj Government to provide, for the following:

1. Fundamental rights of the people, including:

   (i) freedom of association and combination;
   (ii) freedom of speech and of the press;
   (iii) freedom of conscience and the free profession and practice of religion, subject to public order and morality;'
   (iv) protection of the culture, language, and scripts of the minorities;
   (v) equal rights and obligations of all citizens, without any bar on account of sex;
   (vi) no disability to attach to any citizen by reason of his or her religion, caste or creed or sex in regard to public employment, office of power or honour, and in the exercise of any trade or calling;
   (vii) equal right to all citizens in regard to public roads, wells, schools and other places of public resort;
   (viii) right to keep and bear arms in accordance with regulations and reservations made in that behalf;
   (ix) no person shall be deprived of his liberty nor shall his dwelling or property be entered, sequestered or confiscated, save in accordance with law.

2. Religious neutrality on the part of the State.

3. Adult suffrage.
4. Free primary education.
5. A living wage for industrial workers, limited hours of labour, healthy conditions of work, protection against the economic consequences of old age, sickness and unemployment.
6. Labour to be freed from serfdom or conditions bordering on serfdom.
7. Protection of woman workers, and, specially, adequate provisions for leave during maternity period.
8. Prohibition against employment of children of school going age in factories.
9. Right of labour to form unions to protect their interests with suitable machinery for settlement of disputes by arbitration.
10. Substantial reduction in agricultural rent or revenue paid by the peasantry and in case of uneconomic holdings exemption from rent for such period as may be necessary, relief being given to small zamindars wherever necessary by reason of such reduction.
11. Imposition of a progressive income tax on agricultural income above a fixed minimum.
12. A graduated inheritance tax.
13. Military expenditure to be reduced by at least one half of the present scale.
14. Expenditure and salaries in civil department to be largely reduced. No servant of the State, other than specially employed expects and the like, to be paid above a certain fixed figure which should not ordinarily exceed Rs. 500 per month.
15. Protection of indigenous cloth by exclusion of foreign cloth and foreign yarn from the country.
16. Total prohibition of intoxicating drinks and drugs.
17. No duty on salt manufactured in India.
18. Control, over exchange and currency policy so as to help Indian industries and bring relief to the masses.
19. Control by the State of key industries and ownership of mineral resources.
20. Control of usury—direct or indirect.

THE CONSTITUTION OF INDIA

Preamble

WE THE PEOPLE OF INDIA

having solemnly resolved to constitute India into a

[SOVEREIGN SOCIALIST SECULAR DEMOCRATIC REPUBLIC]

and to secure to all its citizens:

JUSTICE, social, economic and political:

LIBERTY of thought, expression, belief, faith and worship:

EQUALITY of status and of opportunity:

and to promote among them all

FRATERNITY assuming the dignity of the individual and the [unity and integrity of the Nation]:

IN OUR CONSTITUENT ASSEMBLY

this twenty-sixth day of November, 1949, do

HEREBY ADOPT, ENACT AND GIVE TO OURSELVES THIS CONSTITUTION.

FUNDAMENTAL RIGHTS, 1950

General

12. Definition. In this Part, unless the context otherwise requires, " the State" includes the Government and Parliament of India and the Government and the Legislature of each of the States and all local or other authorities within the territory of India or under the control of the Government of India.

13. Laws Inconsistent with or in Derogation of the Fundamental Rights. 1. All laws in force in the territory of India immediately before the commencement of this Constitution, in so far as they are inconsistent with the provisions of this Part, shall, to the extent of such inconsistency, be void.

2. The State shall not make any law which takes away or abridges the rights conferred by this Part and any law made in contravention of this clause shall, to the extent of the contravention, be void.

3. In this article, unless the context otherwise requires.—

(a) "law" includes any Ordinance, order, bye-law, rule regulation, notification, custom or usage having in the territory of India the force of law;

(b) "laws in force" includes laws passed or made by a Legislature or other competent authority in the territory of India before the commencement of this Constitution and not previously repealed, notwithstanding that any such law or any part thereof may not be then in operation either at all or in particular areas.

4. Nothing in this article shall apply to any amendment of this Constitution made under Article 368.

Right to Equality

14. Equality Before Law. The State shall not deny to any person equality before the law or the equal protection of the laws within the territory of India.

15. Prohibition of Discrimination on Grounds of Religion, Race, Caste, Sex or Place of Birth. 1. The State shall not discriminate against any citizen on grounds only of religion, race, caste, sex, place of birth or any of them.

2. No citizen shall, on grounds only of religion, race, caste, sex,

place of birth or any of them, be subject to any disability, liability, restriction or conditions with regard to—

(a) access to shops, public restaurants, hotels and places of public entertainment; or

(b) the use of wells, tanks, bathing ghats, roads and places of public resort maintained wholly or party out of State funds or dedicated to the use of the general public.

3. Nothing in this article shall prevent the State from making any special provision for women and children.

4. Nothing in this article or in clause (2) of Article 29 shall prevent the State from making any special provision for the advancement of any socially and educationally backward classes of citizens or for the Scheduled Castes and the Scheduled Tribes.]

16. Equality of Opportunity in Matters of Public Employment. 1. There shall be equality of opportunity for all citizens in matters relating to employment or appointment to any office under the State.

2. No citizen shall, on grounds only of religion, race, caste, sex, descent, place of birth, residence or any of them, be ineligible for, or discriminated against in respect of, any employment or office under the State.

3. Nothing in this article shall prevent Parliament from making any law prescribing, in regard to a class or classes of employment or appointment to an office [under the Government of, or any local or other authority within, a State or Union territory, any requirement as to residence within that State or Union territory] prior to such employment or appointment.

4. Nothing in this article shall prevent the State from making any provision for the reservation of appointments or posts in favour of any backward class of citizens which, in the opinion of the State, is not adequately represented in the services under the State.

5. Nothing in this article shall affect the operation of any law which provides that the incumbent of an office in connection with the affairs of any religious or denominational institution or any member of the governing body thereof shall be a person professing a particular religion or belonging to a particular denomination.

17. Abolition of Untouchability. "Untouchability" is abolished and its practice in any form is forbidden. The enforcement of any disability arising out of "Untouchability" shall be an offence punishable in accordance with law.

18. Abolition of Titles. 1. No title, not being a military or academic distinction, shall be conferred by the State.

2. No citizen of India shall accept any title from any title from any foreign State.

3. No person, who is not a citizen of India shall, while he holds any office of profit or trust under the State, accept without the consent of the President any title from any foreign State.

4. No person holding any office of profit or trust under the State shall, without the consent of the President, accept any present, emolument, or office of any kind from or under any foreign State.

Right to Freedom

19. Protection of Certain Rights Regarding Freedom of Speech, etc. 1. All citizens shall have the right—

(a) to freedom of speech and expression;
(b) to assemble peaceably and without arms;
(c) to form association or unions;
(d) to move freely throughout the territory of India;
(e) to reside and settle in any part of the territory of India; and,
(g) to practise any profession, or to carry on any occupation, trade or business.

[2. Nothing in sub-clause (a) of clause (1) shall affect the operation of any existing law, or prevent the State from making any law, insofar as such law imposes reasonable restrictions on the exercise of the right conferred by the said sub-clauses in the interests of [the sovereignty and integrity of India,] the security of the State , friendly relations with foreign States, public order, decency or morality, or in relation to contempt of court, defamation or incitement to an offence.]

3. Nothing in sub-clause (b) of the said clause shall affect the operation of any existing law insofar as it imposes, or prevent the State from making any law imposing, in the interests of [the sovereignty and integrity of India or] public order, reasonable restrictions on the exercise of the right conferred by the said sub-clause.

4. Nothing in sub-clause (c) of the said clause shall affect the operation of any existing law in so far as it imposes, or prevent the State from making any law imposing, in the interests of [the sovereignty and integrity of India or] public order or morality,

reasonable restrictions on the exercise of the right conferred by the said sub-clause.

5. Nothing in [sub-clauses (d) and (e)] of the said clause shall affect the operation of any existing law in so far as it imposes, or prevent the State from making any law imposing, reasonable restrictions on the exercise of any of the rights conferred by the said sub-clause either in the interests of the general public or for the protection of the interests of any Scheduled Tribe.

6. Nothing in sub-clause (g) of the said clause shall affect the operation of any existing law in so far as it imposes, or prevent the State from making any law imposing, in the interests of the general public, reasonable restrictions on the exercise of the rights conferred by the said sub-clause, and, in particular, [nothing in the said sub-clause shall affect the operation of any existing law in so far as it relates to, or prevent the State from making any law relating to.—

(i) the professional or technical qualifications necessary for practising any profession or carrying on any occupation, trade or business, or

(ii) the carrying on by the State, or by a corporation owned or controlled by the State, of any trade, business, industry or service, whether to the exclusion, complete or partial, of citizens or otherwise].

20. Protection in Respect of Conviction for Offences. 1. No person shall be convicted of any offence except for violation of a law in force at the time of the commission of the act charged as an offence, nor be subjected to a penalty greater than that which might have been inflicted under the laws in force at the time of the commission of the offence.

2. No person shall be prosecuted and punished for the same offence more than once.

3. No person accused of any offence shall be compelled to be a witness against himself.

21. Protection of Life and Personal Liberty. No person shall be deprived of his life or personal liberty except according to procedure established by law.

22. Protection Against Arrest and Detention in Certain Cases. 1. No person who is arrested shall be detained in custody without being informed, as soon as may be, of the grounds for such arrest nor shall he be denied the right to consult, and to be defended by, a legal practitioner of his choice.

2. Every person who is arrested and detained in custody shall be produced before the nearest magistrate within a period of twenty-four hours of such arrest excluding the time necessary for the journey from the place of arrest to the court of the magistrate and no such person shall be detained in custody beyond the said period without the authority of a magistrate.

3. Nothing in clauses (1) and (2) shall apply—

(a) to any person who for the time being is an enemy alien; or

(b) to any person who is arrested or detained under any law providing for preventive detention.

4. No law providing for preventive detention shall authorise the detention of a person for a longer period than three months unless—

(a) an Advisory Board consisting of persons who are, or have been, or are qualified to be appointed as Judges of a High Court has reported before the expiration of the said period of three months that there is in its opinion sufficient cause for such detention:

Provided that nothing in this sub-clause shall authorise the detention of any person beyond the maximum period prescribed by any law made by Parliament under sub-clause (b) of clause (7); or

(b) such person is detained in accordance with the provisions of any law made by Parliament under sub-clauses (a) and (b) of clause (7).

5. When any person is detained in pursuance of an order made under any law providing for preventive detention, the authority making the order shall, as soon as may be, communicate to such person the grounds on which the order has been made and shall afford him the earliest opportunity of making a representation against the order.

6. Nothing in clause (5) shall require the authority making any such order as is referred to in that clause to disclose facts which such authority considers to be against the public interest to disclose.

7. Parliament may by law prescribe—

(a) the circumstances under which, and the class or classes of cases in which, a person may be detained for a period longer than three months under any law providing for preventive detention without obtaining the opinion of an Advisory Board in accordance with the provisions of sub-clause (a) of clause (4):

(b) the maximum period for which any person may in any class or classes of cases be detained under any law providing for preventive detention; and

(c) the procedure to be followed by an Advisory Board in an inquiry under sub-clause (a) of clause (4).

Right Against Exploitation

23. ***Prohibition of Traffic in Human Beings and Forced Labour.*** 1. Traffic in human beings and *begar* and other similar forms of forced labour are prohibited and any contravention of this provision shall be an offence punishable in accordance with law.

2. Nothing in this article shall prevent the State from imposing compulsory service for public purposes, and in imposing such service the State shall not make any discrimination on grounds only of religion, race, caste or class or any of them.

24. Prohibition of Employment of Children in Factories, etc. No child below the age of fourteen years shall be employed to work in any factory or mine or engaged in any other hazardous employment.

Right to Freedom of Religion

25. Freedom of Conscience and Free Profession, Practice and Propagation of Religion. 1. Subject to public order, morality and health and to the other provisions of this Part, all persons are equally entitled to freedom of conscience and the right freely to profess, practise and propagate religion.

2. Nothing in this article shall affect the operation of any existing law or prevent the State from making any law—

(a) regulating or restricting any economic, financial, political or other secular activity which may be associated with religious practice;

(b) providing for social welfare and reform or the throwing open of Hindu religious institutions of a public character to all classes and sections of Hindus.

Explanation I.—The wearing and carrying of *kirpans* shall be deemed to be included in the profession of the Sikh religion.

Explanation II.—In sub-clause (b) of clause (2), the reference to Hindus shall be construed as including a reference to persons professing the Sikh, Jaina or Buddhist religion, and the reference to Hindu religious institutions shall be construed accordingly.

26. Freedom to Manage Religious Affairs. Subject to public order, morality and health, every religious denomination or any section thereof shall have the right—

(a) to establish and maintain institutions for religious and charitable purpose;
(b) to manage its own affairs in matters of religion;
(c) to own and acquire movable and immovable property; and
(d) to administer such property in accordance with law.

27. Freedom as to Payment of Taxes for Promotion of any Particular Religion. No person shall be compelled to pay any taxes, the proceeds of which are specifically appropriated in payment of expenses for the promotion or maintenance of any particular religion or religious denomination.

28. Freedom as to Attendance at Religious Instruction or Religious Worship in Certain Educational Institutions. 1. No religious instruction shall be provided in any educational institution wholly maintained out of State funds.

2. Nothing in clause (1) shall apply to an educational institutions which is administered by the State but has been established under any endowment or trust which requires that religious instruction shall be imparted in such institution.

3. No person attending any educational institution recognised by the State or receiving aid out of State funds shall be required to take part in any religious instruction that may be imparted in such institution or to attend any religious worship that may be conducted in such institution or in any premises attached thereto unless such person or, if such person is a minor, his guardian has given his consent thereto.

Cultural and Educational Rights

29. Protection of Interests of Minorities. 1. Any section of the citizens residing in the territory of India or any part thereof having a distinct language, script or culture of its own shall have the right to conserve the same.

2. No citizen shall be denied admission into any educational institution maintained by the State or receiving aid out of State funds on grounds only of religion, race, caste, language or any of them.

30. Right of Minorities to Establish and Administer Educational Institutions. 1. All minorities, whether based on religion or language, shall have the right to establish and administer educational institutions of their choice.

[(1A) In making any law providing for the compulsory acquisition of any property of an educational institution established and administered by a minority, referred to in clause (1), the State shall ensure that the amount fixed by or determined under such law for the acquisition of such property is such as would not restrict or abrogate the right guaranteed under that clause.]

2. The State shall not, in granting aid to educational institutions, discriminate against any educational institution on the ground that it is under the management of a minority, whether based on religion or language.

31. *[Compulsory acquisition of property] Rep. by the Constitution (Forty-fourth Amendment) Act, 1978,* s. 6 (w.e.f. 20-6-1979).

[Saving of Certain Laws]

[31A. Saving of Laws Providing for Acquisition of Estates, etc. [(1) Notwithstanding anything contained in Article 13, no law providing for—

(a) the acquisition by the State of any estate or of any right therein or the extinguishment or modification of any such rights, or
(b) the taking over of the management of any property by the State for a limited period either in the public interest or in order to secure the proper management of the property, or
(c) the amalgamation of two or more corporations either in the public interest or in order to secure the proper management of any of the corporations, or
(d) the extinguishment or modification of any rights of managing agents, secretaries and treasurers, managing directors, directors or mangers of corporations, or of any voting rights of shareholders thereof, or

(e) the extinguishment or modification of any rights accruing by virtue of any agreement, lease or licence for the purpose of searching for, or winning, any mineral or mineral oil, or the premature termination of cancellation of any such agreement, lease or licence.

shall be deemed to be void on the ground that it is consistent with, or takes away or abridges any of the rights conferred by [Article 14 or Article 19]:

Provided that where such law is a law made by the Legislature of a State, the provisions of this article shall not apply thereto unless such law, having been reserved for the consideration of the President, has received his assent:]

[Provided further that where any law makes any provision for the acquisition by the State of any estate and where any land comprised therein is held by a person under his personal cultivation, it shall not be lawful for the State to acquire any portion of such land as is within the ceiling limit applicable to him under any law for the time being in force or any building or structure standing, thereon or appurtenant thereto, unless the law relating to the acquisition of such land, building or structure, provides for payment of compensation at a rate which shall not be less than the market value thereof.]

(2) In this article—

[(a) the expression "estate" shall, in relation to any local area, have the same meaning as that expression or its local equivalent has in the existing law relating to land tenures in force in that area and shall also include—

(i) any *jagir*, *inam* or *muafi* or other similar grant and in the States of [Tamil Nadu] and Kerala, any *janman* right;
(ii) any land held under ryotwari settlement;
(iii) any land held or let for purposes of agriculture or for purposes ancillary thereto, including waste land, forest land, land for pasture or sites of buildings and other structures occupied by cultivators of land, agricultural labourers and village artisans;]

(b) the expression "rights", in relation to an estate, shall include any rights vesting in proprietor, sub-proprietor, under-proprietor, tenure-holder, *[raiyat, under-raiyat]* or other intermediary and any rights or privileges in respect of land revenue.]

[***31B. Validation of Certain Acts and Regulations.*** Without prejudice to the generality of the provisions contained in Article 31 A. None of the Acts and Regulations specified in the Ninth Schedule nor any of the provisions thereof shall be deemed to be void, or ever to have become void, on the ground that such Act, Regulation or provision is inconsistent with, or takes away or abridge any of the rights conferred by, any provisions of this Part, and notwithstanding any judgment, decree or order of any court or tribunal to the contrary, each of the said Acts and Regulations shall, subject to the power of any competent Legislature to repeal or amend it, continue in force.]

[***31C. Saving of Laws Giving Effect to Certain Directive Principles.*** Notwithstanding anything contained in Article 13, no law giving effect to the policy of the State towards securing [all or any of the principles laid down in Part IV] shall be deemed to be void on the ground that it is inconsistent with, or takes away or abridges any of the rights conferred by [Article 14 or Article 19]; *and no law containing a declaration that it is for giving effect to such policy shall be called in question in any court on the ground that it does not give effect to such policy:*

Provided that where such law is made by the Legislature of a State, lthe provisions of this article shall not apply thereto unless such law, having been reserved for the consideration of the President, had received his assent.]

31D. [*Saving of laws in respect of anti-national activities.*] *Rep. by the Constitution (Forty-third Amendment) Act,* 1977. s. 2 (w.e.f 13-4-1978).

Right to Constitutional Remedies

32. Remedies for Enforcement of Rights Conferred by This Part. 1. The right to move the Supreme Court by appropriate proceedings for the enforcement of the rights conferred by this Part is guaranteed.

2. The Supreme Court shall have power to issue directions or orders or writs, including writs in the nature of *habeas corpus, mandamus, prohibition, quo warranto* and *certiorari,* whichever may be appropriate, for the enforcement of any of the rights conferred by this part.

3. Without prejudice to the powers conferred on the Supreme Court by clauses (1) and (2), Parliament may by law empower any

other court to exercise within the local limits of its jurisdiction all or any of the powers exercisable by the Supreme Court under clause (2).

4. The right guaranteed by this article shall not be suspended except as otherwise provided for by this Constitution.

32.A*[Constitutional validity of State laws not to be considered in proceedings under Article 32.] Rep. by the Constitution (Forty-third Amendment) Act,* 1977, s. 3 (w.e.f. 13-4-1978).

*[33. **Power of Parliament to Modify the Rights Conferred by this Part in Their Application to Forces, etc.*** Parliament may, by law, determine to what extent any of the rights conferred by this Part shall, in their application to—

(a) the members of the Armed Forces; or
(b) the members of the Forces charged with the maintenance of public order; or
(c) persons employed in any bureau or other organisation established by the State for purposes of intelligence or counter-intelligence; or
(d) persons employed in, or in connection with, the telecommunications system set up for the purposes of any Force, bureau or organisation referred to in clauses (a) to (c).

be restricted or abrogated so as to ensure the proper discharge of their duties and the maintenance of discipline among them.]

34. Restriction on Rights Conferred by this Part While Martial Law is in Force in Any Area. Notwithstanding anything in the foregoing provisions of this Part, Parliament may by law indemnify any person in the service of the union or of a State or any other person in respect of any act done by him in connection with the maintenance or restoration of order in any area within the territory of India where martial law was in force or validate any sentence passed, punishment inflicted, forfeiture ordered or other act done under martial law in such area.

35. Legislation to Give Effect to the Provisions of This Part— *Notwithstanding anything in this Consitution—*

(a) Parliament shall have, and the Legislature of a State shall not have, power to make laws—

  (i) with respect to any of the matters which under clause (3) of Article 16, clause (3) of Article 32, Article 33 and Article 34 may be provided for by law made by Parliament; and

(ii) for prescribing punishment for those acts which are declared to be offences under this Part;

and parliament shall, as soon as may be after the commencement of this Constitution, make laws for prescribing punishment for the acts referred to in sub-clause (ii);

(b) any law in force immediately before the commencement of this Constitution in the territory of India with respect to any of the matters referred to in sub-clause (i) of clause (a) or providing for punishment for any act referred to in sub-clause (ii) of that clause shall, subject to the terms thereof and to any adaptations and modifications that may be made therein under Article 372, continue in force until altered or repealed or amended by Parliament

Explanation.—In this article, the expression "law in force" has the same meaning as in Article 372.

DIRECTIVE PRINCIPLES OF STATE POLICY, 1950

36. Definition. In this part, unless the context otherwise requires, "the State" has the same meaning as in Part III.

37. Application of the Principles Contained in This Part. The provisions contained in this Part shall not be enforceable by any court, but the principles therein laid down are nevertheless fundamental in the governance of the country and it shall be the duty of the State to apply these principles in making laws.

38. State to Secure a Social Order for the Promotion of Welfare of the People. 1. The State shall strive to promote the welfare of the people by securing and protecting as effectively as it may a social order in which justice, social, economic and political, shall inform all the institutions of the national life.

[2. The State shall, in particular, strive to minimise the inequalities in income, and endeavour to eliminate inequalities in status, facilities and opportunities, not only amongst individuals but also amongst groups of people residing in different areas or engaged in different vocations.]

39. Certain Principles of Policy to be Followed by the State. The State shall, in particular, direct its policy towards securing—

(a) that the citizens, men and women equally, have the right to an adequate means of livelihood;

(b) that the ownership and control of the material resources of the community are so distributed as best to subserve the common good;

(c) that the operation of the economic system does not result in the concentration of wealth and means of production to the common detriment;

(d) that there is equal pay for equal work for both men and women;

(e) that the health and strength of workers, men and women, and the tender age of children are not abused and that citizens are not forced by economic necessity to enter avocations unsuited to their age or strength;

[(f) that children are given opportunities and facilities to develop in a healthy manner and in conditions of freedom and dignity and that childhood and youth are protected against exploitation and against moral and material abandonment.]

39A. Equal Justice and Free Legal Aid. The State shall secure that the operation of the legal system promotes justice, on the basis of equal opportunity, and shall, in particular, provide free legal aid, by suitable legislation or schemes or in any other way, to ensure that opportunities for securing justice are not denied to any citizen by reason of economic or other disabilities.]

40. Organisation of Village Panchayats. The State shall take steps to organise village panchayat and endow them with such powers and authority as may be necessary to enable them to function as units of self-government.

41. Right to Work, to Education and to Public Assistance in Certain Cases. The State shall, within the limits of its economic capacity and development, make effective provision for securing the right to work, to education and to public assistance in cases of unemployment, old age, sickness and to public assistance in cases of unemployment, old age, sickness and disablement, and in other cases of undeserved want.

42. Provision for Just and Human Conditions of Work and Maternity Relief. The State shall make provision for securing just and humane conditions of work and for maternity relief.

43. Living Wage, etc., for Workers. The State shall endeavour to secure by suitable legislation or economic organisation or in any other way, to all workers, agricultural, industrial or otherwise, work, a living wage, conditions of work ensuring a decent standard of life and full enjoyment of leisure and social and cultural opportunities and, in particular, the State shall endeavour to promote cottage industries on an individual or co-operative basis in rural areas.

[43A. Participation of Workers in Management of Industries. The State shall take steps, by suitable legislation or in any other way, to secure the participation of workers in the management of undertakings, establishments or other organisations engaged in any industry.]

44. Uniform Civil Code for the Citizens. The State shall endeavour to secure for the citizens a uniform civil code throughout the territory of India.

45. Provision for Free and Compulsory E ducation for Children. The State shall endeavour to provide, within a period of ten years from the commencement of this Constitution, for free and compulsory education for all children until they complete the age of fourteen years.

46. Promotion of Educational and Economic Interests of Scheduled Castes, Scheduled Tribes and Other Weaker Sections. The State shall promote with special care the educational and economic interests of the weaker sections of the people, and, in particular, of the Scheduled Castes and the Scheduled Tribes, and shall protect them from social injustice and all forms of exploitation.

47. Duty of the State to Raise the Level of Nutrition and the Standard of Living and to Improve Public Health. The State shall regard the raising of the level of nutrition and the standard of living of its people and the improvement of public health as among its primary duties and, in particular, the State shall endeavour to bring about prohibition of the consumption except for medicinal purposes of intoxicating drinks and of drugs which are injurious to health.

48. Organisation of Agriculture and Animal Husbandry. The State shall endeavour to organise agriculture and animal husbandry on modern and scientific lines and shall, in particular, take steps for preserving and improving the breeds, and prohibiting the slaughter, of cows and calves and other milch and draught cattle.

[48A. Protection and Improvement of Environment and Safeguarding of Forests and Wildlife. The State shall endeavour to protect and improve the environment and to safeguard the forests and wild life of the country.]

49. Protection of Monuments and Places and Objects of National Importance. It shall be the obligation of the State to protect every monument or place or object of artistic or historic interest, [declared by or under law made by Parliament] to be of national importance, from spoilation, disfigurement, destruction, removal, disposal or export, as the case may be.

50. Separation of Judiciary from Executive. The State shall take steps to separate the judiciary from the executive in the public services of the State.

51. Promotion of International Peace and Security. The State shall endeavour to—

(a) promote international peace and security;
(b) maintain just and honourable relations between nations;
(c) foster respect for international law and treaty obligations in the dealings of organised peoples with one another; and
(d) encourage settlement of international disputes by arbitration.

FUNDAMENTAL DUTIES

*51A. **Fundamental Duties.*** It shall be the duty of every citizen of India—

(a) to abide by the Consitution and respect its ideals and institutions, the National Flag and the National Anthem;

(b) to cherish and follow the noble ideals which inspired our national struggle for freedom;

(c) to uphold and protect the sovereignty, unity and integrity of India;

(d) to defend the country and render national service when called upon to do so;

(e) to promote harmony and the spirit of common brotherhood amongst all the people of India transcending religious, linguistic and regional or sectional diversities; to renounce practices derogatory to the dignity of women;

(f) to value and preserve the right heritage of our composite culture;

(g) to protect and improve the natural environment including forests, lakes, rivers and wild life, and to have compassion for living creatures;

(h) to develop the scientific temper, humanism and the spirit of inquiry and reform;

(i) to safeguard public property and to abjure violence;

(j) to strive towards excellence in all spheres of individual and collective activity so that the nation constantly rises to higher levels of endeavour and achievement.

CONSTITUTION OF INDIA

(Extracts)

5. Citizenship at the Commencement of the Constitution. At the commencement of this Constitution, every person, who has his domicile in the territory of India and—

(a) who was born in the territory of India; or

(b) either of whose parents was born in the territory of India; or

(c) who has been ordinarily resident in the territory of India for not less than five years immediately preceding such commencement, shall be a citizen of India.

6. Rights of Citizenship of Certain Persons who have Migrated to India from Pakistan. Notwithstanding anything in Article 5, a person who has migrated to the territory of India from the territory now included in Pakistan shall be deemed to be a citizen of India at the commencement of this Constitution if—

(a) he or either of his parents or any of his grand-parents was born in India as defined in the Government of India Act, 1935 (as originally enacted); and

(b) (i) in the case, where such a person has so migrated, before the nineteenth day of July 1948, he has been ordinarily resident in the territory of India since the date of his migration, or

(ii) in the case, where such person has so migrated on or after the nineteenth day of July 1948, he has been registered as a citizen of India by an officer appointed in that behalf by the Government of the Dominion of India on an application made by him therefor to such officer before the commencement of this Constitution in the form and manner prescribed by that Government:

Provided that no person shall be so registered unless he has been resident in the territory of India for at least six months immediately preceding the date of his application.

7. Rights of Citizenship of Certain Migrants to Pakistan. Notwithstanding anything in Articles 5 and 6, a person who has after the first day of March 1947, migrated from the territory of India to the territory now included in Pakistan shall not be deemed to be a citizen of India:

Provided that nothing in this Article shall apply to a person who, after having so migrated to the territory now included in Pakistan, has returned to the territory of India under a permit for resettlement of permanent return issued by or under the authority of any law and every such person shall for the purposes of clause (b) of Article 6 be deemed to have migrated to the territory of India after nineteenth day of July, 1948.

8. Rights of Citizenship of Certain Persons of Indian Origin Residing Outside India. Notwithstanding anything in Article 5, any person who or either of whose parents or any of whose grandparents was born in India as defined in the Government of India Act, 1935, (as originally enacted) and who is ordinarily residing in any country outside India as so defined shall be deemed to be a citizen of India if he has been registered as a citizen of India by the diplomatic or consular representative of India in the country where he is for the time being residing on an application made by him therefor to such diplomatic or consular representative whether or after the commencement of this Constitution, in the form and manner prescribed by the Government of the Dominion of India or the Government of India.

9. Persons Voluntarily Acquiring Citizenship of a Foreign State not to be Citizens. No person shall be a citizen of India by virtue of Article 5, or be deemed to be a citizen of India by virtue of Article 6 and Article 8, if he has voluntarily acquired the citizenship of any foreign State.

10. Continuance of the Rights of Citizenship. Every person who is or is deemed to be a citizen of India under any of the foregoing provisions of this Part shall, subject to the provisions of any law that may be made by Parliament, continue to be such citizen.

11. Parliament to Regulate the Right of Citizenship by Law. Nothing in the foregoing provisions of this Part shall derogate from the power of Parliament to make any provision with respect to the acquisition and termination of citizenship and all other matters relating to citizenship.

12. Definition. In this Part, unless the context otherwise requires, "the State" includes the Government.and Parliament of India and the Government and the Legislature of each of the States and all local or other authorities within the territory of India or under the control of the Government of India.

13. Laws Inconsistent with or in Derogation of the Fundamental Rights. 1. All laws in force in the territory of India immediately before the commencement of this Constitution, in so far as they are inconsistent with the provisions of this Part, shall, to the extent of such inconsistency, be void.

2. The State shall not make any law which takes away or abridge the rights conferred by this Part and any law made in contravention of this clause shall, to the extent of the contravention, be void.

3. In this Article, unless the context otherwise requires,—

(a) "law" includes any ordinance, order, by-law, rule, regulation, notification, custom or usage having in the territory of India, the force of law;

(b) "laws in force" includes laws passed or made by a Legislature or other competent authority in the territory of India before the commencement of this Constitution and not previously repealed, notwithstanding that any such law or any part thereof may not be then in operation either at all or in particular areas.

4. Nothing in this Article shall apply to any amendment of this Constitution made under Article 368.

15. Prohibition of Discrimination on Grounds of Religion, Race, Caste, Sex or Place of Birth. 1.The State shall not discriminate against any citizen on grounds only of religion, race, caste, sex, place of birth or any of them.

2. No citizen shall, on grounds only of religion, race, caste, sex, place of birth or any of them, be subject to any disability, liability, restriction or condition with regard to—

(a) access to shops, public restaurants, hotels and places of public entertainment; or

(b) the use of wells, tanks, bathing *ghats*, roads and places of public resort maintained wholly or partly out of State funds or dedicated to the use of the general public.

3. Nothing in this Article shall prevent the State from making any special provision for women and children.

4. Nothing in this Article or in clause (2) of Article 29 shall prevent the State from making any special provision for the

advancement of any socially and educationally backward classes of citizens or for the Scheduled Castes and the Scheduled Tribes.

16. Equality of Opportunity in Matters of Public Employment. 1. There shall be equality of opportunity for all citizens in matters relating to employment or appointment to any office under the State.

2. No citizen shall, on grounds only of religion, race, caste, sex, descent, place of birth, residence or any of them, be ineligible for, or discriminated against in respect of, any employment or office under the State.

3. Nothing in this Article shall prevent Parliament from making any law prescribing, in regard to a class or classes of employment or appointment to an office, under the Government of, or any local or other authority within a State or Union Territory, any requirement as residence within that State or Union Territory, prior to such employment or appointment.

4. Nothing in this Article shall prevent the State from making any provision for the reservation of appointments or posts in favour of any Backward Class of citizens which, in the opinion of the State, is not adequately represented in the services under the State.

4-A. Nothing in this Article shall prevent the State from making any provision for reservation in matters of promotion to any class or classes of posts in the service under the State in favour of the Scheduled Castes and the Scheduled Tribes which, in the opinion of the State, are not adequately represented in the services under the State.

5. Nothing in this Article shall affect the operation of any law which provides that the incumbent of an office in connection with the affairs of any religious or denominational institution or any member of the governing body thereof, shall be a person professing a particular religion or belonging to a particular denomination.

17. Abolition of Untouchability. "Untouchability" is abolished and its practice in any form is forbidden. The enforcement of any disability arising out of 'untouchability' shall be an offence punishable in accordance with law.

18. Abolition of Titles. 1. No title, not being a military or academic distinction, shall be conferred by the State.

2. No citizen of India shall accept any title from any foreign States.

3. No person, who is not a citizen of India shall, while he holds

any office of profit or trust under the State, accept without the consent of the President any title from any foreign State.

4. No person holding any office of profit or trust under the State shall without the consent of the President, accept any present, emolument, or office of any kind from or under any foreign State.

19. Protection of Certain Rights Regarding Freedom of Speech, etc. 1. All citizens shall have the right—

(a) to freedom of speech of expression;
(b) to assemble peaceably and without arms;
(c) to form associations of unions;
(d) to move freely throughout the territory of India;
(e) to reside and settle in any part of the territory of India; and
(f) [Omitted by Consitution (Forty-fifth Amendment) Act, 1978, Section 2 (w.e.f. 20-6-1979)].
(g) to practise any profession, or to carry on any occupation, trade or business.

2. Nothing in sub-clause (a) of clause (1) shall affect the operation of any existing law, or prevent the State from making any law, in so far as such law imposes reasonable restrictions on the exercise of the right conferred by the said sub-clause in the interests of (the sovereignty and integrity of India), the security of the State, friendly relations with foreign States, Public order, decency or morality, or in relation to contempt of Court, defamation or incitement to an offence.

3. Nothing in sub-clause (b) of the said clause shall affect the operation of any existing law in so far as imposes, or prevents the State from making any law imposing, the interests of, the sovereignty and integrity of India or, Public order, reasonable restrictions on the exercise of the right conferred by the said sub-clause.

4. Nothing in sub-clause (c) of the said clause shall affect the operation of any existing law in so far as it imposes, or prevent the State from making any law imposing, in the interests of the sovereignty and integrity of India, or public order or morality, reasonably restrictions on the exercise of the right conferred by the said sub-clause.

5. Nothing in [sub-clauses (d) and (ee)], of the said clause shall affect the operation of any existing law in so far as imposes, or prevent, the State from making any law imposing, reasonable restrictions of the exercise of any of the rights conferred by the said

sub-clause either in the interests of the general public or for the protection of the interests of any Scheduled Tribe.

6. Nothing in sub-clause (g) of the said clause shall affect the operation of any existing law in so far as it imposes, or prevent the State from making any law imposing, in the interests of the general public, reasonable restrictions on the exercise of the right conferred by the said sub-clause, and, in particular, (nothing in the said sub-clause shall affect the operation of any existing law in so far as it relates to, or prevent the State from making any law relating to,—

(i) the professional or technical qualification necessary for practising any profession or carrying on any occupation, trade or business, or

(ii) the carrying on by the State or by a Corporation owned or controlled by the state, or any trade, business, industry or service, whether to the exclusion, complete or partial, of citizens or otherwise.

20. Protection in Respect of Conviction for Offences. 1. No person shall be convicted of any offence except for violation of a law in force at the time of the commission of the act charged as an offence, nor be subjected to a penalty greater than that which might have been inflicted under the law in force at the time of the commission of the offence.

2. No person shall be prosecuted and punished for the same offence more than once.

3. No person accused of any offence shall be compelled to be a witness against himself.

21. Protection of Life and Personal Liberty. No person shall be deprived of his life or personal liberty except according to procedure established by law.

22. Protection Against Arrest and Detention in Certain Cases. 1. No person, who is arrested shall be detained in custody without being informed, as soon as may be, of the grounds for such arrest nor shall he be denied the right to consult, and to be defended by, a legal practitioner of his choice.

2. Every person who is arrested and detained in custody shall be produced before the nearest Magistrate within a period of twenty-four hours of such arrest excluding the time necessary for the journey from the place of arrest to Court of the Magistrate and no such person shall be detained in custody beyond the said period without the

authority of a Magistrate.

3. Nothing in clauses (1) and (2) shall apply—

(a) to any person who for the time being is an enemy alien; or

(b) to any person who is arrested or detained under any law providing for preventive detention.

4. No law providing for preventive detention shall authorise the detention of a person for a longer period than three months unless—

(a) an Advisory Board consisting of persons who are, or have been, or are qualified to be appointed as Judges of a High Court has reported before the expiration of the said period of three months that there is in its opinion sufficient cause for such detention:

Provided that, nothing in this sub-clause shall authorise the detention of any person beyond the maximum period prescribed by any law made by Parliament under sub-clause (b) of clause (7); or

(b) such person is detained in accordance with the provisions of any law made by Parliament under sub-clauses (a) and (b) and (7).

5. When any person is detained in pursuance of an order made under any law providing for preventive detention, the authority making the order shall, as soon as may be, communicate to such person the grounds on which the order has been made and shall afford him the earliest opportunity of making a representation against the order.

6. Nothing in clause (5) shall require the authority making any such order as it referred to in that clause to disclose facts which such authority considers to be against the public interest to disclose.

7. Parliament may by law prescribe—

(a) the circumstances under which, and the class or classes of cases in which, a person may be detained for a period longer than three months under any law providing for preventive detention without obtaining the opinion of an Advisory Board in accordance with the provisions of sub-clause (a) of clause (4);

(b) the maximum period for which any person may in any class or classes of cases be detained under any provision for preventive detention; and

(c) the procedure to be followed by an Advisory Board in an inquiry under sub-clause (a) of clause (4).

*23. **Prohibition of Traffic in Human Beings and Forced Labour.*** 1. Traffic in human beings and *begar* and other similar forms of forced labour are prohibited and any contravention of this provision shall be an offence punishable in accordance with law.

2. Nothing in this Article shall prevent the State from imposing compulsory service for public purposes, and in imposing such service the State shall not make any discrimination on grounds only of religion, race, caste or class or any of them.

*24. **Prohibition of Employment of Children in Factories, etc.*** No child below the age of fourteen years shall be employed to work in any factory or mine or engaged in any other hazardous employment.

*25. **Freedom of Conscience and Free Profession, Practice and Propagation of Religion.*** 1. Subject to public order, morality and health and to the other provisions of this Part, all persons are equally entitled to freedom of conscience and the right freely to profess, practice and propagate religion.

2. Nothing in this Article shall affect the operation of any existing law or prevent the State from making any law—

(a) regulating or restricting any economic, financial, political or other secular activity which may be associated with religious practice;

(b) providing for social welfare and reform or the throwing open of Hindu religious institutions of a public character to all classes and sections of Hindus.

Explanation I— The wearing and carrying of *kirpans* shall be deemed to be included in the profession of the Sikh religion.

Explanation II— In sub-clause (b) of clause (2), the reference to Hindus shall be construed as including a reference to persons professing the Sikh, Jaina or Buddhist religion, and the reference to Hindu religious institutions shall be construed accordingly.

*26. **Freedom to Manage Religious Affairs.*** Subject to public order, morality and health, every religious denomination or any section thereof shall have the right—

(a) to establish and maintain institutions for religious and charitable purposes;

(b) to manage its own affairs in matters of religion;

(c) to own and acquire movable and immovable property; and

(d) to administer such property in accordance with law.

27. Freedom as to Payment of Taxes for Promotion of any Particular Religion. No person shall be compelled to pay any taxes, the proceeds of which are specifically appropriate in payment of expenses for the promotion or maintenance of any particular religion or religious denomination.

28. Freedom as to Attendance at Religious Instruction or Religious Worship in Certain Educational Institutions. 1. No religious instruction shall be provided in any educational institution wholly maintained out of State funds.

2. Nothing in clause (1) shall apply to an educational institution which administered by the State but has been established under any endowment or trust which requires that religious instruction shall be imparted in such institution.

3. No person attending any educational institution recognised by the State or receiving aid out of State funds shall be required to take part in any religious instruction that may be conducted in such institution or in any premises attached thereto unless such person or, if such person is a minor his guardian has given his consent thereto.

29. Protection of Interests of Minorities. 1. Any section of the citizens residing in the territory of India or any part thereof having a distinct language, script or culture of its own shall have the right to conserve the same.

2. No citizens shall be denied admission into any educational institution maintained by the State or receiving aid out of State funds on grounds only of religion, race, caste, language or any of them.

30. Right of Minorities to Establish and Administer Educational Institutions. 1. All minorities, whether based on religion or language, shall have the right to establish and administer educational institutions of their choice.

1-A. In making any law providing for the compulsory acquisition of any property of an educational institution established and administered by a minority, referred to in clause (1), the State shall ensure that the amount fixed by or determined under such law for the acquisition of such property is such as would not restrict or abrogate the right guaranteed under that clause.

2. The State shall not, in granting aid to educational institutions, discriminate against any educational institution on the ground that it is under the management of a minority, whether based on religion or language.

31-A. Saving of Laws Providing for Acquisition of Estates, etc. 1. Notwithstanding anything contained in Article 13, no law providing for —

(a) the acquisition by the State of any estate or of any rights therein or the extinguishment or modification of any such rights, or

(b) the taking over the management of any property by the State for a limited period either in the public interest or in order to secure the proper management of the property, or

(c) the amalgamation of two or more corporations either in the public interest or in order to secure the proper management of any of the corporations, or

(d) the extinguishment or modification of any rights of managing agents, secretaries and treasurers, managing directors, directors or managers of corporations, or of any voting rights of shareholders thereof, or

(e) the extinguishment or modification of any rights accruing by virtue of any agreement, leases or licence for the purpose of searching for, or winning any mineral or mineral oil, or the premature termination or cancellation of any such agreement, leases or licence,

shall be deemed to be void on the grounds that it is inconsistent with, or takes away or abridges any of the rights conferred by Article 14 or Article 19:

Provided that where such law is a law made by the Legislature of a State, the provisions of this Article shall not apply thereto, unless such law, having been reserved for the consideration of the President, has received his assent:

Provided further that where any law makes any provision for the acquisition by the State of any estate and where any land comprised therein is held by a person under his personal cultivation, it shall not be lawful for the State to acquire any portion of such land as is within the ceiling limit application to him under any law for the time being in force or any building or structure standing thereon or appurtenant thereto, unless the law relating to the acquisition of such land, building or structure, provides for payment of compensation at a rate which shall not be less than the market value thereof.

2. In this Article—

(a) the expression "estate" shall, in relation to any local area, have the same meaning as that expression or his local equivalent has in the existing law relating to land tenures in force in that area and shall also include—

(i) any *Jagir, Inam* or *Muafi* or other similar grant and in the States of (Tamil Nadu) and Kerala, any *janmam* right;

(ii) any land held under *Ryotwari* settlement;

(iii) any land held or let for purposes of agriculture or for purposes ancillary thereto, including waste land, forest land, land for pasture or sites of buildings and other structures occupied by cultivators of land, agricultural labourers and village artisans;

(b) the expression "rights", in relation to an estate, shall include any rights vesting in a proprietor, sub-proprietor, under-proprietor, tenure-holder, *raiyat* under-*raiyat* or other intermediary and any rights or privileges in respect of land revenue.

131- B, Validation of Certain Acts and Regulations. Without prejudice to the generality of the provisions contained in Article 31-A, none of the Acts and Regulations specified in the Ninth Schedule nor any of the provisions thereof, shall be deemed to be void, or ever to have become void, on the ground that such Act, Regulation or provision is inconsistent with, or takes away or abridges any of the rights conferred by, any provisions of this part, and notwithstanding any judgment, decree or order of any Court or tribunal to the contrary, each of the said Acts and Regulations shall, subject to the power of any competent. Legislature to repeal or amend it, continue in force.

31-C. Saving of Laws Giving Effect to Certain Directive Principles. Notwithstanding anything contained in Article 13, no law giving effect to the policy of the State towards securing all or any of the principles laid down in Part IV shall be deemed to be void on the ground that it is inconsistent with, or takes away or abridges any of the rights conferred by, Article 14 or Article 19; and no law containing a declaration that it is for giving effect to such policy shall be called in question in any Court on the ground that it does not give effect to such policy:

Provided that where such law is made by the Legislature of a State, the provisions of this article shall not apply thereto unless such law, having been reserved for the consideration of the President, has received his assent.

32. Remedies for Enforcement of Rights Conferred by This Part. 1. The right to move the Supreme Court by appropriate proceedings for the enforcement of the rights conferred by this Part is guaranteed.

2. The Supreme Court shall have power to issue directions or orders or writs, including writs in the nature of *habeas corpus, mandamus, prohibition, quo warranto* and *certiorari,* whichever may be appropriate, for the enforcement of any of the rights conferred by this Court.

3. Without prejudice to the powers conferred on the Supreme Court by clauses (1) and (2), Parliament may by law empower any other Court to exercise within the local limits of its jurisdiction all or any of the powers exercisable by the Supreme Court under clause (2).

4. The right guaranteed by this Article shall not be suspended except as otherwise provided for by this Constitution.

39-A. Equal Justice and Free Legal Aid. The State shall secure that the operation of the legal system promotes justice, on a basis of equal opportunity and shall, in particular, provide free legal aid, by suitable legislation or schemes or in any other way, to ensure that opportunities for securing justice are not denied to any citizen by reason of economic or other disabilities..

41. Right to Work, to Education and to Public Assistance in Certain Cases. The State shall, within the limits of its economic capacity and development, make effective provision for securing the right to work, to education and to public assistance in cases of unemployment, old age, sickness and disablement, and in other cases of undeserved want.

48-A. Protection and Improvement of Environment and Safeguarding of Forests and Wildlife. The State shall endeavour to protect and improve the environment and to safeguard the forests and wildlife of the country.

50. Separation of Judiciary from Executive. The State shall take steps to separate the judiciary from the executive in the public services of the State.

51-A. Fundamental Duties. It shall be the duty of every citizen of India—

(a) to abide by the Constitution and respect its ideals and institutions, the National Flag and the National Anthem;
(b) to cherish and follow the noble ideals which inspired our national struggle for freedom;
(c) to uphold and protect the sovereignty, unity and integrity of India;
(d) to defend the country and render national service when called upon to do so;
(e) to promote harmony and the spirit of common brotherhood amongst all the people of India transcending religious, linguistic and regional or sectional diversities, to renounce practices derogatory to the dignity of women;
(f) to value and preserve the rich heritage of our composite culture;
(g) to protect and improve the natural environment including forests, lakes, rivers and wildlife, and to have compassion for living creatures;
(h) to develop the scientific temper, humanism and the spirit of inquiry and reform;
(i) to safeguard public property and to abjure violence;
(j) to strive towards excellence in all spheres of individual and collective activity so that the nation constantly rises to higher levels of endeavour and achievement.

300-A. Persons not to be Deprived of Property Save by Authority of Law. No person shall be deprived of his properly save by authority of law.

330. Reservation of Seats for Scheduled Castes and Scheduled Tribes in the House of the People. 1. Seats shall be reserved in the House of People for—

(a) The Schedule Castes;
(b) the Scheduled Tribes except the Scheduled Tribes in the autonomous districts of Assam; and
(c) the Scheduled Tribes in the autonomous districts of Assam.

2. The number of seats reserved in any State of Union Territory

for the Scheduled Castes or the Scheduled Tribes under clause (1) shall bear, as nearly as may be, the same proportion to the total number of seats allotted to that State or Union Territory in the House of the People as the population of the Scheduled Castes in the State or Union Territory or of the Scheduled Tribes in the State or Union Territory or part of the State or Union Territory, as the case may be, in respect of which seats are so reserved bears to the total population of the State or Union Territory.

3. Notwithstanding anything contained in clause (2), the number of seats reserved in the House of the People for the Scheduled Tribes in the autonomous districts of Assam shall bear to the total number of seats allotted to that State a proportion not less than the population of the Scheduled Tribes in the autonomous districts bears to the total population of the State.

Explanation—In this Article and in Article 332, the expression "population" means the population as ascertained at the last preceding census of which the relevant figures have been published.

Provided that the reference in the *Explanation* to the last preceding census of which the relevant figures have been published shall, until the relevant figures for the first census taken after the year 2000 have been published, be construed, as a reference to the 1971 Census.

331. Representation of the Anglo-Indian Community in the House of the People. Notwithstanding anything in Article 81, the President may, if he is of opinion that Anlgo-Indian community is not adequately represented in the House of the People, nominate not more than two members of that community to the House of the People.

332. Reservation of Seats for Scheduled Castes and Scheduled Tribes in the Legislative Assemblies to the States. 1. Seats shall be reserved for the Scheduled Castes and Scheduled Tribes except the Scheduled Tribes in the autonomous districts of Assam, in the Legislative Assembly of every State.

2. Seats shall be reserved also for the autonomous districts in the Legislative Assembly of the State of Assam.

3. The number of seats reserved for the Scheduled Castes or the Scheduled Tribes in the Legislative Assembly of any State under clause (1) shall bear, as nearly as may be, the same proportion to the total number of seats in the Assembly as the population of the Scheduled Castes in the State or of the Scheduled Tribes in the State or part of the State, as the case may be, in respect of which seats are

so reserved, bears to the total population of the State.

3-A. Notwithstanding anything contained in clause (3), until the taking effect, under Article 170, of the re-adjustment, on the basis of the first census after the year 2000, of the member of seats in the Legislative Assemblies of the States of Arunachal Pradesh, Meghalaya, Mizoram and Nagaland, the seats which shall be reserved for the Scheduled Tribes in the Legislative Assembly of any such State shall be,—

(a) if all the seats in the Legislative Assembly of such State in existence on the date of coming into force of the Constitution (Fifty-seventh Amendment) Act, 1987 (hereafter in this clause referred to as the existing Assembly) are held by members of the Scheduled Tribes, all the seats except one;

(b) in any other case, such number of seats as bears to the total number of seats, a proportion not less than the number (as on the said date) of members belonging to the Scheduled Tribes in the existing Assembly bears to the total number of seats in the existing Assembly.

3-B. Notwithstanding anything contained in clause (3), until the readjustment, under Article 170, takes effect on the basis of the first census after the year 2000, of the number of seats in the Legislative Assembly of the State of Tripura, the seats which shall be reserved for the Scheduled Tribes in the Legislative Assembly shall be, such number of seats as bears to the total number of seats, a proportion not less than the number, as on the date of coming into force of the Constitution (Seventy-Second Amendment) Act, 1992, of members belonging to the Scheduled Tribes in the Legislative Assembly in existence on the said date bears to the total number of seats in that Assembly.

4. The number of seats reserved for the autonomous district in the Legislative Assembly of the State of Assam shall bear to the total number of seats in that Assembly a proportion not less than the population of the district bears to the total population of the State.

5. The constituencies for the seats reserved for any autonomous district of Assam shall not comprise any area outside that district.

6. No person who is not a member of a Scheduled Tribe of any autonomous district of the State of Assam shall be eligible for election to the Legislative Assembly of the State from any constituency of that district.

333. Representation of the Anglo-Indian Community in the

Legislative Assemblies of the States. Notwithstanding anything in Article 170, the Governor of a State may if he is of opinion that the Anglo-Indian community needs representation in the Legislative Assembly of the State and is not adequately represented therein, nominate one member of that community to the Assembly.

334. Reservation of Seats and Special Representation to Cease After Fifty Years. Notwithstanding anything in the foregoing provisions of this Part, the provisions of this Constitution relating to—

(a) the reservation of seats for the Scheduled Castes and the Scheduled Tribes in the House of the People and in the Legislative Assemblies of the States; and

(b) the representation of the Anglo-Indian community in the House of the People and in the Legislative Assemblies of the States by nomination,

shall cease to have effect on the expiration of a period of fifty years from the commencement of this Constitution:

Provided that, nothing in this Article shall effect any representation in the House of the people or in the Legislative Assembly of a State until the dissolution of the then existing House of Assembly, as the case may be.

335. Claims of Scheduled Castes and Scheduled Tribes to Services and Posts. The claims of the members of Scheduled Castes and Scheduled Tribes shall be taken into consideration, consistently with the maintenance of efficiency of administration, in the making of appointments to services and posts in connection with the affairs of the Union or of a State.

336. Special Provision for Anglo-Indian Community in Certain Services. 1. During the first two years after the commencement of this Constitution, appointments of members of the Anglo-Indian community to posts in the Railway, Customs, Postal and Telegraph Services of the Union shall be made on the same basis as immediately before the fifteenth day of August, 1947.

During every succeeding period of two years, the number of posts reserved for the members of the said community in the said services shall, as nearly as possible, be less by ten per cent than the numbers so reserved during the immediately preceding period of two years:

Provided that at the end of ten years from the commencement

of this Constitution all such reservations shall cease.

2. Nothing in clause (1) shall bar the appointment of members of the Anglo-Indian community to posts other than, or in addition to, those reserved for the community under that clause if such members are found qualified for appointment on merit as compared with the members of other communities.

337. Special Provision with Respect to Educational Grants for the Benefit of Anglo-Indian Community. During the first three financial years after the commencement of this Constitution, the same grants, if any, shall be made by the Union and by each State for the benefit of the Anglo-Indian community in respect of education as were made in the financial year ending on the thirty first day of March, 1948.

During the every succeeding period of three years the grants may be less by ten per cent than those for the immediately preceding period of three years:

Provided that at the end to ten years from the commencement of this Constitution such grants, to the extent to which they are a special concession to the Anglo-Indian community, shall cease:

Provided further that no educational institution shall be entitled to receive any grant under this Article unless at least forty per cent of the annual admissions therein are made available to members of communities other than the Anglo-Indian Community.

338. National Commission for Scheduled Castes and Scheduled Tribes. 1. There shall be a Commission for the Scheduled Castes and Scheduled Tribes to be known as the National Commission for the Scheduled Castes and Scheduled Tribes.

2. Subject to the provisions of any law made in this behalf by Parliament, the Commission shall consist of a Chairperson, Vice-Chairperson and five other Members and the conditions of the service and tenure of office of the Chairperson, Vice-Chairperson and other Members so appointed shall be such as the President may by rule determine.

3. The Chairperson, Vice-Chairperson and other Members of the Commission shall be appointed by the President by warrant under his hand and seal.

4. The Commission shall have the power to regulate its own procedure.

5. It shall be the duty of Commission—

(a) to investigate and monitor all matters relating to the safeguards provided for the Scheduled Castes and Scheduled Tribes under this Commission or under any other law for the time being in force or under any order of the Government and to evaluate the working of such safeguards;

(b) to inquire into specific complaints with respect to the deprivation of rights and safeguards of the Scheduled Castes and Scheduled Tribes;

(c) to participate and advise on the planning process of socio-economic development of the Scheduled Castes and Scheduled Tribes and to evaluate the progress of their development under the Union and any States;

(d) to present to the President, annually and at such other times as the Commission may deem fit, reports upon the working of those safeguard;

(e) to make in such reports recommendations as to the measures that should be taken by the Union or any State for the effective implementation of those safeguards and other measures for the protection, welfare and socio-economic development of the Scheduled Castes and Scheduled Tribes; and

(f) to discharge such other functions in relation to the protection, welfare and development and advancement of the Scheduled Castes and Scheduled Tribes as the President may, subject to the provisions of any law made by Parliament by rule specify.

6. The President shall cause all such reports to be laid down before such House of Parliament along with a memorandum explaining the action taken or proposed to be taken on the recommendation relating to the Union and the reasons for the non-acceptance, if any, or any such recommendations.

7. Where any such report, or any part thereof, relates to any matter with which any State Government is concerned, a copy of such report shall be forwarded to the Governor of the State who shall cause it to be laid for before the Legislature of the State along with a memorandum explaining the action taken or proposed to be taken on the recommendations relating to the States and the reasons for the non-acceptance, if any, or any of such recommendations.

8. The Commission shall, while investigating any matter referred to in sub-clause (a) or inquiring into any complaint referred to in

sub-clause (b) of clause (5), have all the powers of a civil Court trying a suit and in particular in respect of the following matters, namely—

(a) summoning and enforcing the attendance of any person from any part of India and examining him on oath;
(b) requiring the discovery and production of any document;
(c) receiving evidence of affidavits;
(d) requisitioning any public record or copy thereof from any Court or office;
(e) issuing commissions for the examination of witnesses and documents;
(f) any other matter which the President may, by rule determine.

9. The Union and every State Government shall consult the Commission on all major policy matters affecting Scheduled Castes and Scheduled Tribes.

10. In this Article, references to the Scheduled Castes and Scheduled Tribes shall be construed as including references to such other backward classes as the President may, on receipt of the report of a Commission appointed under clause (1) of Article 340, by order specify and also to the Anglo-Indian community.

339. Control of the Union over the Administration of Scheduled Areas and the Welfare of Scheduled Tribes 1. The President may at any time and shall, at the expiration of ten years from the commencement of this Constitution by order appoint a Commission to report on the administration of the Scheduled Areas and the welfare of the Scheduled Tribes in the States.

The order may define the composition, powers and procedure of the Commission and may contain such incidental or ancillary provisions as the President may consider necessary or desirable.

2. the executive power of the Union shall extend to the giving of directions to a State as to the drawing up and execution of schemes specified in the direction to be essential for the welfare of the Scheduled Tribes in the State.

340. Appointment of a Commission to Investigate the Conditions of Backward Classes. 1. The President may by order appoint a Commission consisting of such persons as he thinks fit to investigate the conditions of socially and educationally backward classes within the territory of India and the difficulties under which they labour and to make recommendations as to the steps that should be taken by the Union or any State to remove such difficulties and to improve their condition and as to the grants that should be made for the purpose by the Union or any State and the conditions subject to which such grants should be made, and the order appointing such Commission shall define the procedure to be followed by the Commission.

2. A Commission so appointed shall investigate the matters referred to them and present to the President a report setting out the facts as found by them and making such recommendations as they think proper.

3. The President shall cause a copy of the report so presented together with a memorandum explaining the action taken thereon to be laid before each House of Parliament.

341. Scheduled Castes. 1. The President may with respect to any State or Union Territory, and where it is a State, after consultation with Governorthereof by public notification, specify the castes, races or tribes or parts of or groups within castes, races or tribes which shall for the purposes of this Constitution be deemed to be Scheduled Castes in relation to that State or Union Territory, as the case may be.

2. Parliament may by law include in the, or exclude from the, list of Scheduled Castes specified in a notification issued under clause (1) and caste, race or tribe, or part or group within any castes, race or tribe, but save as aforesaid a notification issued under the said clause shall not be varied by any subsequent notification.

342. Scheduled Tribes. 1. The President (may with respect to any State, or Union Territory), and where it is a State, after consultation with the Governor (thereof by public notification, specify the tribes or tribal communities or parts of or groups within tribes or tribal communities which shall for the purposes of this Constitution be deemed to be Scheduled Tribes in relation to that State (or Union Territory, as the case may be).

2. Parliament may by law include in or exclude from the list of Scheduled Tribes specified in a notification issued under clause (1) any tribe of tribal community or part of or group within any tribe or tribal community, but, save as aforesaid a notification issued under the said clause shall not be varied by any subsequent notification.

3

The Protection of Human Rights Act, 1993

PROTECTION OF HUMAN RIGHTS ACT, 1993
No. 10 of 1994
((8th January, 1994)

An act to provide for the constitution of a National Human Rights Commission, State Human Rights Commission in States and Human Rights courts for better protection of human rights and for matters connected therewith or incidental thereto.

Be it enacted by Parliament in the Forty-fourth Year of the Republic of India as follows:

PRELIMINARY

1. ***Short Title, Extent and Commencement.*** 1. This Act may be called the Protection of Human Rights Act, 1993.

2. It extends to the whole of India:

Provided that it shall apply to the State of Jammu and Kashmir only in so far as it pertains to the matters relatable to any of the entries enumerated in List I or List III in the Seventh Schedule to the Constitution as applicable to that State.

3. It shall be deemed to have come into force on the 28th day of September, 1993.

2. ***Definitions.*** 1. In this Act, unless the context otherwise requires:

(a) "armed forces" means the naval, military and air forces and includes any other armed forces of the Union;
(b) "Chairperson" means the Chairperson of the Commission or of the State Commission, as the case may be;
(c) "Commission" means the National Human Rights Commission constituted under section 3;

(d) "Human rights" means the rights relating to life, liberty, equality and dignity of the individual guaranteed by the Constitution or embodied in the International Covenants and enforceable by courts in India;

(e) "Human Rights Court" means the Human Rights Court Specified under section 30;

(f) "International Covenants" means the International Covenant on Civil and Political Rights and The International Covenant on Economic; Social and Cultural Rights adopted by the General Assembly of the United Nations on the 16th December 1966;

(g) "Member" means a Member of the Commission or of the State Commission, as the case may be and includes the Chairperson.

(h) "National Commission for Minorities" means the National Commission for Minorities constituted under Section 3 of the National Commission for Minorities Act, 1992 (9 of 1992);

(i) "National Commission for the Scheduled Castes and Scheduled Tribes" means the National Commission for the Scheduled Castes and Scheduled Tribes referred to in Article 338 of the Constitution.

(j) "National Commission for Women" means the National Commission for Women constituted under Section 3 of the National Commission for Women Act, 1990 (20 of 1990);

(k) "Notification" means a notification published in the official Gazette;

(l) "Prescribed" means prescribed by rules made under this Act;

(m) "Public servant" shall have the meaning assigned to it in section 21 of the Indian Penal Code (45 of 1860); and

(n) "State Commissions" means a State Human Rights Commission constituted under section 21.

2. Any reference in this Act to a law which is not in force in the State of Jammu and Kashmir, shall in relation to that State, be construed as a reference to a corresponding law, if any, in force in that State.

THE NATIONAL HUMAN RIGHTS COMMISSION

3. Constitution of a National Human Rights Commission. 1. The Central Government shall constitute a body to be known as the National Human Rights Commission to exercise the powers conferred upon and to perform the functions assigned to it, under this Act,

2. The Commission shall consist of:

(a) a Chairperson who has been a Chief Justice of the Supreme Court;
(b) one member who is or has been a judge of the Supreme Court;
(c) one Member who is, or has been, the Chief Justice of a High Court; and
(d) two Members to be appointed from amongst persons having knowledge of, or practical experience in, matters relating to human rights.

3. The Chairpersons of the National Commission for Minorities, the National Commission for the Scheduled Castes and Scheduled Tribes and the National Commission for Women shall be deemed to be Member of the Commission for the discharge of functions specified in clauses (b) to (j) of section 12.

4. There shall be a Secretary-General who shall be the Chief Executive Officer of the Commission and shall exercise such powers and discharge such functions of the Commission as it may delegate to him.

5. The headquarter of the Commission shall be at Delhi and the Commission may, with the previous approval of the Central Government establish offices at other places in India.

4. Appointment of Chairperson and other Members. 1. The Chairperson and other Members shall be appointed by the President by warrant under his hand and seal:

Provided that every appointment under this sub-section shall be made after obtaining the recommendation of a Committee consisting of:

(a)	the Prime Minister	Chairperson
(b)	Speaker of the House of the People	Member
(c)	Minister-in-charge of the Ministry of Home Affairs in the Government of India	Member
(d)	Leader of the Opposition of the House of the People	Member

(e) Leader of the Opposition in the Council of States — Member

(f) Deputy Chairman of the Council of States — Member

Provided further that no sitting judge of the Supreme Court or sitting Chief Justice of a High Court shall be appointed except after consultation with the Chief Justice of India.

2. No appointment of a Chairperson or a Member shall be invalid merely by reason of any vacancy in the Committee.

*5. **Removal of a Member of the Commission.*** 1. Subject to the provisions of sub-section (2) the Chairperson or any other Member of the Commission shall only be removed from his office by order of the President on the ground of proved misbehaviour or incapacity after the Supreme Court, on reference being made to it by the President has, on inquiry held in accordance with the procedure prescribed in that behalf by the Supreme Court, reported that the Chairperson or such other Member as the case may be, ought on any such ground to be removed.

2. Notwithstanding anything in sub-section (1), the President may by order remove from office the Chairperson or any other Member if the Chairperson or such other Member, as the case may be—

(a) is adjudged an insolvent; or

(b) engages during his term of office in any paid employment outside the duties of his office; or

(c) is unfit to continue in office by reason of infirmity of mind or body; or

(d) is of unsound mind and stands so declared by a competent court; or

(e) is convicted and sentenced to imprisonment for an offence which in the opinion of the President involves moral turpitude.

*6. **Term of Office of Members.*** 1. A person appointed as Chairperson shall hold office for a term of five years from the date on which he enters upon his office or until he attains the age of seventy years, whichever is earlier.

2. A person appointed as a Member shall hold office for a term of five years from the date on which he enters upon his office and shall be eligible for re-appointment for another term of five years:

Provided that no Members shall hold office after he has attained the age of seventy years.

3. On ceasing to hold office, a Chairperson or a Member shall be ineligible for further employment under the Government of India or under the Government of any State.

7. Member to Act as Chairperson or to Discharge his Functions in Certain Circumstances. 1. In the event of the occurrence of any vacancy in the office of the Chairperson by reason of his death, resignation or otherwise, the president may by notification, authorize one of the Members to act as the Chairperson until the appointment of a new Chairperson to fill such vacancy.

2. When the Chairperson is unable to discharge his functions owing to absence on leave or otherwise, such one of the Members as the President may, by notification, authorize in this behalf, shall discharge the function of the Chairperson until the date on which the Chairperson resumes his duties.

8. Terms and Conditions of Service of Members. The salaries and allowances payable to, and other terms and conditions of service of, the Members shall be such as may be prescribed:

Provided that neither the salary and allowances nor the other terms and conditions of service of a Member shall be varied to his disadvantage after his appointment.

9. Vacancies, etc. not to Invalidate the Proceedings of the Commission. No act to proceedings of the Commission shall be questioned or shall be invalidated merely on the ground of existence of any vacancy or defect in the constitution of the Commission.

10. Procedure to be Regulated by the Commission. 1. The Commission shall meet at such time and place as the Chairperson may think fit.

2. The Commission shall regulate its own procedure.

3. All orders and decisions of the Commission shall be authenticated by the Secretary-General or any other of the Commission duly authorized by the Chairperson in this behalf.

11. Officers and other Staff of the Commission. 1. The Central Government shall make available to the commission:

(a) an officer of the rank of the Secretary to the Government of India who shall be the Secretary-General of the Commission; and

(b) such police and investigative staff under an officer not below the rank of a Director-General of Police and such other officers and staff as may necessary for the efficient performance of the functions of the Commission.

2. Subject to such rules as may be made by the Central Government in this behalf, the Commission may appoint such other administrative, technical and scientific staff as it may consider necessary.

3. The salaries, allowances and conditions of service of the officers and other staff appointed under sub-section (2) shall be such as may be prescribed.

FUNCTIONS AND POWERS OF THE COMMISSION

12. Functions of the Commission. The Commission shall perform all or any of the following functions, namely;

(a) inquire, *suo motu* or on a petition presented to it by a victim or any person on his behalf, into complaint of—

  (i) violation of human rights or abatement thereof, or

  (ii) negligence in the prevention of such violation;

  by a public servant;

(b) intervenes in any proceedings involving any allegation of violation of human rights pending before a court with the approval of such court;

(c) visit, under intimation to the State Government, any jail or any other institution under control of the State Government, where persons are detained or lodged for purposes of treatment, reformation or protection to study the living condition of the inmates and make recommendations thereon;

(d) review the safeguards provided by or under the Constitution or any law for the time being in force for the protection of human rights and recommend measures for their effective implementation;

(e) review the factors including acts of terrorism that inhibit the enjoyment of human rights and recommend appropriate remedial measures;

(f) study treaties and other international instruments on human rights and make recommendations for their effective implementation;

(g) undertake and promote research in the field of human rights;
(h) spread human rights literacy among various sections of society and promote awareness of the safeguards available for the protection of these rights through publication, the media, seminars and other available means;
(i) encourage the efforts of non-governmental organizations and institutions working in the field of human rights; and
(j) such other functions as it may consider necessary for the promotion of human rights.

13. Powers Relating to Inquiries. 1. The Commission shall, while inquiring into complaints under this Act, have all the powers of a civil court trying a suit under the Code of Civil Procedure, 1908 (5 of 1908) and in particular in respect of the following matters, namely—

(a) summoning and enforcing the attendance of witnesses and examining them on oath;
(b) discovery and production of any document;
(c) receiving evidence on affidavits;
(d) requisitioning any public record or copy thereof from any court of office;
(e) issuing commissions for the examination of witnesses or documents; and
(f) any other matter which may be prescribed.

2. The Commission shall have power to require any person, subject to any privilege which may be claimed by that person under any law for the time being in force, to furnish information on such points or matters as, in the opinion of the commission, may be useful for, or relevant to, the subject matter of the inquiry and any person so required shall be deemed to be legally bound to furnish such information within the meaning of Section 176 and Section 177 of the Indian Penal Code (45 of 1860).

3. The Commission or any other officer, not below the rank of a Gazetted Officer, specially authorized in this behalf by the Commission may enter any building or place where the Commission has reason to believe that any document relating to the subject matter of the inquiry may be found and may seize any such document or take extracts or copies therefrom subject to the

provisions of section 100 of the Code of Criminal Procedure, 1973, insofar as it may be applicable.

4. The Commission shall be deemed to be a civil court and when any offence as is described in Section 175, Section 178, Section 179, Section 180 or Section 228 of the Indian Penal Code is committed in the view or presence (45 of 1980) of the Commission, the Commission may, after recording the facts constituting the offence and the statement of the accused as provided for in the Code of Criminal Procedure, 1973, forward the case to a Magistrate having jurisdiction to try the same and the Magistrate to whom any such case is forwarded shall proceed to hear the complaint against the accused as if the case has been forwarded to him under section 346 of the Code of Criminal Procedure, 1973 (2 of 1974).

5. Every proceeding before the commission shall be deemed to be a judicial proceeding within the meaning of sections 193 and 228 and for the purposes of section 196, of the Indian Penal Code (45 of 1960) and the Commission shall be deemed to be a civil court for all the purposes of section 195 and Chapter XXVI of the Code of Criminal Procedure, 1973 (2 of 1974)

14. Investigation. 1. The Commission may, for the purpose of conducting any investigation pertaining to the inquiry, utilize the services of any officer or investigation agency of the Central Government or any State Government with the concurrence of the Central Government or the State Government, as the case may be.

2. For the purpose of investigating into any matter pertaining to the inquiry, any officer or agency whose services are utilized under sub-section (1) may, subject to the direction and control of the Commission:

(a) summon and enforce the attendance of any person and examine him;
(b) require the discovery and production of any document; and
(c) requisition any public record or copy thereof from any office.

3. The provisions of section 15 apply in relation to any statement made by a person before any officer or agency whose services are utilized under sub-section (1) as they apply in relation to any statement made by person in the course of giving evidence before the Commission.

4. The officer or agency whose services are utilized under sub-section (1) shall investigate into any matter pertaining to

the inquiry and submit a report thereon to the Commission within such period as may be specified by the Commission in this behalf.

5. The Commission shall satisfy itself about the correctness of the facts stated and the conclusion, if any, arrived at in the report submitted to it under sub-section (4) and for this purpose the Commission may make such inquiry (including the examination of the person or persons who conducted or assisted in the investigation) as it thinks fit.

15. *Statement Made by Persons to the Commission.* No Statement made by a person in the course of giving evidence before the Commission shall subject him, to or be used against him in, any civil or criminal proceedings except a prosecution for giving false evidence by such statement.

Provided that the statement:

(a) is made in reply to the question which he is required by the Commission to answer; or

(b) is relevant to the subject matter of the inquiry.

16. Persons Likely to be Prejudicially Affected to be Heard. If at any stage of the inquiry, the Commission:

(a) considers it necessary to inquire into the conduct of any person; or

(b) is of the opinion that the reputation of any person is likely to be prejudicially affected by the inquiry;

it shall give to that person a reasonable opportunity of being heard in the inquiry and to produce evidence in his defence:

Provided that nothing in this section shall apply where the credit of a witness is being impeached.

PROCEDURE

17. Inquiry into Complaints. The Commission while inquiring into the complaints of violations of human rights may:

(i) call for information or report from the Central Government or any State Government or any other authority or organisation subordinate thereto within such time as may be specified by it: provided that

(a) if the information or report is not received within the

time stipulated by the Commission, it may proceed to inquire into the complaint on its own.

(b) if, on receipt of information or report, the Commission is satisfied either that no further inquiry is required or that the required action has been initiated or taken by the concerned Government or authority, it may not proceed with the complaint and inform the complainant accordingly;

(ii) without prejudice to any thing contained in clause (i), if it considers necessary, having regard to the nature of the complaint, initiate an inquiry.

18. Steps after Inquiry. The Commission may take any of the following steps upon the completion of an inquiry held under this Act. namely:

1. Where the inquiry discloses, the Commission of violation of human rights or negligence in the prevention of violation of human rights by a public servant, it may recommend to the concerned Government or authority the initiation of proceedings for prosecution or such other action as the Commission may deem fit against the concerned person or persons.

2. Approach the Supreme Court or the High Court concerned for such directions, orders or writs as that Court may deem necessary.

3. Recommend to the concerned Government or authority for the grant of such immediate interim relief to the victim or the members of his family as the Commission may consider necessary.

4. Subject to the provision of clause (5) provide a copy of the inquiry report to the petitioner or his representative.

5. The Commission shall send a copy of its inquiry report together with its recommendations to the concerned Government or authority and the concerned Government or authority shall, within a period of one month, or such further time as the Commission may allow, forward its comments on the report, including the action taken or proposed to be taken thereon, to the Commission.

6. The Commission shall publish its inquiry report together with the comments of the concerned Government or authority, if any, and the action taken or proposed to be taken by the concerned

Government or authority on the recommendations of the Commission.

19. Procedure with Respect to Armed Forces. 1. Notwithstanding anything contained in this Act, while dealing with complaints of violation of human rights by members of the armed forces, the Commission shall adopt the following, namely:

(a) it may, either on its own motion or on receipt of a petition, seek a report from the Central Government; and

(b) after the receipt of the report, it may, either not proceed with the complaint or, as the case may be, make its recommendations to that Government.

2. The Central Government shall inform the Commission of the action taken on the recommendations within three months or such further time as the Commission may allow.

3. The Commission shall publish its report together with its recommendations made to the Central Government and the action taken by that Government on such recommendations.

4. The Commission shall provide a copy of the report published under sub-section (3) to the petitioner or his representative.

20. Annual and Special Report of the Commission. 1. The Commission shall submit an annual report to the Central government and to the State Government concerned and may at any time submit special reports on any matter which, in its opinion, is of such urgency or importance that it should not be deferred till submission of the annual report.

2. The Central Government and the State Government, as the case may be shall be annual and special reports of the Commission to be laid before each house of Parliament or the State Legislature respectively as the case may be, along with a memorandum of action taken or proposed to be taken on the recommendations of the Commission and the reasons for non-acceptance of the recommendations, if any.

NATIONAL HUMAN RIGHTS COMMISSION (PROCEDURE) REGULATIONS, 1994

In exercise of the powers conferred by sub-section (2) of Section 10 of the Protection of Human Rights Act, 1993 (No. 10 of 1994), the National Human Rights Commission hereby makes the following regulations, namely:

1. Short Title and Commencement. 1. These Regulations may be called the National Human Rights Commission (Procedure) Regulations, 1994.

2. They shall come into force with effect from the 1st day of March, 1994.

2. Definitions. In these Regulations unless the context otherwise requires,—

(a) "Act" means the Protection of Human Rights Act, 1993.
(b) "Chairperson" means the Chairperson of the Commission.
(c) "Commission" means the National Human Rights Commission.
(d) "Member" means a Member of the Commission and includes the Chairperson.

3. Headquarters of the Commission. The Headquarters of the Commission shall be located at Delhi.

4. Venue of the Meetings. The Commission shall ordinarily hold its meetings and sittings in its office located at Delhi. However, it may, in its direction, hold its meetings and sittings at any other place in India if it considers it necessary and expedient.

5. Periodicity of Meetings. The Commission shall normally have its regular sittings in the first and third weeks of every month, excepting holidays. However, the Chairperson by himself or at the instance of one or more of the members may direct a special sitting of the Commission to be convened to consider any specific matter of urgency.

6. Secretariat Assistance. The Secretary-General, along with such other officers of the Commission as may be directed by the Chairperson, or considered necessary, shall attend the meetings of the Commission.

7. Agenda. The Secretary-General shall, in consultations with the Chairperson prepare the agenda for each meeting of the Commission and shall cause notes thereon to be prepared by the Secretariat. Such notes shall, as far as possible, be self-contained.

Specific files covering the agenda items shall be made readily available to the Commission for reference. The agenda paper shall ordinarily be circulated to the Members at least two clear days in advance of every meeting; but when matters are set down only for hearing, cause list of the day of sitting shall be prepared and circulated.

8. Procedure for Dealing with Complaints. 1. All complaints in whatever form received by the Commission shall be registered and assigned a number and place for admission before a Bench of two Members constituted for the purpose not later than two weeks of receipt thereof. Ordinarily complaints of the following nature are not entertainable by the Commission.

(a) in regard to events which happened more than one year before the making of complaints;
(b) with regard to matters which are *sub judice;*
(c) which are vague, anonymous or pseudonymous;
(d) which are of frivolous nature; or
(e) those which are outside the purview of the Commission.

2. No fee is chargeable on complaints.

3. Every attempt should be made to disclose a complete picture of the matter leading to the complaint and the same may be made in English or Hindi to enable the Commission to take immediate action. To facilitate the filling of complaints, the Commission shall, however, entertain complaints in any language included in English Schedule of the Constitution. It shall be open to the Commission to ask for further information and affidavits to be filed in support of allegations whenever considered necessary.

4. The Commission may, in its discretion, accept telegraphic complaints and complaints conveyed through fax.

5. The Commission shall have power to dismiss a complaint in limini.

6. Upon admission of a complaint, the Chairperson/ Commission shall direct whether the matter would be set down for inquiry by it or should be investigated into.

7. On every complaint on which a decision is taken by the Chairperson/Commission to either hold an inquiry or investigation, the Secretariat shall call for reports/comments from the concerned Government/authority giving the latter a reasonable time therefor.

8. On receipt of the comments of the concerned authority, a detailed note on the merits of the case shall be prepared for consideration of the Commission.

9. The directions and recommendations of the Commission shall be communicated to the concerned Government/authority and the petitioner as provided for in Sections 18 and 19 of the Act.

10. The Commission may, in its discretion, afford a personal hearing to the petitioner or any other person on his behalf and such other person or persons as in the opinion of the Commission should be heard for appropriate disposal of the matter before it and, where necessary, call for records and examine witnesses in connection with it. The Commission shall afford a reasonable hearing, including opportunity of cross-examining witnesses, if any, in support of the complaint and leading of evidence in support of his stand, to a person whose conduct is enquired into by it or where in its opinion the reputation of such person is likely to be prejudicially affected.

11. Where investigation is undertaken by the team of the Commission or by any other person under its discretion, the report shall be submitted within a week of its completion of such further time as the Commission may allow. The Commission may, in its discretion, direct further investigation in a given case if it is of opinion that investigation has not been proper or the matter requires further investigation for ascertaining the truth or enabling it to properly dispose of the matter. On receipt of the report, the Commission on its own motion, or if moved in the matter, may direct inquiry to be carried by it and receive evidence in course of such inquiry.

12. The Commission or any of its Members when requested by the Chairperson may undertake visits for an on-the-spot study and where such study is undertaken by one or more Members, a report thereon shall be furnished to the Commission as early as possible.

9. Minutes of the Meetings.

(a) The minutes of each meeting of the Commission shall be recorded during the meeting itself or immediately thereafter by the Secretary-General or by any other officer as directed. Such minutes shall be submitted to the Chairperson for his approval and, upon approval, be circulated to all the Members of the Commission at the earliest and in any case, sufficiently before the commencement of the next morning.

(b) The conclusions of the Commission in every matter undertaken by it shall be recorded in the form of an opinion. Dissenting opinions, if given, shall also form part of and be kept on record. Action shall be taken on the basis of the majority opinion where there be any difference.

(c) Follow-up action:

Unless specifically authorised, no action shall be taken by the Secretariat of the Commission on the minutes of the meetings until the same are confirmed by the Chairperson.

10. Record of Minutes. A master copy of the minutes of every meeting and opinions of the Commission shall be maintained duly authenticated by the Secretary-General and a copy of the minutes pertaining to each item shall be added to the relevant file for appropriate action. Opinions shall be kept in the respective records and for convenience, copies thereof with appropriate indexing shall be kept in guard files.

11. Report of Action Taken. Report of follow-up action shall be submitted to the Commission at every subsequent sitting indicating therein the present stage of action on each item on which the Commission had taken a decision in any of its earlier meetings, excepting the items on which no further action is called for.

12. Transaction of Business Outside the Headquarters. The Commission or some of the Members may transact business at places outside its Headquarters as and when previously approved by the Chairperson, provided that if parties are to be heard in connection with any inquiry under the Act at least two Members shall continue the bench of the Commission for such purpose.

13. Authentication of Orders and Decisions. 1. Orders and decision of the Commission shall be authenticated by the Secretary-General or any officer of the Commission (authorised by the Chairperson) not below the rank of an Under-Secretary.

2. Copies of enquiry reports or orders passed finally disposing of matters by the Commission shall be furnished free of cost to the petitioner or his representative.

3. Unless any document is classified by the Commission as confidential, copy thereof would be available to the parties in the

matter on payment of a reasonable fee raised to meet the cost. Every effort should be made to provide the copies with utmost expedition and, in any case, not later than one week of the date of request.

14. Annual Report. The Commission shall furnish its annual report for the period commencing from 1st April of the year to 31st March of the succeeding year to the Central Government and to the State Government concerned as provided in Section 20(1) of the Act. The original report shall be signed by the Chairperson and Members of the Commission and appropriately preserved and a duly authenticated copy shall be sent to the appropriate Government by end of May of every year.

15. Special Reports. The Commission may furnish such Special Reports on specific matters as may be considered necessary in terms of Section 20(1) of the Act.

16. Reports on Complaints and Inquiries. Every report to which section 18 or 19 of the Act applies shall be sent to the concerned Government, authority or person, as the case may be, within one week of completion of the proceedings before the Commission and on receipt of the comments of the concerned Government or authority. The Commission shall publish the report in the manner provided in sections 18(6) or 19(3) of the Act, as the case may be, within one week of the receipt of the appropriate intimation.

17. Printing of the Report. The Secretariat of the Commission shall be responsible for the printing of the Annual Report and Special Reports with utmost expedition and in any case, not later than one month of finalisation of the same.

18. Investigation Team. The Commission shall have its own team of investigation to be headed by a person not below the rank of a Director-General of Police appointed by it and such team shall consist of one Deputy Inspector General of Police, 2 Superintendents of Police, 6 Deputy-Superintendents of Police and 24 Inspectors of Police and such other categories of officers as the Commission from time to time decides. The Commission may in any given case appoint an appropriate number of outsiders to be associated with the investigation either as Investigators or Observers.

19. As and when any matter which is not covered by these Regulations arises, it shall be competent for the Commission to make appropriate directions and the Commission may add, delete, amplify and amend these Regulations from time to time.

BASIC STANDARDS RECOMMENDED BY AMNESTY INTERNATIONAL RELATING TO NATIONAL HUMAN RIGHTS COMMISSION, 1994

The creation of a National Human Rights Commission can be an important mechanism to strengthen human rights protection but can never replace, nor should it in any way diminish, the safeguards inherent in comprehensive and effective legal structures enforced by an independent, impartial, adequately resourced and accessible judiciary. In India, the creation of such a human rights commission should go hand in hand with a thorough review of existing institutions and mechanism including legal aid programmes-in order to make these more effective instruments of human rights protection. These initiatives should be accompanied by a determined government policy aimed at holding the perpetrators of human rights violations fully accountable, thus ending the impunity now effectively granted to virtually all those who violate human rights.

The Commission on Human Rights adopted by consensus Resolution 1992/54 concerning the Principles relating to the status national institutions and has transmitted these through the Economic and Social Council to the 47th regular session of the General Assembly for adoption. These internationally recognised Principles should serve as the basic minimum guidelines for the establishment of a national institution for the promotion and protection of human rights. In addition, Amnesty International would like to put forward in this discussion document the following key recommendations relating to the establishment and functioning of a National Human Rights Commission.

Mandate and Composition

The Commission should be independent from Government and its Charter should reflect this. The Commission should be established by law or, preferably, by Constitutional amendment .

The Commission should consist of men and women known for their integrity and impartiality of judgment who shall decide matters before them on the basis of facts and in accordance with the law, without any restrictions, improper influences, inducements, pressures, or threats or interferences from any quarter or for any reason. Its members should be independent of Government, have a proven expertise and competence in the field of protecting and promoting human rights and should be drawn from a variety of different backgrounds, including relevant professional groups and the non-governmental sector. The method of selection of its members should be fair and transparent and should afford all necessary guarantees of independence and broad representation. Commission members should serve in their individual capacity and should be able to serve the Commission effectively. The terms of their appointment, tenure and removal should be clearly specified, laid down in the Charter and should afford the strongest possible guarantees of competence, impartiality and independence.

The Commission should be mandated to monitor and report on compliance with and implementation of relevant international human rights standards, including the Universal Declaration of Human Rights, the International Covenant on Civil and Political Rights, the UN Declaration and Convention against Torture, as well as the UN Code of Conduct for Law Enforcement Officials, the UN Body of Principles for the Protection of All Persons under Any Form of Detention or Imprisonment and the UN Principles on the Effective Prevention and Investigation of Extra-Legal Arbitrary or Summary Executions.

The Commission should be mandated to review the effectiveness of existing legislation and/or administrative provisions in protecting human rights and should be able to make recommendations for the amendment of such legislation or the introduction of new legislation as necessary. The Commission should also examine bills and proposals for new legislation put forward by the Government or Parliament to verify its conformity with international human rights standards and to ensure the State's compliance with the above international human rights instruments.

Following from the recommendation that the scope of the Commission's concerns be defined in terms of State obligations under international human rights law, Amnesty International believes that the Commission should exclude from its mandate criminal actions by criminal organisations, by political groups which have resorted to arms as a means to achieve their goals and criminal actions occurring in the context of domestic violence, to which separate mechanism can devote special attention.

The Commission should have precisely defined powers to investigate on its own initiative situations and cases of reported human rights violations and set clear priorities for its work in accordance with the seriousness of the violations alleged. Priority should be given to alleged violations of the right to life and security of the person and the right not be the tortured (rights from which no derogation can be made by any Government under any circumstances) as well as the right not to be arbitrarily arrested or detained.

The Commission should be directed to establish effective cooperation with non-governmental organisation with first-hand information about reports of human rights violations.

The Commission should also have the powers to conduct wide-ranging national inquiries on human rights concerns of fundamental importance to the nation. One critical analysis which Amnesty International recommends be made is an in-depth study of the factors which have contributed to the persistence of human rights violations in India, including the failure of existing institutions and legal mechanisms adequately to protect human rights. Such a study, which could draw upon authoritative investigations already carried out, such as by the National Police Commission, could recommend institutional and other changes necessary to bring about effective reform to halt these violations.

The Commission should be empowered to investigate the conduct of the police as well as the army and paramilitary security forces in all Indian States. In order to do this effectively, the Commission should have adequate facilities to conduct thorough investigations independent of the police and other security forces, whose conduct it will be called upon to assess.

Facilities and Methodology

The Commission should have all necessary human and material resources to examine, thoroughly, effectively, speedily and throughout the country, the evidence and other case material concerning specific allegations of violations put before it. The Commission should have its own investigative machinery and should have access to expert assistance whenever required to verify alleges violations. It should have adequate facilities to carry out on the spot investigations. The Commission should have immediate and unhindered access to all places where detained persons are held or are suspected to be held. Officials should be obliged to co-operate with the Commission's investigations.

The Commission should have powers to initiate investigations on its own motion. It should be able to receive communications not only from the complainants themselves but also, if they themselves are unable or prevented from doing so, from lawyers, relatives or others acting on their behalf and non-governmental groups. Investigations initiated by the Commission should be adequately published especially in the state concerned to enable and encourage witnesses to come forward to testify.

The Commission should have full and effective powers to compel the attendance of witnesses and the production of documents.

The Commission should have full and effective powers to protect witnesses, complainants or others providing evidence to the Commission, including bringing about the suspension or transfer of officials allegedly involved to other duties where they would have no power over witnesses or complainants without prejudice pending completion of investigations. Victims or relatives should have access to all relevant information and documents relating to the investigation and be granted all necessary facilities to present evidence. The Commission should be able to provide financial assistance to witnesses enabling them to travel and be accommodated in order to present their evidence before the Commission.

The Commission should work in an open way with its hearings generally open to the public. Private hearings should be an exceptional measure and be resorted to only in specific pre-established circumstances. The Commission's methodology and the result of its investigations, together with official reports, including post-mortem and other expert reports as well as police and Court records, should in each case be published in full, in an easily accessible and comprehensible form. The Commission should also prepare regular reports documenting all the complaints it has received, together with the action taken in each case, as well as an account of all its other activities for and protection of human rights. The Commission's reports should be presented periodically to representative bodies such as the National and State Assemblies.

The result of the Commission's investigations should be referred to appropriate judicial bodies without delay. Anyone the Commission alleges to have been responsible for committing human rights violations or for ordering, encouraging or permitting them, should automatically be brought to justice. The Government should ensure that any prosecutions for human rights related offences are brought by authorities which are distinctly independent from the police or security forces or other bodies allegedly implicated in the human rights violations.

The Commission should have powers to ensure that superior officers are held accountable for acts committed under their authority and should be mandated to closely follow subsequent legal proceedings in the case, for example by serving as a 'watchdog' at trials, if necessary appearing before the court to make legal submission to press for appropriate legal action to be taken within a reasonable time.

The Commission should have powers to ensure that effectively remedies including interim measures to protect the life and safety of an individual and free medical treatment where necessary; it should ensure that full and prompt compensation is paid and other measures of redress and rehabilitation are taken in all cases it has taken up in which the police or the security forces are found to have perpetrated human rights violations.

The Government should undertake an obligation to respond, within a reasonable time, to the case specific as well as the more general findings, conclusions and recommendations made by the Commission. The Government's response should be made public.

FORMATION OF STATE HUMAN RIGHTS COMMISSION, 1993

21. *Constitution of State Human Rights Commissions.* 1. A State Government may constitute a body to be known as the . . . (name of the State) Human Rights Commission to exercise the powers conferred upon, and to perform the functions assigned to, a State Commission under this chapter.

2. The State Commission shall consist of—

(a) a chairperson who has been a Chief Justice of a High Court;
(b) one Member who is, or has been a Judge of a High Court;
(c) one Member who is, or has been, a District Judge in that State; and
(d) two Members to be appointed from amongst persons having knowledge of, or practical experience in, matters relating to human rights.

3. There shall be a Secretary who shall be the Chief Executive Officer of the State Commission and shall exercise such powers and discharge such functions of the State Commission as it may delegate to him.

4. The headquarters of the State Commission shall be at such place as the State Government may, by notification, specify.

5. A State Commission may inquire into violation of human rights only in respect of matters relatable to any of the entries enumerated in List II and List III in the Seventh Schedule to the Constitution:

Provided that if any such matter is already being inquired into by the Commission or any other Commission duly constituted under any law for the time being in force, the State Commission shall not inquire into the said matter.

Provided further that in relation to the Jammu and Kashmir Human Rights Commission, this sub-section shall have effect as if for the words and figures "List II and List III in the Seventh Schedule to the Constitution" the words and figures "List III in the Seventh Schedule to the Constitution as applicable to the State of Jammu and Kashmir and in respect of matters in relation to which the Legislature of that State has power to make laws" had been substituted.

22. ***Appointment of Chairperson and other Members of State Commission.*** 1. The Chairperson and other Member shall be appointed by the Governor by warrant under this hand and seal.

Provided that every appointment under this sub-section shall be made after obtaining the recommendation of a Committee consisting of:

(a)	the Chief Minister	Chairperson
(b)	Speaker of the Legislative Assembly	Member
(c)	Minister-in-charge of the Department of Home in that State	Member
(d)	Leader of the Opposition in the Legislative Assembly	Member

Provided further that where there is a Legislative Council in a State, the Chairman of that Council and the Leader of the Opposition in that Council shall also be members of the Committee:

Provided also that no sitting judge of a High Court or a sitting District Judge shall be appointed except after consultation with the Chief Justice of the High Court of the concerned State.

2. No appointment of a Chairperson or a Member of the State Commission shall be invalid merely by reason of any vacancy in the Committee.

23. ***Removal of a Member of the State Commission.*** 1. Subject to the provisions of sub-section (2), the Chairperson or any other member of the State Commission shall only be removed from his office by order of the President on the ground of proved misbehaviour or incapacity after the Supreme Court, on a reference being made to it by the President, has, on inquiry held in accordance with the procedure prescribed in that behalf by the Supreme Court, reported that the Chairperson or such other Member, as the case may be, ought on any such ground to be removed.

2. Notwithstanding anything in sub-section (1), the President may by order remove from office the Chairperson or any other Member if the Chairperson or such other Member, as the case may be—

(a) is adjudged an insolvent; or

(b) engages during his term of office in any paid employment outside the duties of his office; or

(c) is unfit to continue in office by reason of infirmity of mind or body; or

(d) is of unsound mind and stands so declared by a competent court; or

(e) is convicted and sentenced to imprisonment for an offence which in the opinion of the President involves moral turpitude.

24. Term of Office of Member of the State Commission. 1. A person appointed as Chairperson shall hold office for a term of five years from the date on which he enters upon his office or until he attains the age of seventy years, whichever is earlier.

2. A person appointed as a Member shall hold office for a term of five years from the date on which he enters upon his office and shall be eligible for re-appointment for another term of five years:

Provided that no Member shall hold office after he has attained the age of seventy years.

3. On ceasing to hold office, a Chairperson or a Member shall be ineligible for further employment under the Government of a State or under the Government of India.

25. Member to Act as Chairperson or to Discharge his Functions in Certain Circumstances. 1. In the event of the occurrence of any vacancy in the office of the Chairperson by reason of his death, resignation or otherwise, the Governor may by notification, authorize one of the Members to act as the Chairperson until the appointment of a new Chairperson to fill such vacancy.

2. When the Chairperson is unable to discharge his functions owing to absence on leave or otherwise, such one of the Members as the Governor may, by notification, authorize in this behalf, shall discharge the functions of the Chairperson until the date on which the Chairperson resumes his duties.

26. Terms and Conditions of Service of Members of the State Commission. The salaries and allowances payable to, and other terms and conditions of service of, the Members shall be such as may be prescribed by the State Government:

Provided that neither the salary and allowances nor the other terms and conditions of service of a Member shall be varied to his disadvantage after his appointment.

27. Officers and other Staff of the State Commission. 1. The State Government shall make available to the Commission—

(a) an officer not below the rank of a Secretary to the State Government who shall be the Secretary of the State Commission; and

(b) such police and investigative staff under an officer not below the rank of an Inspector-General of Police and such other officers and staff as may be necessary for the efficient performance of the functions of the State Commission.

2. subject to such rules as may be made by the State Government in this behalf, the State Commission may appoint such other administrative technical and scientific staff as it may consider necessary.

3. The salaries, allowances and conditions of service of the officers and other staff appointed under sub-section (2) shall be such as may be prescribed by the State Government.

28. Annual and Special Reports of State Commission. 1. The State Commission shall submit an annual report to the State Government and may at any time submit special reports on any matter which, in its opinion, is of such urgency or importance that it should not be referred till submission of the annual report.

2. The State Government shall cause the annual and special reports of the State Commission to be laid before each House of State Legislature where to consists of two Houses, or where such Legislature consists of one House, before that House along with a memorandum of action taken or proposed to be taken on the recommendations of the State Commission and the reasons for non-acceptance of the recommendations, if any.

29. Application of Certain Provisions Relating to National Human Rights Commission to State Commissions. The provisions of sections 9, 10, 12, 13, 14, 15, 16, 17 and 18 shall apply to a State Commission and shall have effect, subject to the following modifications, namely:

(a) references to "Commission" shall be construed as references to "State Commission";

(b) in Section 10, in sub-section (3), for the word "Secretary General", the word "Secretary" shall be substituted;

(c) in section 12, clause (f) shall be omitted; and

(d) in section 17, in clause (i), the words "Central Government or any" shall be omitted.

HUMAN RIGHTS COURTS

30. For the purpose of providing speedy trial of offences arising out of violation of human rights, the State Government may, with the concurrence of the Chief Justice of the High Court, by notification, specify for each district a Court of Session to be a Human Rights court to try the said offences.
Provided that nothing in this section shall apply it:

(a) a Court of Session is already specified as a special court, or
(b) a special court is already constituted, for such offences under any other law for the time being in force.

31. Special Public Prosecutor. For every Human Rights Court, the State Government shall, by notification, specify a Public Prosecutor or appoint an advocate who has been in practice as an advocate forgot less than seven years, as a Special Public Prosecutor for the purpose of conducting cases in that Court.

FINANCE, ACCOUNTS AND AUDIT

32. Grants by the Central Government. 1. The Central Government shall after due appropriation made by Parliament by law in this behalf, pay to the Commission by way of grants such sums of money as the Central Government may think fit for being utilized for the purposes of the Act.

2. The Commission may spend such sums as it thinks fit for performing the functions under this Act, and such sums shall be treated as expenditure payable out of the grants referred to in sub-section (1).

33. Grants by the State Government. 1. The State Government shall, after due appropriation made by Legislature by law in this behalf, pay to the State Commission by way of grants such sums of money as the State Government may think fit for being utilized for the purposes of this Act.

2. The State Commission may spend such sums as it thinks fit for performing the functions under Chapter V, and such sums shall be treated as expenditure payable out of the grants referred to in sub-section (1).

34. Accounts and Audit. 1. The Commission shall maintain proper accounts and other relevant records and prepare an annual statement of accounts in such form as may be prescribed by the Central Government in consultation with the Comptroller and Auditor-General of India.

2. The Accounts of the Commission shall be audited by the Comptroller and Auditor-General at such intervals as may be specified by him and any expenditure incurred in connection with such audit shall be payable by the Commission to the Comptroller and Auditor-General.

3. The Comptroller and Auditor-General and any person appointed by him in connection with the audit of the accounts of the Commission under this Act shall have the same rights and privileges and the authority in connection with such audit as the comptroller and Auditor-General generally has in connection with the audit of Government accounts and, in particular, shall have the right to demand the production of books, accounts, connected vouchers and other documents and papers and to inspect any of the offices of the Commission.

4. The accounts of the Commission as certified by the Comptroller and Auditor-General or any other person appointed him in this behalf, together with the audit report thereon shall be forwarded annually to the Central Government be the Commission and the Central Government shall cause the audit report to be laid, as soon as may be after it is received, before each House of Parliament.

35. Accounts and Audit of State Commissioner. 1. The State Commission shall maintain proper accounts and other relevant records and prepare an annual statement of accounts in such form as may be prescribed by the State Government in consultation with the Comptroller and Auditor-General of India.

2. The accounts and Audit of State commission shall be audited by the Comptroller and Auditor-General at such interval as may be specified by him and any expenditure incurred in connection with such audit shall be payable by the State Commission to the Comptroller and Auditor-General.

3. The Comptroller and Auditor-General and any person appointed by him in connection with the audit of the accounts of the State Commission under this act shall have the same rights and privileges and the authority in connection with such audit as the Comptroller and Auditor-General has in connection with the

audit of Government accounts and in particular, shall have the right to demand the production of books, accounts, connected vouchers and other documents and papers and to inspect any of the offices of the State Commission.

4. The accounts of the State Commission, as certified by the Comptroller and Auditor-General or any other person appointed by him in this behalf, together with the audit report thereon, shall be forwarded annually to the State Government by the State Commission and the State Government shall cause the audit report to be laid, as soon as may be after it is received, before the State Legislature.

MISCELLANEOUS

36. Matters not Subject to Jurisdiction of the Commission. 1. The Commission shall not inquire into any matter which is pending before a State Commission or any other Commission fully constituted under any law for the time being in force.

2. The Commission or the State Commission shall not inquire into any matter after the expiry of one year from the date on which the act constituting violation of human rights is alleged to have been committed.

37. Constitution of Special Investigation Teams. Notwithstanding any thing contained in any other law for the time being in force, where the Government considers it necessary so to do. It may constitute one or more special investigation teams, consisting of such police officers as it thinks necessary for purposes of investigation and prosecution of offences arising out of violations of human rights.

38. Protection of Action Taken in Good Faith. No suit or other legal proceeding shall lie against the Central Government, State Government, Commission, the State Commission or any Member thereof or any person acting under the direction either of the Central Government, State Government, Commission or the State Commission in respect of any thing which is in good faith done or intended to be done in pursuance of this Act or of any rules or any order made thereunder or in respect of the publication by or under the authority of the Central Government, State Government, Commission or the State Commission of any report, paper or proceedings.

39. Member and Officers to be Public Servants. Every Member of the Commission, State Commission, and every officer appointed or authorized by the Commission of the State Commission to exercise functions under this Act shall be deemed to be a public servant within the meaning the meaning of section 21 of the Indian Penal Code.

40. Power of Central Government to Make Rules. 1. The Central Government may, by notification, make rules to carry out the provisions of this Act.

2. In particular and without prejudice to the generality of the foregoing power, such rules may provide for all or any of the following matters, namely,

(a) the salaries and allowances and other terms and conditions of service of the Members under section 8;
(b) the conditions subject to which other administrative, technical and scientific staff may be appointed by the Commission and the salaries and allowances of officers and other staff under sub-section (3) of section 11;
(c) any other power of a civil court required to be prescribed under clause (f) of sub-section (1) of section 13;
(d) the form in which the annual statement of accounts is to be prepared by the Commission under sub-section (1) of section 34; and
(e) any other matter which has to be, or may be prescribed.

3. Every rule made under this Act shall be laid, as sin as may be after it is made, before each House of Parliament, while it is in session, for a total period of thirty days which may be comprised in one session or in two or more successive session, and if, before the expiry of the sessions immediately following the session or the successive sessions aforesaid both Houses agree in making any modification in the rule or both Houses agree that the rule should not be made, the rule shall thereafter have effect only in such modified form or be of no effect, as the case may be; so however that any such modification or annulment shall be without prejudice to the validity of anything previously done under that rule.

41. Power of State Government to Make Rules. 1. The State Government may, by notification, make rules to carry out the provisions of this Act.

2. In the particular and without prejudice to the generality of the foregoing power; such rules may provide for all or any of the following matters, namely:

(a) the salaries and allowances and other terms and conditions of service of the members under section 26;

(b) the conditions subject to which other administrative, technical and scientific staff may be appointed by the State Commission and the salaries and allowances of officers and other staff under sub-section (3) of section 27; and

(c) the form in which the annual statement of accounts is to be prepared under sub-section (1) of section 35.

3. Every rule made by the State Government under this section shall be laid, as soon as may be after it is made before each House of the State Legislature where it consists of two Houses, or where such Legislature consists of one House, before that House.

42. Power to Remove Difficulties. 1. If any difficulty arises in giving effect to the provisions of this Act the Central Government may by order published in the Official Gazette make such provisions, not inconsistent with the provisions of this Act as appear to it to be necessary or expedient for removing the difficulty.

Provided that no such order shall be made after the expiry of the period of two years from the date of commencement of this Act.

2. Every Order made under this section shall, as soon as may be after it is made, by laid before each House of Parliament.

43. Repeal and Savings. 1. the Protection of Human Rights Ordinance, 1993 is hereby repeated.

2. Notwithstanding such repeal, anything done or any action taken and under the said Ordinance, shall be deemed to have been done or taken under the corresponding provisions of this Act.

THE PROTECTION OF CIVIL RIGHTS ACT, 1955
(Act No. 22 of 1955)
(As amended by Act No. 106 of 1976)

An Act to prescribe punishment for the preaching and practice of "Untouchability", for the enforcement of any disability arising therefrom and for matters connected therewith.

Be it enacted by Parliament in the Sixth Year of the Republic of India as follows:

1. Short Title, Extent and Commencement. 1. This Act may be called the Protection of Civil Rights Act, 1955.

2. It extends to the whole of India.

3. It shall come into force on such date as the Central Government may, by notification in the official Gazette, appoint.

2. *Definitions.* In this Act, unless the context otherwise requires:

(a) "civil rights" means any right accruing to a person by reason of the abolition of untouchability by Article 17 of the Constitution;

(aa) "hotel' includes a refreshment room, a boarding house, a lodging house, a coffee house and a cafe;

(b) "place" includes a house, building and other structure and premises, and also includes a tent, vehicle and vessel;

(c) "place of public entertainment" includes any place to which the public are admitted and in which an entertainment is provided or held;

Explanation: "Entertainment" includes any exhibition, performance game, sport and any other form of amusement;

(d) "place of public worship" means a place by whatever name known, which is used as a place of public religious worship or which is dedicated generally to, or is used generally by persons professing any religion or belonging to any religious denomination or any section thereof, for the performance of any religious service or for offering prayers therein and includes—

(i) all lands and subsidiary shrines appurtenant or attached to any such place,

(ii) convately owned place of worship which is, in fact allowed by the owner thereof to be used as a place of public worship, and

(iii) such land or subsidiary shrine appurtenant to such privately owned place of worship as is allowed by the owner thereof to be used as a place of public religious worship];

[(da) "Prescribed" means prescribed by rules made under this Act;

(db) "Scheduled Castes" has the meaning assigned to it in Clause (24) of Art. 166 of the Constitution];

(e) "show" means any premises where goods are sold either wholesale or by retail or both wholesale and by retail and includes—

(i) any place from where goods are sold by a hawker or vendor or from a mobile van or cart;

(ii) a laundry and a hair-cutting saloon,

(iii) any other place where services are rendered to customers;]

3. ***Punishment for Enforcing Religious.*** Whoever on the ground of "untouchability" prevents any person—

(a) from entering any place of public worship which is open to other persons professing the same religion or any section thereof as such person; or

(b) from worshiping or offering prayers or performing any religious service in any place of public worship, or bathing in, or using the waters of, any sacred tank, well, spring or water-course, river or lake or bathing at any *ghat* of such tank, water course, river or lake in the same manner and to the same manner and to the same extent as is permissible to the other person professing the same religion or any section thereof, as such person

[shall be punishable with imprisonment for a term of not less than one month and not more than six months and also with fine which shall be not less than one hundred rupees and not more than five hundred rupees.]

Explanation: For the purposes of this Section and Section 4 persons professing the Buddhist, Sikh and Jaina religion or persons professing the Hindu religion in any of its forms or developments including Virashaivas, Lingayats, Adivasis, followers of Brahmo, Prarthana, Arya Samaj and the Swaminarayana Smoradaya shall be deemed to be Hindus.

4. *Punishment for Enforcing Social Disabilities.* Whoever on the ground of "untouchability" enforces against any person any disability with regard to—

(i) access to any shop, public restaurant, hotel or place of public entertainment, or
(ii) the use of any utensils, and other Articles kept in any public restaurant, hotel, *dharmasala, sarai* or *musafirkhana* for the use of the general public or of any section thereof; or
(iii) the practice of any profession or the carrying on of any occupation, trade or business or employment in any job; or
(iv) the use of or access to, any river, stream, spring, well, tank, cistern, water-tap or other watering place, or any bathing *ghat*, burial or cremation ground, any sanitary convenience, any road, or passage, or any other place of public resort which other members of the public, or any section thereof, have a right to use or have access to; or
(v) the use of or access to, any place used for a charitable or a public purpose maintained wholly or partly out of State funds or dedicated to the use of the general public or any section thereof; or
(vi) the enjoyment of the benefit under a charitable trust created for the benefit of the general public or of any section thereof; or
(vii) the use of, or access to, any public conveyance; or
(viii) the construction, acquisition, or occupation of any residential premises in any locality, whatsoever, or
(ix) the use of any *dharmasala, sarai,* or *musafirkhana* which is open to general public, or to any section thereof; or
(x) the observance of any social or religious custom, usage or ceremony or taking part in, or taking out, any religious, social or cultural processing; or
(xi) the use of jewelry and finery.

[shall be punishable with imprisonment for a term of not less than one month and not more than six months and also with fine which shall be not less than one hundred rupees and not more than five hundred rupees.]

Explanation: For the purposes of this Section, enforcement of any disability includes any discrimination on the ground of "untouchability".

5. *Punishment for Refusing to Admit Persons to Hospitals, etc.* Whoever on the ground of "untouchability"—

(a) refuses admission to any person to any hospital, dispensary, educational institution or any hotel [x x x] if such hospital, dispensary, educational institution or hotel is established or maintained for the benefit of the general public or any section thereof; or

(b) does any act which discriminates against any such person after admission to any of aforesaid institution;

[shall be punishable with imprisonment for a term of not less than one month and not more than six months and also with fine which shall be not less than one hundred rupees and not more than five hundred rupees.]

6. *Punishment for Refusing to Sell Goods or Render Services.* Whoever on the ground of "untouchability" refuses to sell any goods or refuses to render any service to any person at the same time and place and on the same terms and conditions at/on which such goods are sold or services are rendered to other persons in the ordinary course of business shall be punishable with imprisonment for a term of not less than one month and not more than six months and also with fine which shall be not less than one hundred rupees and not more than five hundred rupees.

7. *Punishment for other Offences Arising out of "Untouchability".* Whoever:

(a) prevents any person from exercising any rights accruing to him by reason of the abolition of "untouchability" under Article 17 of the Constitution; or

(b) molests, injures, annoys, obstructs or causes or attempts to cause obstruction to any person in the exercise of any such right or molests, injures, annoys or boycotts any person by reason of his having exercised any such rights; or

(c) by words, either spoken or written, or by signs or by visible representations or otherwise, incites or encourages any person or class of persons or the public generally to practice "untouchability" in any form whatsoever; or

(d) insults or attempts to insult on the ground of "untouchability" a member of a Scheduled Caste;

[shall be punishable with imprisonment for a term of not less than one month and not more than six months, and also with fine which shall be not less than one hundred rupees and not more than five hundred rupees.]

Explanation 1. A person shall be deemed to boycott another person who—

(a) refuses to such other person or refuses to permit such other person, to use or occupy any house or land or refuses to deal with, work for hire for, or do business with, such other person or to render to him, receive from him any customary service, or refuses to do any of the said things on the terms on which such things would be commonly done in the ordinary course of business; or

(b) abstains from such social, professional or business relations as he would ordinarily maintain with other person.

Explanation 2. For the purpose of clause (c) a person shall be deemed to incite or encourage the practice of "untouchability"—

(i) if he directly or indirectly, preaches "untouchability" or it practices in any form; or

(ii) if he justifies whether on historical, philosophical or religious grounds or on the ground of any trading of the caste system or on any other ground, the practice of "untouchability" in any form.

1-A. Whoever commits any offence against the person or property of any individual as a reprisal or revenge for his having exercised any right accruing to him by reason of the abolition of "untouchability" under Article 17 of the constitution, shall, where the offence is punishable with imprisonment for a term proceeding two years, be punishable with imprisonment for a term which shall be of less than two years and also with fine

2. Whoever:

(i) demise to any person belonging to his community or any section thereof any right or privilege to which such person would be entitled as a member of such community or section; or

(ii) takes any part in the ex-communication of such person, on the ground that such person has refused to practice "untouchability" that such person has done any act in furtherance of the objects of this Act;

shall be punishable with imprisonment for a term of not less than one month and not more than six months, and also with fine which shall be not less than one hundred rupees and not more than five hundred rupees.

7. (a) ***Unlawful Compulsory Labour when to be Deemed to be a Practice of "Untouchability".*** 1. Whoever compels any person, on the ground of "untouchability" to do any scavenging or sweeping or to remove any carcass or a flay any animal, or to remove the umbilical cord or to do any other job of a similar nature shall be deemed to have enforced a disability arising out of "untouchability".

2. Whoever is deemed under sub-section (1) to have enforced a disability arising out of "untouchability" shall be punishable with imprisonment for a term which shall be not less than three months and not more than six months and also with fine which shall be not less than one hundred rupees and not more than five hundred rupees.

Explanation. For the purposes of the section "compulsion" includes a threat of social or economic boycott.

8. Cancellation or Suspension of Licenses in Certain Cases. When a person who is convicted of an offence under Section 6, holds any license under any law for the time being in force in respect of any profession, trade, calling or employment in relation to which the offence is committed the court trying the offence may, without prejudice to any other penalty to which such person may be liable under that section, direct that the license shall stand cancelled or to be suspended for such period, as the Court may deem fit, and every order of the Court to cancelling or suspending a license shall have effect as if it had been passed by the authority competent to cancel or suspend the license under any such law.

Explanation. In this section, "license" includes a permit or permission.

9. Resumption or Suspension of Grants made by Government. Where the manager or trustee of a place of public worship or any educational institution or hostel which is in respect of a grant of land or money from the Government is convicted of an offence under this Act and such conviction is not reversed or quashed in any appeal or revision, the Government may, if in its opinion the circumstances of the case warrant such a course, direct the suspension or resumption of the whole or any part of such grant.

10. Abatement of Offence. Whoever abets any offence under this Act shall be punishable with the punishment provided for the offence.

Explanation. A public servant who willfully neglects the investigation of any offence punishable under this Act shall be deemed to have abetted an offence punishable under this Act.

10.A. Power to State Government to Impose Collective Fine. 1. If after an inquiry in the prescribed manner the State Government is satisfied that the inhabitants of an area are concerned in, or abetting the commission of, any offence punishable under this Act, or labouring persons concerned in the commission of such offence or failing to render all the assistance in their power to discover or apprehend the offender or offenders or suppressing material evidence of the commission of such offence, the State Government may, by notification in the Official Gazette, impose a collective fine on such inhabitants and apportion such fine amongst the inhabitants who are able collectively to pay it, and such apportionment shall be made according to the State Government's judgment of the respective means of such inhabitants and in making any such apportionment the Government may assign a portion of such fine to a Hindu undivided family to be payable by it:

Provided that the fine apportioned to an inhabitant shall not be realized until the petition, if any, filed by him under sub-section (3) is disposed of.

2. The notification made under sub-section (1) shall be proclaimed in the area by beat of drum or in such other manner as the State Government may think best in the circumstances to bring the imposition of the collective fine to the notice of the inhabitants of the said area.

3. (a) Any person aggrieved by the imposition of the collective fine under sub-section (1) or by the order of apportionment, may within the prescribed period file a petition before the State Government or such other authority as that Government may specify in this behalf for being exempted from such fine or for modification of the order ot apportionment:

Provided that no fee shall be charged for filing such petition.

(b) The State Government or the authority specified by it shall, after giving to the petitioner a reasonable opportunity of being heard, pass such order as it may think fit:

Provided that the amount of the fine exempted or reduced under this section shall not be realizable from any person, and the total fine imposed on the inhabitants of an area under sub-section (1) shall be deemed to have been reduced to that extent.

4. Notwithstanding anything contained in sub-section (4), the State Government may exempt the victims of any offence punishable under this Act or any person who does not, in its opinion, fall within the category of persons specified in sub-section (1), or any portion thereof.

5. The portion of collective fine payable by any person (including a Hindu undivided family) may be recovered in the manner provided by the Code of Criminal Procedure, 1973 (2 of 1974), for the recovery of fines imposed by a Court as if such portion were a fine imposed by a Magistrate.

11. Enhanced Penalty on Subsequent Conviction. Whoever having already been convicted of an offence under this Act or of an abatement of such offence is again convicted of any such offence or abatement shall, on conviction, be punishable:

(a) for the second offence, with imprisonment for a term of not less than six months and not more than one year, and also with fine which shall be not less than two hundred rupees and not more than five hundred rupees;

(b) for the third offence subsequent to the third offence with imprisonment for a term of not less than one year and not more than two years, and also with fine which shall be not less than five hundred rupees and not more than one thousand rupees.

12. Presumption by Courts in Certain Cases. Where any act constituting an offence under this Act is committed in relation to a member of a Scheduled Caste [xx], the Court shall presume, unless the contrary is proved, that such Act was committed on the ground of "untouchability".

13. Limitation of Jurisdiction of Civil Courts. 1. No Civil Court shall entertain or continue any suit or proceeding or shall pass any decree or order or executive wholly or partially any decree or order if the claim involved in such suit or proceeding or if the passing of such decree or order or if such execution would, in any way, be contrary to the provisions of this Act.

2. No Court shall, in adjudicating any matter or executing any decree or order, recognize any custom or usage imposing any disability on any person on the ground of "untouchability".

14. Offences by Companies. 1. If the person committing an offence under this Act is a company, every person who at the time the offence was committed was in-charge of and was responsible to, the company for the conduct of the business of the company, shall be deemed to be guilty of the offences and shall be liable to be proceeded against and punished accordingly:

Provided that nothing contained in this sub-section shall render any such person liable to any punishment, if he proves that the offence was committed without his knowledge or that he exercised all due diligence to prevent the commission of such offence.

2. Notwithstanding anything contained in sub-section (1) where an offence under this Act has been committed with consent of any director or manager, secretary or other officer of the company such director, manager, secretary or other officer shall also be deemed to be guilty of that offence and shall be liable to be proceeded against and punished accordingly.

Explanation. For the purposes of this section—

(a) "company" means any body corporate and includes a firm or other association of individuals; and

(b) "director" in relation to a firm means a partner in the firm.

*[**14. Protection of Action Taken in Good Faith.*** 1. No suit, prosection or other legal proceeding shall lie against the Central Government or a State Government for anything which in good faith done or intended to be done under this Act.

2. No suit or other legal proceeding shall lie against the Central Government or a State Government for any damage cause or likely to be caused by anything which is in good faith done or intended to be done under this Act.]

15. Offences to be Cognizable and Triable Summarily. 1. Notwithstanding anything contained in the Code of Criminal Procedure, 1973 (2 of 1974) every offence punishable under this Act shall be cognizable and every such offence except where it is a punishable with imprisonment for a minimum term exceeding three months may be tried summarily by a Judicial Magistrate of the first class or in a Metropolitan area by a Metropolitan Magistrate in accordance with the procedure specified in the said code.

2. Notwithstanding anything contained in the Code of Criminal Procedure, 1973 (2 of 1974) when any public servant is alleged to have committed the offence of abatement of an offence punishable under this Act while acting or purporting to act in the discharge of his official duty, no court shall take cognizance of such offence of abatement except with the previous sanction—

(a) of the Central Government, in the case of a person employed in connection with the affairs of the Union; and

(b) of the State Government, in the case of a person employed in connection with the affairs of a State.

15-A. *Duty of State Government to Ensure that the Rights Accruing from the Abolition of "Untouchability" may be Availed of by the Concerned Persons:* 1. Subject to such rules as the Central Government may make in this behalf, the State Government shall take such measures as may be necessary for ensuring that the rights from the abolition of "untouchability" or made available to and are availed of by, the persons subjected to any disability arising out of "untouchability".

2. In particular, and without prejudice to the generality of the provisions of sub-section (1) such measures may include—

(i) the provision of adequate facilities including legal aid, to the persons subjected to any disability arising out of "untouchability" to enable them to avail themselves of such rights;

(ii) the appointment of officer for initiating exercising supervision over prosecution for the contravention of the provision of this Act;

(iii) the setting up of Special Courts for the trial of offences under this Act;

(iv) the setting up of Committees at such appropriate levels as the State Government may think fit to assist the State Government in formulating or implementing such measures;

(v) provision for periodic survey of the working of the

provisions of this Act with a view to suggesting measures for the better implementation of the provisions of this Act; and

(vi) the identification of the areas where persons are under any disability arising out of "untouchability" and adoption of such disability from such areas.

3. The Central Government shall take such steps as may be necessary to co-ordinate the measures taken by the State Government under sub-Section (1).

4. The Central Government shall, every year, place on the Table of each House of Parliament, report on the measures taken by itself and by the State Governments in pursuance of the provisions of this section.

16. Act to override other laws. Save as otherwise expressly provided in this Act, the provisions of this Act shall have effect notwithstanding anything inconsistent therewith contained in any other law for the time being in force, or any custom or usage or any instrument having effect by virtue of any such law or any decree or order of any Court or other authority.

16-A. Probation of Offenders Act, 1958, not to apply to persons above the age of fourteen years. The provisions of the probation of Offenders Act, 1958, (20 of 1958) shall not apply to any person above the age of fourteen years who is found guilty of having committed any offence punishable under this Act.

16-B. Power to make rules. 1. The Central Government may by notification in the Official Gazette, make rules to carry out the provisions of this Act.

2. Every rule made by the Central Government under this Act shall be laid as soon as may be after it is made, before each House of Parliament while it is in session for a total period of thirty days which may be comprised in one session or in two or more successive sessions, and if, before the expiry of the session immediately following the session or the successive session aforesaid, both Houses agree in making any modification in the rule or both Houses agree that the rule should not be made, the rule shall thereafter have effect only in such modified form or to be of no effect, as the case may be, so however, that any such modification or annulment shall be without prejudice to the validity of anything previously done under that rule.

17. Repeal. The enactments specified in the Schedule are hereby repealed to the extent to which they or any of the provisions contained therein correspond or are repugnant to this Act or to any of the provisions contained therein.

THE PROTECTION OF CIVIL RIGHTS RULES, 1977

S.O. 3006, 15.9.1977. In exercise of the powers conferred by Section 16-B of the Protection of Civil Rights Act, 1955 (22 of 1955), the Central Government hereby makes the following rules, namely:

1. Short Title and Commencement. 1. These rules may be called the Protection of Civil Rights Rules, 1977.

2. They shall come into force on the date of their publication in the Official Gazette.

2. Definition. In these rules unless the context otherwise requires,

(a) "Act" means the Protection of Civil Rights Act, 1955 (22 of 1955);

(b) "Section" means a section of the Act.

3. Manner of Inquiry under Sub-section (1) of Section 10-A. 1. The State Government may appoint an officer not below the rank of a Sub-Divisional Magistrate for the purpose of making an inquiry referred to in sub-section (1) of Section 10-A.

2. The officer appointed under sub-rule (1) (hereinafter in this rule referred to as the inquiry officer) shall issue a public notice specifying the date, time, place and the purpose of such inquiry and calling upon all the residents of the area in respect of which the inquiry is to be held to furnish such information and materials including documents in their possession, as may be relevant for the purposes of the enquiry, or

3. The public notice referred to in sub-rule (2) shall be in the local language or languages of the area and the same shall be,-

(i) published on the notice board in the Offices of the District Magistrate, the District Superintendent of Police, The Village Panchayat or Municipal Committee of the area and such other places as the enquiry officer deems fit and at least in one daily newspaper circulating in the area; and

(ii) proclaimed in the area by beat of drum or in such other manner as the inquiry officer may think best in the circumstance to bring the contents of the public notice to the notice of the inhabitants of the area.

4. The inquiry officer, while making such inquiry shall follow as nearly as practicable, the procedure for summary trials including

the recording of evidence as laid down in Chapter XXI of Code of Criminal Procedure, 1973 (2 of 1974).

5. The inquiry officer shall complete the inquiry as expeditiously as possible and submit his report to the State Government within such period, not exceeding six weeks as may be specified by the State Government in the order appointing the inquiry officer:

Provided that the State Government may having regard to the nature of the inquiry, extend the period of submission of the report by such period not exceeding two months in total as it may consider necessary.

4. ***Period for Filing a Petition under Sub-section (3) of Section 10-A.*** Any person aggrieved by the imposition of a collective fine under sub-section (1) of Section 10-A or by the order of apportionment, may within a period of thirty days from the date of proclamation of the notification under sub-section (2) of that section file a petition before the State Government or the authority specified by it:

Provided that where the State Government or the authority, as the case may be, may entertain the petition after the expiry of the said period if it is satisfied that the petitioner was prevented by sufficient cause from filing the petition in time.

2. The State Government or the authority before which the petition is filed shall dispose of the petition as expeditiously as possible.

5. **Reports by the Government.-** Every State Government shall, for the purpose of enabling the Central Government, place the report referred to in sub-section (4) of Section 15-A on the Table of each house of Parliament, furnish to the Government before the 15th day of February each year, a summary of the measures taken by it under sub-sections (1) and a (2) of the section during the preceding calendar year and shall also furnish such other information as may be required by the Central Government from time to time.

4

Scheduled Castes, Scheduled Tribes, Backward Classes, *Safai Karamcharis*, Minorities and Human Rights

THE SCHEDULED CASTES AND THE SCHEDULED TRIBES (PREVENTION OF ATROCITIES) ACT, 1989

(No. 33 of 1989)

(11th September, 1989)

Received the assent of the President on September 11, 1989 and published in the Gazette of India, Extra, Part II, Section 1, Dt. 12th September, 1989, Sl. No. 39.

An act to prevent the commission of offences of atrocities against the members of the Scheduled Castes and the Scheduled Tribes, to provide for Special Courts for the trial of such offences and for the relief and rehabilitation of the victims of such offences and for matters connected therewith or incidental thereto.

Be it enacted by Parliament in the Fortieth Year of the Republic of India as follows:

The Scheduled Castes and the Scheduled Tribes (Prevention of Atrocities) Act, 1989 is an Act to prevent the Commission of offences of atrocities against the member of the Scheduled Castes and the Scheduled Tribes and to provide for special courts for the trial of such offences.

PRELIMINARY

1. *Short Title, Extent and Commencement.* 1. This Act may be called the Scheduled Castes and the Scheduled Tribes (Prevention of Atrocities) Act, 1989.

2. It extends to the whole of India except the State of Jammu and Kashmir.

It shall come into force on such date as the Central Government may by notification in the Official Gazette, appoint.

2. *Definitions.* 1. In this Act unless the context otherwise requires—

(a) "Atrocity" means an offence punishable under Section 3;
(b) "Code" means the Code of Criminal Procedure 1973 (2 of 1974);
(c) "Scheduled Castes and Scheduled Tribes" shall have the meanings assigned to them respectively under Clause (24) and Clause (25) of Article 366 of the Constitution;
(d) "Special Court" means a Court of Session specified as a Special Court in Section 14;
(e) "Special Public Prosecutor" means a Public Prosecutor specified as Special Public Prosecutor or an advocate referred to in Section 15;
(f) Words and expressions used but not defined in this Act, and defined in the Code or the Indian Penal Code (45 of 1860) shall have the meanings assigned to them respectively in the Code, or as the case may be, in the Indian Penal Code.

2. Any reference in this Act to any enactment or any provision thereof shall, in relation to an area in which such enactment or such provision is not in force, be construed as a reference to the corresponding law, if any, in force in that area.

OFFENCES AT ATROCITIES

3. ***Punishment for Offences of Atrocities.*** 1. Whoever, not being a member of a Scheduled Caste or a Scheduled Tribe

(i) forces a member of a Scheduled Caste or a Scheduled Tribe to drink or eat any inedible or obnoxious substance;
(ii) acts with intent to cause injury, insult or annoyance to any member of a Scheduled Caste or a Scheduled Tribe by dumping excreta, waste matter, carcasses or any other obnoxious substance in his premises or neighbourhood;
(iii) forcibly removes clothes from the person of a member of a Scheduled Caste or a Scheduled Tribe or parades him naked or with painted face or body or commits any similar act which is derogatory to Human Dignity;
(iv) wrongfully occupies or cultivates any land owned by, or allotted to, or notified by any competent authority to be allotted to, a member of a Scheduled Caste or Scheduled Tribe or gets the land allotted to him transferred;
(v) wrongfully dispossesses a member of a Scheduled Caste or a Scheduled Tribe from his land or premises or

interferes with the enjoyment of his rights any land, premises or water;

(vi) compels or entices a member of a Scheduled Caste or Scheduled Tribe to do 'begging' or other similar forms of forced or bonded labour other than any, compulsory service for public purpose imposed by Government;

(vii) forces or intimidates a member of a Scheduled Caste or a Scheduled Tribe not to vote or to vote to a particular candidate or to vote in a manner other than that provided by law;

(viii) institutes false, malicious or vexatious suit or criminal or other legal proceedings against a member of a Scheduled Caste or a Scheduled Tribe;

(ix) gives any false or frivolous information to any public servant and thereby causes such public servant to use his lawful power to the injury or annoyance of a member of a Scheduled Caste or a Scheduled Tribe;

(x) internationally insults or intimidates with extent to humiliate a member of a Scheduled Caste or a Scheduled Tribe in any place within public view;

(xi) assaults or uses force to any woman belonging to a. Scheduled Caste or a Scheduled Tribe with intent to dishonour or outrage her modesty;

(xii) being in a position to dominate the will of a woman belonging to Scheduled Caste or a Scheduled Tribe and uses that position to exploit her sexually to which she would not have otherwise agreed;

(xiii) corrupts or fouls the water of any spring reservoir or any other source ordinarily used by members of the Scheduled Castes or the Scheduled Tribes so as to render it less fit for the purpose for which it is ordinarily used;

(xiv) denies a member of a Scheduled Caste or a Scheduled Tribe any customary right to passage to place of public resort or obstructs such member so as to prevent him from using or having access to a place of public resort to which other members of public or any section thereof have a right to use or access to;

(xv) forces or causes a member of a Scheduled Caste of Scheduled Tribe to leave his house, village, or other place or residence;

shall be punishable with imprisonment for a term which shall not be less that six months but which may extend to five years and with fine.

2 Whoever, not being a member of a Scheduled Caste or a Scheduled Tribe.

(i) gives or fabricates false evidence intending thereby to cause, or knowing it to be likely that he will thereby cause any member of a Scheduled Caste or a Scheduled Tribe to be convicted of an offence which is capital by the law for the time being in force shall be punished with imprisonment for life and with fine and if an innocent member of a Scheduled Caste or a Scheduled Tribe be convicted and executed in consequence of such false or fabricated evidence the person who gives or fabricates such false evidence shall be punished with death.

(ii) gives or fabricates false evidence intending thereby to cause, or knowing it to be likely that he will thereby cause, any member of a Scheduled Caste or a Scheduled Tribe to be convicted of an offence which is not capital but punishable with imprisonment for a term of seven years or upwards, shall be punishable with imprisonment for a term which shall not be less than six months but which may extend to seven years or upwards and with fine;

(iii) commits mischief by fire or any explosive substance intending to cause or knowing it to be likely that he will thereby cause damage to any property belonging to a member of a Scheduled Castes or a Scheduled Tribes, shall be punishable with imprisonment for a term which shall not be less than six months but which may extend to seven years and with fine;

(iv) commits mischief by fire or any explosive substance intending to cause or knowing it to be likely that he will thereby cause destruction of any building which is ordinarily used as a place of worship or as a place for human dwelling or as a place for custody of the property by a member of a Scheduled Caste or a Scheduled Tribe, shall be punishable with imprisonment for life and with fine;

(v) commits any offence under the Indian Penal Code (45 of 1860) punishable with imprisonment for a term of 10 years or more against a person or property on the ground that such person is a member of a Scheduled Caste or a Scheduled Tribe, or such propert belongs to such member, shall be punishable with imprisonment for life and with fine;

(vi) knowingly or having reason to believe that an offence has been committed under this Chapter, causes any evidence of the commission of that offence to disappear with the intention of screening the offender from legal punishment, or with the intention gives any information respecting the offence which he knows or believes to be false, shall be punishable with the punishment provided for that offence; or

(vii) being a public servant, commits any offence under this section shall be punishable with imprisonment for a term which shall not be less than one year but which may extend to the punishment provided for their offence.

4. ***Punishment for Neglect of Duties.*** Whoever, being public servant but not being a member of a Scheduled Caste or a Scheduled Tribe, willfully neglects his duties required to be performed by him under this Act, shall be punishable with imprisonment for a term which shall not be less than six months but which may extend to one year.

5. ***Enhanced Punishment for Subsequent Conviction.*** Whoever, having already been convicted of an offence under this Chapter is convicted for the second offence or any offence subsequent to the second offence, shall be punishable with imprisonment for a term which shall not be less than one year which may extend to the punishment provided for that offence.

6. ***Application of Certain Provisions of the Indian Penal Code.*** Subject to the other provisions of this Act, the provisions of Sec. 34, Chapter III, Chapter IV, Chapter V, Chapter V-A, Section 149 and Chapter XXIII of the Indian Penal Code (45 of 1860), shall, so far as may be, apply for the purposes of this Act as they apply for the purposes of the Indian Penal Code.

7. ***Forfeiture of Property of Certain Persons.*** 1. Where a person has been convicted any offence punishable under this Chapter, the Special Court may, in addition to awarding any punishment, by

order in writing, declare that any property, movable or immovable or both belonging to the person, which has been sued for the commission of that offence, shall stand forfeited to Government.

2. Where any person is accused of any offence under this Chapter, it shall be open to the Special Court trying him to pass an order that all or any of the period of such trial, be attached, and where such trial ends in conviction, the property so attached shall be liable to forfeiture to the extent it is required for the purpose of realization of any fine imposed under this Chapter.

8. ***Presumption as to Offences.*** In a prosecution for an offence under this Chapter, if it is proved that—

(a) the accused rendered any financial assistance to a person accused of, or reasonably suspected of committing an offence under this Chapter, the special Court shall presume, unless the contrary proved, that such person had abetted the offence;

(b) a group of persons committed an offence under this Chapter and if it is proved that the offence committed was a sequel to any existing dispute regarding land or any other matter, it shall be presumed that the offence was committed in furtherance of the common intention or in prosecution of the common object.

9. ***Conferment of Powers.*** 1. Notwithstanding anything contained in the Code or in any other provision of this Act, the State Government may, if it considers it necessary or expedient so to do—

(a) for the prevention of and for copying with any offence under this Act, or

(b) for any case or class or group of cases this Act, on any district or part thereof, confer by notification in the Official Gazette, on any district or part thereof, as the case may be, for such case or class or group of cases, and in particular, the powers of arrest, investigation and prosecution of persons before any Special Court.

2. All officers of police and all other officers of Government shall assist the officer referred to in sub-section (1) in the execution of the provisions of this Act or any rule, scheme or order made hereunder.

3. The provisions of the Code shall, so far as may be apply to the exercise of the powers by an officer under sub-section (1).

EXTERNMENT

10. Removal of Person Likely to Commit Offence. 1. Where the Special Court is satisfied, upon a complaint or a police report that a person is likely to commit an offence under Chapter II of this Act in any area included in 'Scheduled Area' or 'tribal areas', as referred to in Article 244 of the Constitution, it may by order in writing, direct such person to remove himself beyond the limits of such area, by such route and within such time as may be specified in the order, and not to return to that area from which he was directed to remove himself for such period, not exceeding two years, as may be specified in the order;

2. The Special Court shall, along with the order under sub-section (1), communicate to the persons directed under that sub section the grounds on which such order has been made.

3. The Special Court may revoke or modify the order made under sub-section (1) for the reasons to be recorded in writing, on the representation made by the person against whom such order has been made or by any other person on his behalf within thirty days from the date of the order.

11. Procedure and Failure of Person to Remove Himself from Area and Enter thereon after Removal. 1. If a person to whom direction has been issued under Section 10 to remove himself from any area—

(a) fails to remove himself as directed; or

(b) having so removed himself enters such area within the period specified in the order.

Otherwise than with the permission in writing of the Special Court under sub-section (2) the Special Court may cause him to be arrested and removed in police custody to such place outside such area as the Special Court may specify.

2. The Special Court may, by order in writing, permit any person in respect of whom an order under Section 10 has been made, to return to the area from which he was directed to remove himself for such temporary period and subject to such conditions as may be specified in such order and may require him to execute a bond with or without surety for the due observation of the conditions imposed.

3. The Special Court may at any time revoke any such permission.

4. Any person who, with such permission returns to the area from which he was directed to remove himself shall observe the

conditions imposed and at the expiry of the temporary period for which he was permitted to return or on the revocation of such permission before the expiry of such temporary period, shall remove himself outside such area and shall not return thereto within the unexpired portion specified under Section 10 without a fresh permission.

5. If a person fails to observe any of the conditions imposed or to remove himself accordingly having so removed himself enters or returns to such area without fresh permission the Special Court may cause him to be arrested and removed in police custody to such place outside area as the Special Court may specify.

12. Taking Measurements and Photographs, etc. of Persons Against Whom Order Under Section 10 is Made. 1. Every person against whom an order has been made under Section 10 shall, if so required by the Special Court, allow, his measurement and photographs to be taken by a police officer.

2. If any person referred to in sub-section (1), when required to his measurements or photographs to be taken resists or refuses to allow his taking of such measurements or photographs, it shall be lawful to use all necessary means to secure the taking thereof.

3. Resistance to or refusal to allow the taking of measurements or photographs under sub-section (2) shall be deemed to an offence under Section 186 of the Indian Penal Code (45 of 1860).

4. Where an order under Section 10 is revoked, all measurements and photographs (including negatives) taken under sub-section (2) shall be destroyed or made over to the person against whom such order is made.

13. Penalty for Non-compliance with Order Under Section 10. Any person contravening an order of the Special Court made under Section 10 shall be punishable with imprisonment for a term which may extend to one year and with fine.

SPECIAL COURTS

14. Special Court. For the purpose of providing for speedy trial, the State Government shall, with the concurrence of the Chief Justice of the High Court, by notification in the Official Gazette, specify for each district a Court of Session to be a Special Court to try the offences under this Act.

15. Special Public Prosecutor. For every Special Court, the State Government shall, by notification in the Official Gazette, specify a Public Prosecutor or appoint an advocate who has been in practice as an advocate for not less than seven years, as a Special Public Prosecutor for the purpose of conducting cases in that Court.

MISCELLANEOUS

16. Power of State Government to Impose Collective Fine. The provision of Section 10-A of the Protection of Civil Rights, Act, `1955 (22 of 1955) shall so far as may, apply for the purpose of imposition and realization of collective fine and for all other matters connected therewith under this Act.

17. Preventive Action to be Taken by the Law and Order Machinery. 1. A District Magistrate or a Sub-Divisional Magistrate or any other Executive Magistrate or any Police Officer not below the rank of a Deputy Superintendent of Police may on receiving information and after such inquiry as he may think necessary has reason to believe that a person or a group of persons not belonging to the Scheduled Castes or the Scheduled Tribes, residing in or frequenting any place within the local limits of his jurisdiction is likely to commit an offence or has threatened to commit any offence under this Act and is of the opinion that there are sufficient grounds for proceeding declare such an area to be an area prone to atrocities and take necessary action for keeping the peace and good behaviour and maintenance of public order and tranquility and may take preventive action.

2. The provisions of Chapter VII, X and XI of the Code shall, so far as may be apply for the purposes of sub-section (1).

3. The State Government may, by notification, in the Official Gazette, make one or more schemes specifying the manner in which the officers referred to sub-section (1) shall take appropriate action specified in such scheme or schemes to prevent atrocities and to restore the feeling of security amongst the members of the Scheduled Castes and the Scheduled Tribes.

18. Section 438 of the Code not to Apply to Person Committing an Offence Under the Act. Nothing in Section 438 of the Code shall apply in relation to any case involving the arrest of any person on an accusation of having committed an offence under this Act.

19. Section 360 of the Code or the Provision of the Probation of Offenders Act not Apply to Persons Guilty of an Offence Under the Act. The provisions of Section 360 of the Code and the provisions of the Probation of Offenders Act, 1958 (20 of 1958) shall apply to any person above the age of eighteen years who is found guilty having committed an offence under this Act.

20. Act to Override other Laws. Save as otherwise provided in this Act, the provisions of this Act shall have effect notwithstanding anything inconsistent therein contained in any other law for the time being in force or any custom or usage or any instrument having effect by virtue of any such law.

21. Duty of Government to Ensure Effective Implementation of the Act. 1. Subject to such rules as the Central Government may make in this behalf, the State Government shall take such measures as may be necessary for the effective implementation of this Act.

2. In particular, and without prejudice to the generality of the foregoing provisions, such measures may include—

- (i) the provision for adequate facilities, including legal aid, to the persons subjected to atrocities to enable them to avail themselves of justice;
- (ii) the provisions for travelling and maintenance expenses to witness, including the victims of atrocities, during investigation and trial of offences under this Act;
- (iii) the provision for the economic and social rehabilitation or the victims of the atrocities;
- (iv) the appointment of officers of initiating or exercising supervision over prosecution for the contravention of the provisions of this Act;
- (v) the setting up of committees at such appropriate levels as the State Government may think fit to assist that Government in formulation or implementation of such measures;
- (vi) provision for a periodic survey of the working of the provisions this Act with a view to suggesting measures for the better implementation of the provisions of this Act;
- (vii) the identification of the areas where the members of the Scheduled Castes and the Scheduled Tribes are likely to

be subjected to atrocities and adoption of such measures so as to ensure safety for such members.

3. The Central Government shall take such steps as may be necessary to co-ordinate the measures taken by the State Government under sub-section (1)

4. The Central Government shall, every year, place on the table of each House of Parliament a report on the measures taken by itself and by the State Governments in pursuance of the provisions of this section.

22. Protection of Action Taken in Good Faith. No suit, prosecution of other legal proceedings shall lie against the Central Government or against the State Government or any officer or authority of Government or any other person for anything which is in good faith done or intended to be done under this Act

23. Power to Make Rules. 1. The Central Government may, by notification in the Official Gazette, make rules for carrying out the purposes of this Act.

2. Every rule made under this Act shall be laid, as soon as may be after it is made, before each House of Parliament, while it is in session for a total period of thirty days which may be comprised in one session or in two or more successive sessions and if, before the expiry of the session immediately following the session of successive sessions aforesaid, both Houses agree in making any modification in the rule or both Houses agree that the rule should not be made, the rule shall thereafter have effect only in such modified form or be of no effect, as the case may be; so however, that any such modification or annulment shall be without prejudice to be validity of any thing previously done under that rule.

THE SCHEDULED CASTES AND THE SCHEDULED TRIBES (PREVENTION OF ATROCITIES) RULES, 1995

G.S.R. No. 316(E), dated 31st March, 1995—In exercise of the power conferred by sub-section (1) of Section 23 of the Scheduled Castes and the Scheduled Tribes (Prevention of Atrocities) Act, 1989 (33 of 1989), the Central Government hereby makes the following rules namely.

1. Short Title and Commencement. 1. These rules may be called the Scheduled Castes and Scheduled Tribes (Prevention of Atrocities) Rules, 1995.

2. They shall come into force on the date of their publication in the Official Gazette.

2. *Definitions.* In these rules, unless the context otherwise requires,—

(a) "Act" means the Scheduled Castes and the Scheduled Tribes (Prevention of Atrocities) Act, 1989 (33 of 1989);

(b) "dependent", with its grammatical variations and cognate expression, includes wife, children, whether married or unmarried, dependent parents, widowed sister, widow and children of predeceased son of a victim of atrocity;

(c) "identified area" means such area where State Government has reason to believe that atrocity may take place or there is an apprehension of re-occurrence of an offence under the Act or an area prone to victim of atrocity;

(d) "Non-Government Organisation" means a voluntary organisation engaged in the welfare activities relating to the Scheduled Castes and the Scheduled Tribes and registered under the Societies Registration Act, 1860 (21 of 1860) or under any law for the registration of documents or such organisation for the time being in force;

(e) "Schedule" means the Schedule annexed to these rules;

(f) "Section" means section of the Act;

(g) "State Government", in relation to a Union Territory, means the Administrator of that union Territory appointed by the President under Article 239 of the Constitution;

(h) words and expressions used herein and not defined but defined in the Act shall have the meaning, respectively, assigned to them in the Act.

3. Precautionary and Preventive Measures. 1. With a view to prevent atrocities on the Scheduled Castes and the Scheduled Tribes, the State Government shall,

(i) identify the area where it has reasons to believe that atrocity may take place or there is an apprehension of re-occurrence of an offence under the Act;

(ii) order the District Magistrate and Superintendent of Police or any other officer to visit the identified area and review the law and other situation;

(iii) if deem necessary, in the identified area cancel the arms licences of the persons, not being member of the Scheduled Castes or Scheduled Tribes, their near relations, servants or employees and family friends and get such arms deposited in the Government Armoury;

(iv) seize all illegal firearms and prohibit an illegal manufacture of firearms;

(v) with a view to ensure the safety of person and property, if deem necessary, provide arms licences to the members of the Scheduled Castes and the Scheduled Tribes;

(vi) constitute a high power State-level committee, district and divisional level committees or such number of committees as deem proper and necessary for assisting the Government in implementation of the provisions of the Act;

(vii) set-up a vigilance and monitoring committee to suggest effective measures to implement the provisions of the Act;

(viii) set-up Awareness Centres and organise Workshops in the identified area or at some other place to educate the persons belonging to the Scheduled Castes and the Scheduled Tribes about their rights and the protection available to them under the provisions of various Central and State enactments or rules, regulations and schemes framed thereunder;

(ix) encourage Non-Government Organisations for establishing and maintaining Awareness Centres and organising Workshops and provide them necessary financial and other sort of assistance;

(x) deploy special Police force in the identified area;

(xi) by the end of every quarter, review the law and order situation, functioning of different committees, performanc of Special Public Prosecutors, Investigating Officers and other Officers responsible for implementing the provisions of the Act and the cases registered under the Act.

4. ***Supervision of Prosecution and Submission of Report.*** 1. The State Government on the recommendation to the District Magistrate shall prepare for each district a panel of such number of eminent senior advocates who have been in practice for not less than seven years, as it may deem necessary for conducting cases in the Special Courts. Similarly, in consultation with the Director of Prosecution, officer-in-charge of the prosecution, a panel of such number of Public Prosecutors as it may deem necessary for conducting cases in the Special Courts, shall also be specified. Both these panels shall be notified in the Official Gazette of the State and shall remain in force for a period of three years.

2. The District Magistrate and the Director of Prosecution, officer-in-charge of the prosecution shall review at least twice in a calendar year, in the month of January and July, the performance of Special Public Prosecutors so specified or appointed and submit a report to the State Government.

3. If the State Government is satisfied or has reason to believe that a Special Public Prosecutor so appointed as specified has not conducted the case to the best of his ability and with due care and caution, his name may be, for reasons to be recorded in writing, denotified.

4. The District Magistrate and the officer-in-charge of the prosecution at the District level, shall review the position of cases registered under the Act and submit a monthly report on or before 20th day of each subsequent month to the Director of Prosecution and the State Government. This report shall specify the actions taken/proposed to be taken in respect of investigation and prosecution of each case.

5. Notwithstanding anything contained in sub-rule (1) the District Magistrate or the Sub-Divisional Magistrate may, if deem necessary or if so desired by the victims of atrocity engage an eminent Senior Advocate for conducting cases in the Special Courts on such payment of fees as he may consider appropriate.

6. Payment of fee to the Special Public Prosecutor shall be fixed by the State Government on a scale higher than the other panel advocates in the State.

5. Information to Police Officer-in-Charge of a Police Station. 1. Every information relating to the commission of an offence under the Act, if given orally to an officer-in-charge of a Police station shall be reduced to writing by him or under his direction, and be read over to the informant, and every such information, whether given in writing or reduced to writing as aforesaid, shall be signed by the person giving it, and the substance thereof shall be entered in a book to be maintained by that police station.

2. A copy of the information as so recorded under sub-rule (1) above shall be given forthwith, free of cost, to the informant.

3. Any person aggrieved by a refusal on the part of a officer-in-charge of a Police station to record the information referred to in sub-rule (1) may send the substance of such information, in writing and by post, to the Superintendent of Police concerned who after investigation either by himself or by a Police officer not below the rank of Deputy Superintendent of Police, shall make an order in writing to the officer-in-charge of the concerned Police station to enter the substance of that information in the book to be maintained by that police station.

6. Spot Inspection by Officers. 1. Whenever the District Magistrate or the Sub-Divisional Magistrate or any other Executive Magistrate or any Police officer not below the rank of Deputy Superintendent of Police receives an information from any person or upon his own knowledge that an atrocity had been committed on the members of the Scheduled Castes or the Scheduled Tribes within his jurisdiction he shall immediately himself visit the place of occurrence to assess the extent of atrocity, loss of life, loss and damage to the property and submit a report forthwith to the State Government.

2. The District Magistrate or the Sub-Divisional Magistrate or any other Executive Magistrate and the Superintendent of Police, Deputy Superintendent of Police after inspecting the place or area shall on the spot,—

(i) draw a list of victims, their family members and dependents entitled of relief,

(ii) prepare a detailed report of the extent of atrocity loss and damage to the property of the victims;

(iii) order for intensive Police patrolling in the area;

(iv) take effective and necessary steps to provide protection to the witnesses and other sympathisers of the victims;

(v) provide immediate relief to the victims.

7. ***Investigating Officer.*** 1. An offence committed under the Act shall be investigated by a Police officer not below the rank of a Deputy Superintendent of Police. The Investigating Officer shall be appointed by the State Government, Director-General of Police, Superintendent of Police after taking into account his past experience, sense of ability and justice to perceive the implications of the case and investigate it along with right lines within the shortest possible time.

2. The Investigating Officer so appointed under sub-rule (1) shall complete the investigation on top priority within thirty days and submit the report to the Superintendent of Police who in turn will immediately forward the report to the Director-General of Police of the State Government.

3. The Home Secretary and the Social Secretary to the State Government, Director of Prosecution, the Officer-in-Charge of Prosecution and the Director General of Police shall review by the end of every quarter the position of all investigations done by the Investigating Officer.

8. ***Setting up of the Scheduled Castes and the Scheduled Tribes Protection Cell.*** 1. The State Government shall set up a Scheduled Castes and the Scheduled Tribes Protection Cell at the State headquarters under the charge of Director of Police, Inspector-General of Police. This Cell shall be responsible for,

(i) conducting survey of the identified area;

(ii) maintaining public order and tranquillity in the identified area;

(iii) recommending to the State Government for deployment of special Police force or establishment of special Police post in the identified area;

(iv) making investigations about the probable causes leading to an offence under the Act;

(v) restoring the feeling of security amongst the members of the Scheduled Castes and the Scheduled Tribes;

(vi) informing the nodal officer and special officer about the law and order situation in the identified area;

(vii) making enquiries about the investigation and spot inspections conducted by various officers;

(viii) making enquiries about the action taken by the Superintendent of Police in the cases where an officer-in-charge of the police station has refused to enter an information in a book to be maintained by that police station under sub-rule (3) of Rule 5;

(ix) making enquiries about the wilful negligence by a public servant;

(x) reviewing the position of cases registered under the Act; and

(xi) submitting a monthly report on or before 20th day of each subsequent month to the State Government nodal officer about the action taken or proposed to be taken in respect of the above.

9. Nomination of Nodal Officer. The State Government shall nominate a nodal officer of the level of a Secretary to the Government preferably belonging to the Scheduled Castes or the Scheduled Tribes, for co-ordinating the functioning of the District Magistrates and Superintendent of Police or other officers authorised by them as Investigating Officers and other officers responsible for implementing the provisions of the Act. By the end of the every quarter, the nodal officer shall review—

(i) the reports received by the State Government under sub-rules (2) and (4) of Rule 4, Rule 6, clause (xi) of rule 8;

(ii) the position of cases registered under the Act;

(iii) law and order situation in the identified area;

(iv) various kinds of measures adopted for providing immediate relief in cash or kind or both to the victim of atrocity or his or her dependent;

(v) adequacy of immediate facilities like rationing, clothing, shelter, legal aid, travelling allowance, daily allowance and transport facilities provided to the victim of atrocity or his or her dependents;

(vi) performance of non-Government organisations, the Scheduled Castes and the Schedule Tribes Protection Cell, various committees and the public servants responsible for implementing the provisions of the Act.

10. Appointment of a Special Officer. In the identified area a Special Officer not below the rank of an Additional District Magistrate shall be appointed to co-ordinate with the District Magistrate,

Superintendent of Police or other officers responsible for implementing the provisions of the Act, various committees and the Scheduled Castes and the Scheduled Tribes Protection Cell.

The Special Officer shall be responsible for—

(i) providing immediate relief and other facilities to the victims of atrocity and initiate necessary measures to prevent or avoid reoccurrence of atrocity;

(ii) setting up an awareness centre and organising workshop in the identified area or at the district headquarters to educate the persons belonging to the Scheduled Castes and the Scheduled Tribes about their rights and the protection available to them under the provisions of various Central and State enactments or rules and schemes etc., framed therein;

(iii) co-ordinating with the Non-Governmental organisations and providing necessary facilities and financial and other type of assistance to Non-Governmental Organisation for maintaining centres or organising workshops.

11. Travelling Allowance, Daily Allowance, Maintenance Expenses and Transport Facilities to the Victim of Atrocity or his or her Dependents and Witnesses. 1. Every victim of atrocity or his/her dependents and witnesses shall be paid to and fro rail fare by second class in express/mail/passenger train or actual bus or taxi fare from his/her place of residence or actual bus or taxi fare from his/her place of residence or place of stay to the place of investigation or hearing of trial of an offence under the Act.

2. The District Magistrate or the Sub-Divisional Magistrate or any other Executive Magistrate shall make necessary arrangements for providing transport facilities or reimbursement of full payment thereof to the victims of atrocity and witnesses for visiting the Investigating Officer, Superintendent of Police/Deputy Superintendent of Police, District Magistrate or any other Executive Magistrate.

3. Every woman witness the victim of atrocity or her dependent being a woman or a minor, a person more than sixty years of age and a person having 40 per cent or more disability shall be entitled to be accompanied by an attendant of her/his choice. The attendant shall also be paid travelling and maintenance expenses as applicable to the witness or the victim of atrocity when called upon during hearing, investigation and trial of an offence under the Act.

4. The witness, the victim of atrocity or his/her dependent and the attendant shall be paid daily maintenance expenses for the days he/she is away from the place of his/her residence or stay during investigation, hearing and trial of an offence, at such rates but not less than the minimum wages, as may be fixed by the State Government for the agricultural labourers.

5. In addition to daily maintenance expenses the witness, the victim of atrocity (or his/her dependent) and the attendant shall also be paid diet expenses at such rates as may be fixed by the State Government from time to time.

6. The payment of travelling allowance, daily allowance, maintenance expenses and reimbursement of transport facilities shall be made immediately or not later than three days by the District Magistrate or the Sub-Divisional Magistrate or any other Executive Magistrate to the victims, their dependents/attendants and witnesses for the days they visit the Investigating Officer or in charge of Police station or hospital authorities or Superintendent of Police, Deputy Superintendent of Police or District Magistrate or any other officer concerned or the Special Court.

7. When an offence has been committed under Section 3 of the Act, the District Magistrate or the Sub-Divisional Magistrate or any other Executive Magistrate shall reimburse the payment of medicines, special medical consultation, blood transfusion, replacement of essential clothings, meals and fruits provided to the victim(s) of atrocity.

12. Measures to be Taken by the District Administration. 1. The District Magistrate and the Superintendent of Police shall visit the place or area where the atrocity has been committed to assess the loss of life and damage to the property and draw a list of victims, their family members and dependents entitled for relief.

2. The Superintendent of Police shall ensure that the First Information Report is registered in the book of the concerned police station and effective measures for apprehending the accused are taken.

3. The Superintendent of Police, after spot inspection, shall immediately appoint an Investigation Officer and deploy such police force in the area and take such other preventive measures as he may deem proper and necessary.

4. The District Magistrate or the Sub-Divisional Magistrate or any other Executive Magistrate shall make arrangements providing

immediate relief in cash or in kind or both to the victims of atrocity, their family members and dependents according to the scale as in the Schedule annexed to these Rules (Annexure I read with Annexure II). Such immediate relief shall also include food, water, clothing, shelter, medical aid, transport facilities and other essential items necessary for human beings.

5. The relief provided to the victim of the atrocity or his/her dependent under sub-rule (4) in respect of death, or injury to, or damage to property shall be in addition to any other right to claim compensation in respect thereof under any other law for the time being in force.

6. The relief and rehabilitation facilities mentioned in sub-rule (4) above shall be provided by the District Magistrate or the Sub-Divisional Magistrate or any other Executive Magistrate in accordance with the scales provided in the Schedule annexed to these rules.

7. A report of the relief and rehabilitation facilities provided to the victims shall also be forwarded to the Special Court by the District Magistrate or the Sub-Divisional Magistrate or the Executive Magistrate or Superintendent of Police. In case the Special Court is satisfied that the payment of relief was not made to the victim or his/her dependent in time or the amount of relief or compensation was not sufficient or only a part payment of relief or compensation was made, it may order for making in full on part payment of relief or any other kind of assistance.

13. Selection of Officers and Other Staff Members for Completing the Work Relating to Atrocity. 1. The State Government shall ensure that the administrative officers and other staff members to be appointed in an area prone to atrocity shall have the right aptitude and understanding of the problems of the Scheduled Castes and Scheduled Tribes.

2. It shall also be ensured by the State Government that persons from the Scheduled Castes and the Scheduled Tribes are adequately represented in the administration and in the Police force at all levels, particularly at the level of police posts and police station.

14. Specified Responsibility of the State Government. The State Government shall make necessary provisions in its annual budget for providing relief and rehabilitation facilities to the victims of atrocity. It shall review at least twice in a calendar year, in the month of January and July the performance of the Special Public Prosecutor specified or appointed under Section 15 of the Act, various reports received, investigation made and preventive steps taken by the District Magistrate, Sub-Divisional Magistrate and Superintendent of Police, relief and rehabilitation facilities provided to the victims and the reports in respect of lapses on behalf of the concerned officers.

15. Contingency Plan by the State Government. 1. State Government shall prepare a model contingency plan for implementing the provisions of the Act and notify the same in the Official Gazette of the State Government. It should specify the role and responsibility of various departments and their officers at different levels, the role and responsibility of Rural/Urban Local Bodies and Non-Government Organisation. *Inter alia* this plan shall contain a package of relief measures including the following:

(a) scheme to provide immediate relief in cash or in kind or both;
(b) allotment of agricultural land and house-sites;
(c) the rehabilitation packages;
(d) scheme for employment in Government or Government Undertaking to the dependent or one of the family members of the victim;
(e) pension scheme for widows, dependent children of the deceased, handicapped or old age victims of atrocity;
(f) mandatory compensation for the victims;
(g) scheme for strengthening the socio-economic condition of the victim;
(h) provision for providing brick/stone masonry house to the victims;
(i) such other elements as health care, supply of essential commodities, electrification, adequate drinking water facility, burial/cremation ground and link roads to the Scheduled Castes and the Scheduled Tribes habitates.

2. The State Government shall forward a copy of contingency plan or a summary thereof and a copy of the scheme, as soon as may be, to the Central Government in the Ministry of Welfare and to all the District Magistrates, Sub-Divisional Magistrates, Inspector Generals of Police and Superintendents of Police.

16. Constitution of State Level Vigilance and Monitoring Committee. 1. The State Government shall constitute a high power vigilance and monitoring committee of not more than 25 members consisting of the following—

(i) Chief Minister/Administrator-Chairman (in case of a State under President's Rule Governor); —*Chairman*

(ii) Home Minister, Finance Minister and Welfare Minister (in case of a State under the President's Rule Advisors); —*Members*

(iii) all elected Members of Parliament and the State Legislative Assembly and Legislative Counsel from the State belonging to the Scheduled Castes and the Scheduled Tribes. —*Members*

(iv) Chief Secretary, the Home Secretary, the Director-General of Police, Director/Deputy Director of National Commission for the Scheduled Castes and the Scheduled Tribes. —*Members*

(v) the Secretary-in-Charge of the welfare and development of the Scheduled Castes and the Scheduled Tribes. —*Convenor*

2. The high power vigilance and monitoring committee shall meet at least twice in a calendar year, in the months of January and July to review the implementation of the provisions of the Act, relief and rehabilitation facilities provided to the victims and other matters connected therewith, prosecution of cases under the Act, rule of different officers/agencies responsible for implementing the provisions of the Act and various reports received by the State Government.

17. Constitution of District Level Vigilance and Monitoring Committee. 1. In each district within the State, the District Magistrate shall set up a vigilance and monitoring committee in his district to review the implementation of the provisions of the Act, relief and rehabilitation facilities provided to the victims and other matters connected therewith, prosecution of cases under the Act, role of different officers/agencies responsible for implementing the provisions of the Act and various reports received by the District Administration.

2. The district level vigilance and monitoring committee shall consist of the elected Members of the Parliament and State Legislative Assembly and Legislative Council, Superintendent of Police, three group 'A' Officers, Gazetted Officers of the State Government belonging to the Scheduled Castes and the Scheduled Tribes not more than 5 non-official members belonging to the Scheduled Castes and the Scheduled Tribes and not more than 3 members from the

categories other than the Scheduled Castes and the Scheduled Tribes having association with Non-Government Organisations. The District Magistrate and District Social Welfare Officer shall be Chairman and Member-Secretary, respectively.

3. The district level committee shall meet at least once in three months.

18. Material for Annual Report. The State Government shall, before every 31st March, forward the report to the Central Government about the measures taken for implementing provisions of the Act and various schemes/plans framed by it during the previous calendar year.

RULES OF PROCEDURE OF THE NATIONAL COMMISSION FOR SCHEDULED CASTES AND SCHEDULED TRIBES

GENERAL

1. *Constitution of the Commission.* The National Commission for Scheduled Castes and Scheduled Tribes (hereinafter called the Commission) has been constituted under Article 338 of the Constitution of India as amended by the Constitution (Sixty-fifth Amendment) Act, 1990. The Commission shall consist of a Chairperson, a Vice-Chairperson and five other Members.

2. *Headquarters of the Commission.* The Headquarters of the Commission shall be located at New Delhi.

3. *State Offices of the Commission.* The Commission shall have under its control the following State Offices:

	Location	Jurisdiction
1.	Agartala	Tripura
2.	Ahmedabad	Gujarat, and UT of Dadra and Nagar Haveli
3.	Bangalore	Karnataka
4.	Bhopal	Madhya Pradesh
5.	Bhubaneshwar	Orissa
6.	Kolkata	West Bengal, Sikkim and UT of A&N Islands
7.	Chandigarh	Punjab, Haryana, Himachal Predesh, J&K and UT of Chandigarh

8. Guwahati	Assam, Arunachal Pradesh, Manipur and Nagaland
9. Hyderabad	Andhra Pradesh
10. Jaipur	Rajasthan
11. Lucknow	Uttar Pradesh and Uttaranchal
12. Madras	Tamil Nadu and UT of Pondicherry
13. Patna	Bihar
14. Pune	Maharashtra, Goa, and UT of Daman and Diu
15. Shillong	Meghalaya and Mizoram
16. Thiruvananthapuram	Kerala and UT of Lakshadweep and Minicoy Islands

4. The Commission may, if considered necessary, open new offices and sub-offices and upgrade or downgrade the status and change the jurisdiction of any of its State Offices.

5. The function and responsibilities of the Commission as laid down in the Constitution are:

(a) to investigate and monitor all matters relating to the safeguards provided for the Scheduled Castes and Scheduled Tribes under the Constitution or under any other law for the time being in force or under any order of the Government and to evaluate the working of such safeguards;

(b) to inquire into specific complaints with respect to the deprivation of rights and safeguards of the Scheduled Castes and Scheduled Tribes;

(c) to participate and advise on the planning process of socio-economic development of the Scheduled Castes and Scheduled Tribes and to evaluate the progress of their development under the Union and any State;

(d) to present to the President, annually and at such other times as the Commission may deem fit, reports upon the working of those safeguards;

(e) to make in such reports recommendation as to the measures that should be taken by the Union or any State for the effective implementation of those safeguards and other measures for the protection, welfare and socio-economic development of the Scheduled Castes and Scheduled Tribes; and

(f) to discharge such other functions in relation to the protection, welfare and development and advancement of the Scheduled Castes and Scheduled Tribes as the President may, subject to the provisions of any law made by Parliament, by rule specify.

6. The Commission shall function by holding 'sittings' and 'meetings' at any place within the country and also through its officers at the Headquarters and in the State Offices. The Members of the Commission including the Chairperson and the Vice-Chairperson shall function in accordance with the procedure prescribed under these rules.

DIVISION OF RESPONSIBILITIES AND ALLOCATION OF WORK

Chairperson

7. The Chairperson shall be the head of the Commission and shall have the residuary powers to decide on all questions and matters arising in the Commission excepting such matters where specific provision has been made in these rules.

8. The Chairperson shall allocate subject and responsibilities among the Members of the Commission. The Order allocating the subjects and responsibilities shall be circulated to all concerned by the Secretariat of the Commission.

9. The Chairperson shall be the authority to sanction leave and approve tours of the Members.

10. The Chairperson shall preside over the meetings of the Commission.

11. All important decisions in the Commission pertaining to the subjects allotted to the Members shall be taken with the approval of the Chairperson.

12. The Chairperson may call for any records on any matter which he considers important any may take a decision on it himself or, if necessary, place it at the meeting of the Commission.

Vice-Chairperson

13. The Vice-Chairperson shall preside over the meetings of the Commission in the absence of the Chairperson.

14. The Vice-Chairperson shall perform such functions as are entrusted to him by the Chairperson.

Members

15. The Members of the Commission shall have collective responsibility and shall function by participating in the 'meetings' and 'sittings' of the Commission and looking after the subjects allocated to them. Important actions and decisions of a Member may be brought at a meeting of the Commission which may review for same.

16. Any Members may suggest items for inclusion in the agenda of a meeting of the Commission and the same shall be so included after obtaining the consent of the Chairperson.

17. Each member shall have overall responsibility of subjects and/or regions or State(s) as may be allocated to him.

18. The Members shall play the role of advising the State Governments under their jurisdiction on matters of planning and development relating to the welfare of Scheduled Castes and Scheduled Tribes. The Commission's Secretariat at Headquarters and the State Offices shall assist the Members in keeping them fully informed of the problems and activities of the States and subjects under their respective charge.

19. One or more Members may, in accordance with the procedure specified in the rules elsewhere, hold sittings of the Commission to give hearing to the cases or to collect evidence or information on any matter, issue or case under investigation or inquiry by the Commission.

20. The Members shall communicate their tour programmes well in advance to the State Offices indicating in detail the purpose of the visit and to the State Government Department and others concerned for discussions/inquiry, etc., during the tour/visit. The Members will observe the norms laid down by the State Governments regarding security/travel/accommodation etc., during such tours.

Secretary

21. The Secretary shall be the administrative head of the Commission and shall assist the Commission in the discharge of its functions with the assistance of the officers of the Commission.

22. All important administrative matters shall be placed before the Secretary who may pass general or specific orders on such matters.

23. The Secretary shall be responsible for having the agenda prepared for the meetings of the Commission and for circulating the minutes.

24. The Secretary shall assist the Commission in finalising the Reports.

25. The Secretary may, in his discretion, delegate any of the functions or authority to a subordinate officer of the Secretariat.

INVESTIGATION AND INQUIRY BY THE COMMISSION

Methods of Investigation and Inquiry

26. The Commission may adopt any one or more of the following methods for investigating or inquiring into the matters falling within its authority:

(a) by the Commission directly;
(b) by an Investigating Team Constituted at the Headquarters of the Commission; and
(c) through its State Offices.

Investigation and Inquiry by the Commission Directly

27. The Commission may hold sittings for investigation into matters relating to safeguards, protection, welfare and development of the Scheduled Castes and Scheduled Tribes or for inquiring into specific complaints for which the Commission decides to take up investigation or inquiry directly. Such sittings may be held either at the Headquarters of the Commission or at any other place within the country.

28. The sitting(s) of the Commission would be held after giving due notice to the parties intended to be heard and also due publicity notice to the general public. Care will be taken to see that the members of the Scheduled Castes or Scheduled Tribes who are affected in the matter under investigation or inquiry are given due information through notice or publicity.

29. When a decision for direct investigation is taken, an officer not below the rank of Research Officer/Section Officer along with necessary staff may be attached to the Member(s) entrusted with such investigation or enquiry and they shall take all steps to arrange such sittings.

30. During the course of the investigation or inquiry the Commission, acting through such a sitting, may make evidence on oath or receive affidavits. When considered necessary, the Commission, for the purpose of taking evidence in the investigation or inquiry, require the presence of any person and may issue summons to him. The summons shall provide at least fifteen days' notice to the person directed to be present before the Commission from the date of receipt of the summons.

31. Where the property, service/employment of SCs and STs and other related matters are under immediate threat and prompt attention of the Commission is required, the matter shall be taken cognizance by issue of telex/fax to the concerned authority for making it known to them that the Commission is seized of the issue. Urgent reply by telegram or fax shall be called from the concerned authority. In case no letter is received within a week, the authority concerned shall be summoned at a short notice for enquiry.

32. The Commission may issue Commission to take evidence in any matter under investigation or inquiry and for this purpose appoint any person by an order in writing. The Commission may make further rules for payment of fee and travelling and other allowances to persons appointed to take evidence on commission.

33. After holding the required sittings, the Member(s) who conducted the investigation shall make a report which shall be sent to the Secretary or any other officer authorised to receive the report. After examination, action may be initiated on the report with the approval of the Chairperson.

Investigation or Inquiry by an Investigation Team Constituted at the Headquarters of the Commission

34. The Commission may decide about the matter that is to be investigated or enquired into by an Investigating Team of officials of the Commission, provided that in case the matter is urgent, the decision for such investigation or inquiry may be taken by the Chairperson.

35. The Investigating Team shall hold the investigation or inquiry, as the case may be, promptly and for this purpose may initiate necessary correspondence including issuance of notices for production of documents in Form I.

36. The Investigating Team may visit the area concerned after observing due formalities for obtaining approval of tours and other administrative requirements and after giving information to the concerned local authorities regarding the matter, purpose, scope and procedure of the investigation or inquiry. The Investigating Team may enlist the help of the officers and staff of the concerned State Office but the responsibility of preparing and presenting the report shall rest with the head of the Investigating Team.

37. The Investigating Team shall submit the report of the investigation or enquiry, as the case may be, to the Secretary or a subordinate officer of the Commission as may be directed by general or specific orders within the stipulated time, if any. If the time limit stipulated is likely to be exceeded the head of the Investigating Team shall obtain the orders of the Secretary through the Officer-in-Charge of the matter. The report shall be examined and put up to the competent authority for decision regarding the action to be taken on the report.

38. The report shall be placed before the Chairperson of the Commission who will take appropriate action in the matter.

Investigation and Inquiry Through the State Offices

39. The Chairperson, the Vice-Chairperson, the Members having jurisdiction over the subject or the Secretary of the Commission may decide about an investigation or inquiry that may be carried out through the State Offices of the Commission. The decision will be conveyed to the Officer-in-Charge of the concerned State Office who will be asked to get the matter investigated or inquired into within a stipulated time and send the report. The State Office shall conduct the investigation or inquiry through interrogation, on the spot visit, discussions and correspondence and examination of documents as may be necessary in the case and shall follow any special or general instructions issued in the matter by the Secretariat of the Commission from time to time.

40. If the investigation or inquiry cannot be completed within the stipulated time the Officer-in-Charge of the State Office may send a communication to the Secretariat of the Commission before the expiry of the stipulated time and explain the circumstances and reasons for non-completion of the investigation or inquiry, as the case may be, within the stipulated time. The Secretary to the Commission or an officer acting under delegated functions may consider the request and communicate a revised date for the completion of the investigation or inquiry.

41. If during the course of investigation or inquiry the head of the State Office feels that it is necessary to invoke the powers of the Commission to require the production of any document or compelling the attendance of a person, he may make a special report with full facts to the Secretariat of the Commission. On receipt of such special report the matter shall be placed before the Secretary/ Member-in-Charge of the subject/State/UT who may make an order that necessary legal processes to compel attendance or to require production of any document may be issued. The summons and warrants issued for the purpose may be served on the person concerned either directly or through the Officer-in-Charge of the State Office as may be directed by the Secretary/Member authorising issue of such legal process.

42. After completion of the investigation or inquiry, as the case may be, the head of the State Office shall submit the report to the Secretary of the Commission suggesting the course of action that could be followed in the matter. The gist or findings of the report may be placed before the Secretary who may decide about further action in the matter.

Confidentiality of Certain Reports

43. The Commission may, through a decision at a meeting or otherwise, direct that the contents of any report made on any matter shall be kept confidential and shall not be revealed to any person other than those who have been authorised access to such report.

Legal Processes

44. All summons and warrants that are required to be issued in pursuance of the exercise of the powers of a Civil Court by the Commission shall be written in the prescribed form and shall bear the seal of the Commission. The legal process shall be issued from the Legal Cell of the Commission and shall bear its seal. The provisions of the Code of Civil Procedure applicable for the service of the legal processes shall be followed by the Commission.

Issue of Letters and Notices

45. Letters and notices requiring production of documents which are issued without exercising the powers of the Civil Court by the Commission may be signed by an officer not below the rank of Research Officer/Section Officer.

Form of Summons and Warrants

46. The summons and warrants shall be as provided in Forms II and III respectively, appended to these rules.

MEETINGS OF THE COMMISSION

Frequency of Meetings

47. The Commission shall meet at least once in two months. The notice for a meeting shall normally be issued two weeks in advance. Emergent meetings may also be called by the Chairperson either on his own or on the request of a Member or the Secretary for disposing of important matters requiring urgent consideration by the Commission.

Quorum

48. The Chairperson or the vice-Chairperson and two other Members shall form the quorum for holding a meeting of the Commission.

Matters Requiring Decisions by the Commission at its Meetings

49. The following matters shall be brought up before the Commission at a meeting for consideration and decision:

- (i) any amendment to these Rules of Procedure;
- (ii) matters to be investigated by the Commission directly;
- (iii) all the reports that are required to be considered by the Commission as provided in these rules;
- (iv) any matters that a Member may like to bring to the meeting, with the approval of the Chairperson;
- (v) importing matters relating to planning and development for the welfare and advancement of the Scheduled Castes and Scheduled Tribes and specially references received under Article 338(9) of the Constitution; and
- (vi) any matter that the Chairperson may direct to be placed at a meeting of the Commission.

Agenda for the Meeting

50. The agenda will normally be circulated to all the Members at least seven days before the date of the meeting, provided that for an Emergent meeting this time limit may not apply.

51. The minutes of a meeting shall be circulated as soon as possible to all the Members.

Place of Meeting of the Commission

52. Normally the place of meeting of the Commission shall be the Headquarters of the Commission at New Delhi. The Commission may, however, decide to hold a meeting at any other place in India.

Fee

53. The Chairperson, the Vice-Chairperson and the Members shall not be entitled to any fee for sitting in the meeting of the Commission. However, the entitlement of Part-time Members, if any, may be determined by the terms of appointment of such Members.

SITTINGS OF THE COMMISSION

Need for Sittings

54. Whenever a matter is to be investigated into directly by the Commission it may do so by holding sittings of the Commission. In the case of such sittings the presence of all the Members may not be necessary.

Officers to be Present

55. Whenever a Member(s) is holding a sitting, an Officer of the Commission, not below the rank of Research Officer/Section Officer, duly deputed for the purpose shall be present to assist the Member(s) holding the sitting to discharge the functions properly and promptly. It shall be the duty of the officer to assist the Member(s) in preparing the report if called upon to do so by the Member(s). The Officer shall also be responsible for assisting the Member(s) in following the prescribed procedure.

Frequency of Sitting(s)

56. Sittings of the Commission may be held as and when necessary. The Commission may hold more than one sitting simultaneously in different parts of the country with different Members functioning separately.

Programme of the Sittings

57. The programme of the sittings, both at the Headquarters and at other places, would normally be worked out each month in advance and duly circulated.

Defraying Expenses to Witnesses

58. The Commission may defray travelling expenses to persons who have been called through summons to appear before the Commission in a sitting, provided that the place of residence of one person is more than 8 kms, from the place of the sittings of the Commission. The amount so defrayed shall be limited to the actual travelling expenses plus Daily Allowance for the number of days that the person has appeared before the Commission in its sitting, provided that the person is not entitled to travelling and daily allowance from any other source. Persons who are employees of the Government/Public Sector Undertaking shall be deemed to be on duty if they are summoned to depose before the Commission or produce documents. The limit of travelling expenses shall be determined on the basis of the rail fare and road mileage calculated on the basis of the rates that may be prescribed by the Commission. In the case of any doubt regarding the entitlement of the person the decision of the Secretary of the Commission shall be final.

59. The officer attached to the Member for the purposes of the sitting shall take steps to ensure that sufficient cash amount is carried if the sitting is held at a place other than the Headquarters of the Commission. The Secretariat of the Commission may devise a suitable procedure to ensure that such claims as above are paid on the spot and in cash to the person(s) so appearing.

60. The claim for travelling expenses as above shall not be admissible in the case of a person who appears before the Commission during any investigation or enquiry on his own accord or in response to a communication or notice which is not a summon issued by the Commission.

DUTIES OF THE STATE OFFICES OF THE COMMISSION

61. It shall be the duty of the State Offices of the Commission:

(i) To act as the "eyes and ears" of the Commission in the State(s) of their jurisdiction.

(ii) To maintain effective interaction and liaison with State Government/UT Administrations on behalf of the Commission.

(iii) To serve on State Level Advisory Councils/Committees/Corporations, etc. on behalf of the Commission.

(iv) To provide information and documentation about the policies and programmes of the Union Government for the welfare and advancement of SCs and STs to the States, NGOs, Media in their respective jurisdiction. Obtain similar information and documentation from such organisation and provide to the Headquarters of the Commission information/documentation about important development, social movements, policy changes. etc. in the State affecting the interest of SCs and STs.

(v) To monitor and assist the working of voluntary and other non-governmental organisations receiving grant-in-aid from the Ministry of Social Justice and Empowerment as also other Ministries/Departments of the Central Government and the concerned State Governments, Foreign Aid Agencies, etc., for Research Studies and any other development work relating to SCs and STs.

(vi) To conduct Research Studies, Seminars, Conferences, Surveys, etc. either on their own or as entrusted to them by Headquarters from time to time.

(vii) To conduct on the spot inquiries into cases of atrocities on SCs and STs either on their own or as entrusted to them by Headquarters and interact with the concerned Administrative/Police authorities having jurisdiction and report to the Headquarters.

(viii) To deal with complaints/representations from individuals, SC/ST Welfare Associations, etc. on various matters.

(ix) To participate and advise in the planning process for socio-economic development of the SCs/STs as envisaged under Clause 5 of Article 338 of the Constitution of India.

(x) To collect, compile, analyse and monitor issues pertaining to development of SCs and STs in the States especially with reference to SCP, TSP and SCA, and prepare drafts of Reports pertaining to the State/UT under their jurisdiction.

(xi) To prepare and maintain a comprehensive and up to date

data base of SC/ST population, education, development, etc. in the State/UT; and

(xii) To perform any other duty specifically assigned/entrusted to the State Office(s) by the Commission or the Secretary or any other officer empowered in this regard.

ADVISORY ROLE OF THE COMMISSION

Interaction of the Commission with the State Governments

62. The Commission shall interact with the State Governments through its Members, Secretariat and the State Offices.

63. The Member in charge of the State/UT would interact with the State Government/UT Administration through meetings, personal contacts, visits and correspondence. The information in this regard may be sent to the concerned Department/Organisations well in advance and the State Offices should also be informed about the same. For this purpose, detailed guidelines may be formulated by the Commission. The Secretariat of the Commission through its concerned Wing(s) would provide necessary assistance and information to the Member for enabling him to discharge his functions effectively. The State Government should provide facilities for transport, security, accommodation etc., to the Member as per his entitlement.

Interaction with the Planning Commission

64. The Commission shall interact with the Planning Commission at appropriate levels through representation in the various Committees, Working Groups or other such bodies set up by the Planning Commission. The Commission shall indicate this requirement through general or specific communication to the Planning Commission.

65. The Commission may request the Planning Commission to forward copies of all the documents concerning the process of planning and development and evaluation of all programmes and schemes touching upon the Scheduled Castes and Scheduled Tribes.

66. The Commission may decide about the manner of interaction between the Chairperson/Members of the Commission and the Deputy Chairman/Members of the Planning Commission.

Interaction of the State Offices with the State Governments

67. The State Offices of the Commission shall work in a manner so as to provide a regular and effective link between the State Governments concerned and the Commission. For this purpose the Commission may send communication to the State Governments suggesting that the officers-in-charge of the State Offices of the Commission may be taken on important Planning, Evaluation and Advisory Bodies including Corporations concerned with the welfare protection and development of the Scheduled Castes and Scheduled Tribes.

68. The officer-in-charge of the State Offices may be directed or authorised by the Commission to convey to any State Authority the formal views, opinion or approach of the Commission on any specific or general matter or issue arising at any meeting or deliberation.

Research/Studies/Surveys/Evaluation

69. The Commission may undertake studies to evaluate the impact of the development schemes on the socio-economic development of the Scheduled Castes and Scheduled Tribes taken up by the Union or State Governments. For this purpose the Commission may constitute Study Teams either at the Headquarters or at the State Offices. The Study Teams may undertake investigations, survey or studies either in collaboration with the Central or State Government authorities or Universities or Research Bodies, as the case may be, or may do so independently.

70. The Commission may entrust surveys or evaluation studies to any professional body or person considered suitable and competent to undertake such work and for this purpose may make any reasonable payment to such body or person towards the cost of the study by way of fee or grant.

71. The studies so undertaken or their gists may form part of the Annual or Special Report of the Commission to be presented to the President or may be published separately by the Commission.

72. The Commission may forward a copy of such a study report to the Union or the State Government concerned, as the case may be, asking for their comments, if any. The comments or action taken reports by the Union/State Government may also form part of the Annual Report of the Commission.

MONITORING FUNCTIONS OF THE COMMISSION

The Commission to Determine Subjects for Monitoring

73. The Commission may determine from time to time the subjects or matters and areas that it would monitor relating to safeguards and other socio-economic development measures provided for the Scheduled Castes and Scheduled Tribes under the Constitution or under any other law for the time being in force or under any order of the Government.

Prescribing Returns and Reports

74. The Commission may prescribe periodical returns or reports to be furnished by any authority responsible for or having control of the subject-matter of which monitoring is being done by the Commission.

75. The Commission may from time to time issue instructions to its State Offices to collect information and data on any particular subject or matter from the State Governments. Local Bodies, Corporate Bodies or any other authorities which is charged with the implementation of the safeguards provided for the Scheduled Castes and Scheduled Tribes.

76. The Commission may direct its State Offices to process the information or data in the State Offices with a view to arriving at conclusion with regard to the deficiencies or shortcoming discovered through such processing or analysis of the data and to bring these to the notice of the concerned authority for comments and rectification, where necessary.

77. The Commission may have data, relating to the subject monitored collected to the headquarters and may prescribe returns and reports for the purpose to be sent directly to its Headquarters by the Ministries/Departments of the Central Government or a State Government or Public Sector Undertaking or any other body or authority which is charged with the responsibility of implementing safeguards relating to the Scheduled Castes and Scheduled Tribes.

Follow-up Action

78. In order to ensure that monitoring is done effectively the Commission, after getting the information as prescribed in the above rules and after reaching conclusions, may as early as possible send out communication to the concerned authority describing the shortcomings that have been noticed in the implementation of the safeguards and suggesting corrective steps. Decisions on sending out such a communication may be taken at a level not lower than that of Joint Secretary/Secretary at Headquarters. Directors-in-Charge of State Offices may take decisions on routine matter whereas they will seek approval of the Secretary and the concerned Member on complex and important matters effecting the interest of SCs and STs, as a group.

79. The Commission may ask for the comments of the concerned authority on the action taken in pursuance of the communication sent under the provisions of Rule 78.

80. The Commission may include in its Annual Report or any Special Report findings and conclusions arrived at through the process of monitoring of the subjects relating to the safeguards and socio-economic development measures provided for the Scheduled Castes and Scheduled Tribes under the Constitution or under any other law for the time being in force or under any order of the Union/State Government.

NON-FORMAL ACTIONS BY THE COMMISSION

81. The Commission may initiate correspondence in special cases in matters or cases which are not strictly covered under the law if the matter is such that the welfare of an individual person belonging to Scheduled Castes or Scheduled Tribes or that of a group of such persons is involved and it is necessary for the Commission in its inherent capacity as the protector of the interests of these classes of persons, to take action. The decision for correspondence on such matter shall be taken at the level of Director or above.

82. All routine formal communications from the Commission shall be issued under the signatures of an Officer not below the rank of Research Officer/Section Officer.

83. The Commission can sue or be sued through its Secretary.

84. The Scheduled Castes and Scheduled Tribes in these rules will have the same connotation as is given in Clause 10 of Article 338 of the Constitution.

Applicability of Rules, etc., of the Central Government

85. All rules, regulations and orders issued by the Central Government and applicable in the Ministries/Departments will also apply in the Commission.

86. The provisions relating to the delegation of financial powers in the Government of India shall apply to the corresponding officers in the Commission.

Use of Staff Cars

87. The Staff Car Rules of the Government of India shall apply for the purposes of utilisation of staff cars in the Commission.

Decision on Matters not Specified in These Rules

88. If a question arises regarding any such matter for which no provision exists in these rules, the decision of the Chairperson shall be sought. The Chairperson may, if deems fit, direct that the matter may be considered at a meeting of the Commission.

FORM I

NATIONAL COMMISSION FOR SCHEDULED CASTES AND SCHEDULED TRIBES

(A Constitutional body under Article 338 of the Constitution of India)

5th Floor, Loknayak Bhawan
New Delhi—110 003

(Notice for collecting basic facts)

To

Whereas a Petition/complaint/information has been received by the National Commission for Scheduled Castes and Scheduled Tribes from .... press news under caption ....appearing in................dated................as enclosed and the Commission has decided to investigate/inquire into the matter in pursuance of the powers conferred upon it under Article 338 of the Constitution of India, you are hereby requested to submit the facts and information on the action taken on the allegations/matters to the undersigned within 30 days of receipt of this notice either by post or in person or by any other means of communication.

Please take notice that in case of the Commission does not receive reply from you within the stipulated time, the Commission may exercise the powers of Civil Courts conferred on it under

Article 338 of the Constitution of India and issue summons for your appearance in person or by a representative before the Commission.

Signature
Director/Under Secretary/Dy. Director/Assistant
Director/Research Officer/Section Officer
National Commission for Scheduled Castes
and Scheduled Tribes

Dated:

FORM II

BEFORE THE NATIONAL COMMISSION FOR SCHEDULED CASTES AND SCHEDULED TRIBES

(A Constitutional body exercising powers of Civil Court under Article 338 of the Constitution of India)

SUMMONS

File No.

5th Floor, Loknayak Bhawan
New Delhi—110 003

To

Whereas the National Commission has decided to investigate into the following matter in pursuance of powers conferred upon it under Article 338 of the Constitution of India, your attendance is hereby required in person to appear before the National Commission on the .... of ....2000...............at...............hours at...............

You are required to bring with you the connected documents for examination by the National Commission.

Case reference

If you fail to comply with this order without lawful excuse, you shall be subjected to the consequences of non-attendance laid down in Rule 12 of Order XVI of Code of Civil Procedure, 1908.

Given under my hand and seal of the National Commission

for SCs & STs exercising powers of Civil Court this................of...............200................

Seal **Court Officer**

FORM III

(WARRANT OF ARREST OF WITNESS)

National Commission for Scheduled Castes and Scheduled Tribes

(A Constitutional body exercising powers of Civil Court under Article 338 of the Constitution of India)

Loknayak Bhawan (Floor V)
New Delhi—110 003

To,

Whereas............................R/o...........................has been duly served with a summons but has failed to attend (absconds and keeps out of the way for the purpose of avoiding service of a summons), the National Commission for Scheduled Castes and Scheduled Tribes exercising powers of a Civil Court under Article 338(8) of the Constitution of India hereby order you to arrest and bring the said....................before the National Commission at New Delhi.

You are further ordered to return this warrant on or before the ....day of....................200....................with an endorsement certifying the day and the manner in which it has been executed, or the reason why it has not been executed.

Given under my hands and the seal of the National Commission exercising powers of Civil Court, this ....day of...................200....................

Seal Signature

THE NATIONAL COMMISSION FOR BACKWARD CLASSES ACT, 1993
(Act 27 of 1993)

[2 April, 1993]

An Act to constitute a National Commission for Backward Classes other than the Scheduled Castes and Scheduled Tribes and to provide for matters connected therewith or incidental thereto.

Be it enacted by Parliament in the Forty-fourth Year of the Republic of India as follows—

Statement of Objects and Reasons. In its judgment dated 16th November, 1992 on matter arising out of Government Orders on reservation of appointments or posts under the Government of India in favour of Backward Classes of citizens under Article 16(4) of the Constitution, the Supreme Court, *inter alia* directed the Government of India to constitute a permanent body within four months from the date of judgment, i.e. by 15th March, 1993 for entertaining and examining and for recommending upon request made to it for, inclusion and complaints of over-inclusion and under-inclusion in the lists of Backward Classes of citizens. The Supreme Court observed that the body so created can also be consulted by the Government in the matter of periodic revision of lists of backward classes. The Supreme Court has also observed that the permanent body must be empowered to examine complaints relating to such matters and pass appropriate orders. Its advice/opinion should ordinarily be binding upon the Government.

As Parliament was not in session, and as the Government was required to comply with the direction of the Supreme Court within the time-frame stipulated in the judgment, the President promulgated the National Commission for Backward Classes Ordinance, 1993 on the 1st day of February, 1993.

The Bill seeks to replace the said Ordinance.

PRELIMINARY

1. Short Title, Extent and Commencement. 1. This Act may be called the National Commission for Backward Classes Act, 1993.

2. It extends to the whole of India except the State of Jammu and Kashmir.

3. It shall be deemed to have come into force on the 1st day of February, 1993.

2. *Definitions.* In this Act, unless the context otherwise requires—

(a) "backward classes" means such backward classes of citizens other than the Scheduled Castes and the Scheduled Tribes as may be specified by the Central Government in the lists;

(b) "Commission" means the National Commission for Backward Classes constituted under Section 3;

(c) "lists" means lists prepared by the Government of India from time to time for purposes of making provision for the reservation of appointments or posts in favour of backward classes of citizens which, in the opinion of that Government, are not adequately represented in the services under the Government of India and any local or other authority within the territory of India or under the control of the Government of India;

(d) "Member" means a Member of the Commission and includes the Chairperson;

(e) "prescribed" means prescribed by rules made under this Act.

THE NATIONAL COMMISSION FOR BACKWARD CLASSES

3. *Constitution of National Commission for Backward Classes.* 1. The Central Government shall constitute a body to be known as the National Commission for Backward Classes to exercise the powers conferred on, and to perform the functions assigned to, it under this Act.

2. The Commission, shall consist of the following Members nominated by the Central Government:

(a) a Chairperson, who is or has been a Judge of the Supreme Court or of a High Court;

(b) a social scientist;

(c) two persons, who have special knowledge in matters relating to backward classes; and

(d) a Member-Secretary, who is or has been an officer of the Central Government in the rank of a Secretary to the Government of India.

4. Term of Office and Conditions of Service of Chairperson and Members. 1. Every Member shall hold office for a term of three years from the date he assumes office.

2. A Member may, by writing under his hand addressed to the Central Government, resign from the office of Chairperson or as the case may be, of Member at any time.

3. The Central Government shall remove a person from the office of Member if that person—

(a) becomes as undischarged insolvent:
(b) is convicted and sentenced to imprisonment for an offence which, in the opinion of the Central Government, involves moral turpitude;
(c) becomes of unsound mind and stands so declared by a competent Court;
(d) refuses to act or becomes incapable of acting;
(e) is, without obtaining leave of absence from the Commission, absent from three consecutive meetings of the Commission; or
(f) has, in the opinion of the Central Government, so abused the position of Chairperson or Member as to render that person's continuance in office detrimental to the interests of backward classes or the public interest:

Provided that, no person shall be removed under this clause until that person has been given an opportunity of being heard in the matter.

4. A vacancy caused under sub-section (2) or otherwise shall be filled by fresh nomination.

5. The salaries and allowances payable to, and the other terms and conditions of service of, the Chairperson and Members shall be such as may be prescribed.

5. ***Officers and Other Employees of the Commission.*** 1. The Central Government shall provide the Commission with such officers and employees as may be necessary for the efficient performance of the functions of the Commission.

2. The salaries and allowances payable to, and the other terms and conditions of service of, the officers and other employee appointed for the purpose of the Commission shall be such as may be prescribed.

6. ***Salaries and Allowances to be Paid out of Grants.*** The salaries and allowances payable to the Chairperson and Members and the administrative expenses, including salaries, allowances and pension payable to the officers and other employees referred to in

Section 5, shall be paid out of the grants referred to in sub-section (1) of Section 12.

7. Vacancies, etc. not to Invalidate Proceedings of the Commission. No act or proceedings of the Commission shall be invalid on the ground merely of the existence of any vacancy or defect in the constitution of the Commission.

8. Procedure to be Regulated by the Commission. 1. The Commission shall meet as and when necessary at such time and place as the Chairperson may think fit.

2. The Commission shall regulate its own procedure.

3. All orders and decisions of the Commission shall be authenticated by the Member-Secretary or any other officer of the Commission duly authorised by the Members-Secretary in this behalf.

FUNCTIONS AND POWERS OF THE COMMISSION

9. Functions of the Commission. 1. The Commission shall examine requests for inclusion of any class of citizens as a backward class in such lists and hear complaints of over-inclusion or under-inclusion of any backward class in such lists and tender such advice to the Central Government as it deems appropriate.

2. The advice of the Commission shall ordinarily be binding upon the Central Government.

10. Powers of the Commission. The Commission shall, while performing its functions under sub-section (1) of Section 9, have all the power of a Civil Court trying a suit and in particular, in respect of the following matters, namely:

(a) summoning and enforcing the attendance of any person from any part of India and examining him on oath;
(b) requiring the discovery and production of any document;
(c) receiving evidence on affidavits;
(d) requisitioning any public record or copy thereof, from any court or office;
(e) issuing commissions for the examination of witnesses and documents; and
(f) any other matter which may be prescribed.

11. Periodic Revision of Lists by the Central Government. 1. The Central Government may at any time, and shall, at the expiration of ten years from the coming into force of this Act and every succeeding period of ten years thereafter, undertake revision of the lists with a view to excluding from such lists those classes who have ceased to be backward classes or for including in such lists new backward classes.

2. The Central Government shall, while undertaking any revision referred to in sub-section (1), consult the Commission.

FINANCE, ACCOUNTS AND AUDIT

12. Grants by the Central Government. 1. The Central Government shall, after due appropriation made by Parliament by law in this behalf, pay to the Commission by way of grants such sums of money as the Central Government may think fit for being utilised for the purposes of this Act.

2. The Commission may spend such sums as it thinks fit for performing the functions under this Act,, and sums shall be treated as expenditure payable out of the grants referred to in sub-section (1).

13. Accounts and Audit. 1. The Commission shall maintain proper accounts and order relevant records and prepare an annual statement of accounts in such form as may be prescribed by the Central Government in consultation with the Comptroller and Auditor-General.

2. The accounts of the Commission shall be audited by the Comptroller and Auditor-General at such intervals as may be specified by him and any expenditure incurred in connection with such audit shall be payable by the Commission to the Comptroller and Auditor-General.

3. The Comptroller and Auditor-General and any person appointed by him in connection with the audit of the accounts of the Commission under this Act shall have the same rights and privileges and the authority in connection with such audit as the Comptroller and Auditor-General generally has in connection with the audit of Government accounts and, in particular, shall have the right to demand the production of books, accounts, connected vouchers and other documents and papers and to inspect any of the offices of the Commission.

14. Annual Report. The Commission shall prepare, in such form and at such time, for each financial year, as may be prescribed, its annual report, giving a full account of its activities during the previous financial year and forward a copy thereof, to the Central Government.

15. Annual Report and Audit Report to be Laid before Parliament. The Central Government shall cause the annual report, together with memorandum of action taken on the advice tendered by the Commission under Section 9 and the reasons for the non-acceptance, if any, of any such advice, and the audit report to be laid as soon as may be after they are received before each House of Parliament.

MISCELLANEOUS

16. Chairperson, Members and Employees of the Commission to be Public Servants. The Chairperson, Members and employees of the Commission shall be deemed to be public servants within the meaning of Section 21 of the Indian Penal Code (45 of 1860).

17. Power to Make Rules. 1. The Central Government may, by notification in the official Gazette, make rules for carrying out the provisions of the Act.

2. In particular, and without prejudice to the generality of the foregoing powers, such rules may provide for all or any of the following matters, namely:

(a) salaries and allowances payable to, and the other terms and conditions of service of, the Chairperson and Members under sub-section (5) of Section 4 and the officers and other employees under sub-section (2) of Section 5;
(b) the form in which the annual statement of accounts shall be prepared under sub-section (1) of Section 13;
(c) the form in, and the time at, which the annual report shall be prepared under Section 14;

Any other matter which is required to be, or may be, prescribed.

3. Every rule made under this Act, shall be laid, as soon as may be after it is made, before each House of Parliament, while it is in session, for a total period of thirty days which may be comprised in one session or in two or more successive sessions, and if, before the expiry of the session immediately following the session or the successive session aforesaid, both houses agree in making any modification in the rule or both Houses agree that the rule should not be made, the rule shall thereafter have effect only in such modified form or be of no effect, as the case may be; so, however, that any such modification or annulment shall be without prejudice to the validity of anything previously done under that rule.

18. Power to Remove Difficulties. 1. If any difficulty arises in giving effect to the provisions of this Act, the Central Government may, by order published in the Official Gazette, make provisions, not inconsistent with the provisions of this Act as appear to it to be necessary or expedient, for removing the difficulty:

Provided that no such order shall be made after the expiry of a period of two years from the date of commencement of this Act.

2. Every order made under this section shall, as soon as may be after it is made, be laid before each House of Parliament.

19. Repeal and Saving. 1. The National Commission for Backward Classes Ordinance, 1993 (Ordinance 23 of 1993) is hereby repealed.

2. Notwithstanding such repeal, anything done or any action taken under the said Ordinance, shall be deemed to have been done or taken under the corresponding provisions of this Act.

THE NATIONAL COMMISSION FOR *SAFAI KARAMCHARIS* ACT, 1993
[Act 64 of 1993]

[4th September, 1993]

An Act to constitute a National Commission for Safai Karamcharis and to provide for matters connected therewith or incidental thereto.

Be it enacted by Parliament in the Forty-fourth year of the Republic of India as follows:

Statement of objects and reasons. 1. The Government of India have taken a number of steps for the social, economic and educational upliftment of *Safai Karamcharis*, special schemes for the liberation and rehabilitation of *Safai karamcharis* have also been formulated by the Government. In spite of these efforts, the obnoxious practice of manual scavenging still continues in many parts of the country. Since this practice is a continuing stigma on our social fabric, Government is determined to eradicate the practice within a fixed time frame, i.e. by the end of the Eighth Five Year Plan. A total plan outlay of Rs. 464 crore has been allocated in the Eighth Five Year Plan for liberation of scavengers. The total cost of the scheme including Bank loans and States' contribution is estimated to be Rs. 905 crore. The scheme is at present being implemented by the Scheduled Castes Development Corporation set up by the State Governments. There is no agency at the Central level to study, evaluate and monitor the scheme of liberation and rehabilitation of *Safai Karamcharis*. Since the scope of the national Commission for Scheduled Castes and Scheduled Tribes is restricted to Scheduled Castes and Scheduled Tribes and since persons other than those belonging to the Scheduled Castes and the Scheduled Tribes also constitute a sizable proportion of *Safai Karamcharis*, it was felt that a separate statutory National Commission needs to be established for monitoring the schemes for the liberation and rehabilitation of *Safai Karamcharies*.

2. The Bill seeks to achieve the aforesaid objects.

PRELIMINARY

1. Short Title, Extent, Application, Commencement, Duration and Savings. 1. The Act may be called the National Commission for *Safai Karamcharis* Act, 1993.

2. It extends to the whole of India except the State of Jammu and Kashmir.

3. It shall come into force on such date as the Central Government may, by notification in the Official Gazette, appoint.

4. It shall cease to have effect after [31st day of March, 2002], except as respects things done or omitted to be done before such cesser, and upon such cesser Section 6 of the General Clauses Act, 1897 (10 of 1897), shall apply as if this Act had then been repealed by a Central Act.

2. ***Definitions.*** In this Act, unless the context otherwise requires,:

(a) "Chairperson" means the Chairperson of the Commission;

(b) "Commission" means the National Commission for *Safai Karamcharis* constituted under Section 3;

(c) "Member" means a Member of the Commission;

(d) "Prescribed' means prescribed by rules made under this Act;

(e) " *Safai Karamcharis*" means a person engaged in, or employed for, manually carrying human excreta or any sanitation work:

(f) "Vice-Chairperson" means the Vice-Chairperson of the Commission.

THE NATIONAL COMMISSION FOR *SAFAI KARAMCHARIS*

3. ***Constitution of National Commission for Safai karamcharis.*** 1. The Central Government shall, by notification in the official Gazette, constitute a body to be known as the National Commission for *Safai Karamcharis* to exercise the powers conferred on, and to perform the functions assigned to it under this Act.

2. The Commission shall consist of—

(a) a Chairperson;

(b) a Vice-Chairperson;

(c) five members,

to be nominated from amongst the persons of eminence connected with the socio-economic development and welfare of *Safai Karamcharis*, by the Central Government:

Provided that at least one of the members shall be a woman.

4. ***Term of Office and Conditions of Service of Chairperson, Vice Chairperson and Members.*** 1. The Chairperson, Vice-Chairperson any every Member shall hold office for such period not exceeding three years as may be specified by the Central

Government in this behalf or upto the 31st day of March, 1997, whichever is earlier:

[Provided that, the Chairperson, Vice-Chairperson and every Member holding office as such immediately before the commencement of the National Commission for *Safai Karamcharis* (Amendment) Act, 1997 shall vacate their respective offices on the 31st day of March, 1997:

Provided further that the Chairperson , Vice-Chairperson and every Member appointed after commencement of the National Commission for *Safai Karamcharis* (Amendment) Act, 1997 shall hold office for such period not exceeding three years as may be specified by the Central Government in this behalf or upto the 31st day of March, 2002, whichever is earlier.]

2. The Chairperson, Vice-Chairperson or a Member may, by notice in writing addressed to the Central Government, resign from the office of Chairperson, Vice-Chairperson, or as the case may be, of the Member at any time.

3. The Central Government shall remove a person from the office of Chairperson, Vice-Chairperson, or a Member if that person,—

(a) becomes an undischarged insolvent;

(b) is convicted and sentenced to imprisonment, for an offence which, in the opinion of the Central Government, involves moral turpitude;

(c) becomes of unsound mind and stands so declared by a competent Court;

(d) refuses to act or becomes incapable of acting;

(e) is, without obtaining leave of absence from the Commission, absent from three consecutive meetings of the Commission; or

(f) in the opinion of the Central Government has so abused the position of Chairperson, Vice-Chairperson or Member as to render that persons' continuance in office detrimental to the public interest:

Provided that no person shall be removed under this clause until that person has been given a reasonable opportunity of being heard in the matter.

4. A vacancy caused under sub-section (2) or sub-section (3) or otherwise shall be filled by fresh nomination and a person so nominated shall hold office for the unexpired period of the term for

which his predecessor in office would have held office if, such vacancy has not arisen.

5. The salaries and allowances payable to, and other terms and conditions of service of, the Chairperson, Vice-Chairperson and Members shall be such as may be prescribed.

*5. **Officers and other Employees of the Commission.*** 1. The Central Government shall provide the Commission with such officers and employees as may be necessary for the efficient performance of the functions of the Commission under this Act.

2. The salaries and allowances payable to, and other terms and conditions of service of, the officers and other employees appointed for the purpose of the Commission shall be such as may be prescribed.

*6. **Vacancy, etc., not to Invalidate the Proceedings of the Commission.*** No act or proceedings of the Commission shall be questioned or shall be invalid on the ground merely of the existence of any vacancy or defect in the constitution of the Commission.

*7. **Procedure to be Regulated by the Commission.*** 1. The Commission shall meet as and when necessary and shall meet at such time and place as the Chairperson may think fit.

2. The Commission shall regulate its own procedure.

3. All orders and decisions of the Commission shall be authenticated by the Chairperson or any other officer of the Commission duly authorised by the Chairperson in this behalf.

FUNCTIONS AND POWERS OF THE COMMISSION

*8. **Functions and Powers of the Commission.*** 1. The Commission shall perform all or any of the following functions, namely:

(a) recommend to the Central Government specific programmes of action towards elimination of inequalities in status, facilities and opportunities for *Safai Karamcharis* under a time-bound action plan;

(b) study and evaluate the implementation of the programmes and schemes relating to the social and economic rehabilitation of *Safai Karamcharis* and make recommendation to the Central Government and State Governments for better co-ordination and implementation of, such programmes and schemes;

(c) investigate specific grievances and take *suo motu* notice of matter relating to non-implementation, of,—

   (i) programmes or schemes in respect of any group of *Safai Karamcharis;*
   (ii) decisions, guidelines or instructions aimed at mitigating the hardship of *Safai Karamcharis;*
   (iii) measures for the social and economic upliftment of *Safai Karamcharis;*
   (iv) the provisions of any law in its application to *Safai Karamcharis,*

and take up such matters with the concerned authorities or with the Central or State Governments;

(d) make periodical reports to Central and State Government on any matter concerning *Safai Karamcharis*, taking into account any difficulties or disabilities being encountered by *Safai Karamcharis;*
(e) any other matter which may be referred to it by the Central Government.

2. In the discharge of its functions under sub-section (1), the Commission shall have power to call for information with respect to any matter specified in that sub-section from any Government of local or other authority.

MISCELLANEOUS

9. Chairperson, Vice-Chairperson and Members and other Employees of the Commission. The Chairperson, Vice-Chairperson, Members, Officers and other employees of the Commission shall be deemed to be public servants within the meaning of Section 21 of the Indian Penal Code (45 of 1860).

10. Central Government to Consult Commission. The Central Government shall consult the Commission on all major policy matters affecting *Safai Karamcharis.*

11. Annual Report. The Commission shall prepare in such form and at such time for each financial year as may be prescribed its annual report giving a full account of its activities during the previous financial year and forward a copy thereof to the Central Government.

12. Annual Report to be Laid before Parliament or the Legislative Assembly. 1. The Central Government shall cause the annual report to be laid before each House of Parliament along with the memorandum explaining the action taken or proposed to be taken on the recommendations contained therein so far as they relate to the Central Government and the reasons for non-acceptance, if any, of such recommendation.

2. Where the said report or any part thereof relates to any matter within which a State Government is concerned, a copy of such report shall be forwarded to the Governor of the State who shall cause it to be laid before the Legislature of the State along with a memorandum explaining the action taken or proposed to be taken on the recommendations relating to the State and the reason for the non-acceptance, if any of any such recommendation or part.

13. Delegation of Powers. The Commission may, by general or special order, delegate to the Chairperson, Vice-Chairperson or any Member or to any officer of the Commission subject to such conditions and limitations, if any, as may be specified there in. Such of its powers and duties under this Act as it may deem fit.

14. Protection of Action Taken in Good Faith. No suit, prosecution or other legal proceeding shall lie against the Central Government, Commission, Chairperson, Vice-Chairperson, Members or any officer or other employee of the Commission for anything which is in good faith done or intended to be done under this Act.

15. Power to Make Rules. 1. The Central Government may, by notification in the Official Gazette, make rules for carrying out the provisions of this Act.

2. In particular, and without prejudice to the generality of the foregoing powers, such rules may provide for all or any of the following matters, namely:

(a) salaries and allowances payable to, and the other terms and conditions of service of, the Chairperson, Vice-Chairperson and Members under sub-section (5) of Section 4 and of officers and other employees of the Commission under sub-section (2) of Section 5;

(b) the form in, and the time at, which the annual report shall be prepared under Section 11;

(c) any other matter which is required to be, or may be, prescribed.

3. Every rule made under this Act shall be laid. As soon as may be after it is made, before such House of Parliament, while it is in

session for a total period of thirty days which may be comprised in one session or in two or more successive sessions, and if, before the expiry of the session immediately following the session or the successive session aforesaid, both Houses agree in making any modification in the rule or both Houses agree that the rule should not be made, the rule shall thereafter, have effect only in such modified form or be of no effect, as the case may be; so, however, that any such modification of annulment shall be without prejudice to the validity of anything previously done under that rule.

THE NATIONAL COMMISSION FOR MINORITIES ACT, 1992

[17th May 1992]

AN ACT to constitute a National Commission for Minorities and to provide for matters connected therewith or incidental thereto.

Be it enacted by Parliament in the Forty-third Year of the Republic of India as follows:

PRELIMINARY

1. ***Short Title, Extent and Commencement.*** 1. This Act may be called the National Commission for Minorities Act, 1992.

2. It extends to the whole of India except the State of Jammu and Kashmir.

3. It shall come into force on such date as the Central Government may, by notification in the Official Gazette, appoint.

2. ***Definitions.*** In this Act, unless the context otherwise requires,—

(a) "Commission" means the National Commission for Minorities constituted under section 3;

(b) "Member" means a Member of the Commission;

(c) "minority", for the purpose of this Act, means a community notified as such by the Central Government;

(d) "prescribed" means prescribed by rules made under this Act.

THE NATIONAL COMMISSION FOR MINORITIES

3. ***Constitution of the National Commission for Minorities.*** 1. The Central Government shall constitute a body to be known as the National Commission for Minorities to exercise the powers conferred on, and to perform the functions assigned to, it under this Act.

2. The Commission shall consist of a Chairperson and six Members to be nominated by the Central Government from amongst persons of eminence, ability and integrity:

Provided that five Members including the Chairperson shall be from amongst the minority communities.

4. ***Term of Office and Conditions of Service of Chairperson and Members.*** 1. The Chairperson and every Member shall hold office for a term of three years from the date he assumes office.

2. The Chairperson or a Member may, by writing under his

hand addressed to the Central Government, resign from the office of Chairperson or, as the case may be, of the Member at any time.

3. The Central Government shall remove a person from the office of Chairperson or a Member referred to in sub-section (2) if that person:

(a) becomes an undischarged insolvent;
(b) is convicted and sentenced to imprisonment for an offence which, in the opinion of the Central Government, involves moral turpitude;
(c) becomes of unsound mind and stands so declared by a competent court;
(d) refuses to act or becomes incapable of acting;
(e) is, without obtaining leave of absence from the Commission, absent from three consecutive meetings of the Commission; or
(f) has, in the opinion of the Central Government, so abused the position of Chairperson or Member as to render that person's continuance in office detrimental to the interests of minorities or the public interest:

Provided that no person shall be removed under this clause until that person has been given a reasonable opportunity of being heard in the matter.

4. A vacancy caused under sub-section (2) or otherwise shall be filled by fresh nomination

5. The salaries and allowances payable to, and the other terms and conditions of service of, the Chairperson and Members shall be such as may be prescribed.

5. Officers and other Employees of the Commission. 1. The Central Government shall provide the Commission with a Secretary and such other officers and employees as may be necessary for the efficient performance of the functions of the Commission under this Act

2. The salaries and allowances payable to, and the other terms and conditions of service of, the officers and other employees appointed for the purpose of the Commission shall be such as may be prescribed.

6. Salaries and Allowances to be Paid out of Grants. The salaries and allowances payable to the Chairperson and Members and the administrative expenses, including salaries, allowances and pensions payable to the officers and other employees referred to in section 5, shall be paid out of the grants referred to in sub-section (1) of section 10.

7. Vacancies, etc., not to Invalidate Proceedings of the Commission. No act or proceeding of the Commission shall be questioned or shall be invalid merely on the ground of the existence of any vacancy or defect in the constitution of the Commission.

8. Procedure to be Regulated by the Commission. 1. The Commission shall meet as and when necessary at such time and place as the Chairperson may think fit.

2. The Commission shall regulate its own procedure.

3. All orders and decisions of the Commission shall be authenticated by the Secretary or any officer of the Commission duly authorised by the secretary in this behalf.

FUNCTIONS OF THE COMMISSION

9. Functions of the Commission. 1. The Commission shall perform all or any of the following functions, namely:

(a) evaluate the progress of the development of minorities under the Union and States;

(b) monitor the working of the safeguards provided in the Constitution and in laws enacted by Parliament and the State Legislatures;

(c) make recommendations for the effective implementation of safeguards for the protection of the interests of minorities by the Central Government or the State Governments;

(d) look into specific complaints regarding deprivation of rights and safeguards of the minorities and take up such matters with the appropriate authorities;

(e) cause studies to be undertaken into problems arising out of any discrimination against minorities and recommend measures for their removal;

(f) conduct studies, research and analysis on the issues relating to socio-economic and educational development of minorities;

(g) suggest appropriate measures in respect of any minority to be undertaken by the Central Government or the State Governments;

(h) make periodical or special reports to the Central Government on any matter pertaining to minorities and in particular difficulties confronted by them; and

(i) any other matter which may be referred to it by the Central Government.

2. The Central Government shall cause the recommendations referred to in clause (c) of sub-section (1) to be laid before each House of Parliament along with a memorandum explaining the action taken or proposed to be taken on the recommendations relating to the Union and the reasons for the non-acceptance, if any, of any of such recommendations.

3. Where any recommendation referred to in clause (c) of sub-section (1) or any part thereof with which any State Government is concerned, the Commission shall forward a copy of such recommendation or part to such State Government who shall cause it to be laid before the Legislature of the State along with a memorandum explaining the action taken or proposed to be taken on the recommendations relating to the State and the reasons for the non-acceptance if any, of any of such recommendation or part.

4. The Commission shall, while performing any of the functions mentioned in sub-clauses (a), (b) and (d) of sub-section (1), have all the powers of a civil court trying a suit and in particular, in respect of the following matters, namely:

(a) summoning and enforcing the attendance of any person from any part of India and examining him on oath;
(b) requiring the discovery and production of any document;
(c) receiving evidence on affidavits;
(d) requisitioning any public record or copy thereof from any court of office;
(e) issuing commissions for the examination of witnesses and documents; and
(f) any other matter which may be prescribed.

FINANCE, ACCOUNTS AND AUDIT

10. Grants by the Central Government. 1. The Central Government shall, after due appropriation made by Parliament by law in this behalf, pay to the Commission by way of grants such sums of money as the Central Government may think fit for being utilised for the purposes of this Act.

2. The Commission may spend such sums as it thinks fit for performing the functions under this Act, and such sums shall be

treated as expenditure payable out of the grants referred to in sub-section (1).

11. Accounts and Audit. 1. The Commission shall maintain proper accounts and other relevant records and prepare an annual statement of accounts in such form as may be prescribed by the Central Government in consultation with the Comptroller and Auditor-General of India.

2. The accounts of the Commission shall be audited by the Comptroller and Auditor-General at such intervals as may be specified by him and any expenditure incurred in connection with such audit shall be payable by the Commission to the Comptroller and Auditor-General.

3. The Comptroller and Auditor-General and any person appointed by him in connection with the audit of the accounts of the Commission under this Act shall have the same rights and privileges and the authority in connection with such audit as the Comptroller and Auditor-General generally has in connection with the audit of Government accounts and, in particular, shall have the right to demand the production of books, accounts, connected vouchers and other documents and papers and to inspect any of the offices of the Commission.

12. Annual Report. The Commission shall prepare, in such form and at such time, for each financial year, as may be prescribed, its annual report, giving a full account of its activities during the previous financial year and forward a copy thereof to the Central Government.

13. Annual Report and Audit Report to be Laid before Parliament. The Central Government shall cause the annual report together with a memorandum of action taken on the recommendations contained therein, in so far as they relate to the Central Government, and the reasons for the non-acceptance, if any, of any of such recommendations and the audit report to be laid as soon as may be after the reports are received, before each House of Parliament.

MISCELLANEOUS

14. Chairperson, Members and Staff of the Commission to be Public Servants. The Chairperson, Members and employees of the Commission shall be deemed to be public servants within the meaning of section 21 of the Indian Penal Code.

15. Power to Make Rules. 1. The Central Government may, by notification in the Official Gazette, make rules for carrying out the provisions of this Act.

2. In particular, and without prejudice to the generality of the foregoing powers, such rules may provide for all or any of the following matters, namely:

(a) salaries and allowances payable to, and the other terms and conditions of service of, the Chairperson and Members under sub-section (5) of section 4 and of officers and other employees under sub-section (2) of section 5;
(b) any other matter under clause (f) of sub-section (4) of section 9;
(c) the form in which the annual statement of accounts shall be maintained under sub-section (1) of section 11;
(d) the form in, and the time at, which the annual report shall be prepared under section 12;
(e) any other matter which is required to be, or may be, prescribed.

3. Every rule made under this Act shall be laid, as soon as may be after it is made, before each House of Parliament, while it is in session, for a total period of thirty days which may be comprised in one session or in two more successive sessions, and if, before the expiry of the session immediately following the session or the successive sessions aforesaid, both houses agree in making any modification in the rule or both Houses agree that the rule should not be made, the rule shall thereafter have effect only in such modified form or be of no effect, as the case may be; so, however, that any such modification or annulment shall be without prejudice to the validity of anything previously done under that rule.

16. Power to Remove Difficulties. 1. If any difficulty arises in giving effect to the provisions of this Act, the Central Government may, by order published in the Official Gazette, make such provisions, not inconsistent with the provisions of this Act as appear to it to be necessary or expedient for removing the difficulty:

Provided that no such order shall be made after the expiry of a period of two years from the date of commencement of this Act.

2. Every order made under this section shall, as soon as may be after it is made, be laid before each House of Parliament.

CHRISTIAN MARRIAGE AND MATRIMONIAL CAUSES BILL, 1994

(a) Marriage. The Bill is a consensus of the Christian people of India to update their laws pertaining to marriage and matrimonial causes bearing in mind the vast social changes that have taken place in the last century. As stated above, the law on the subject comprises of two major enactments. Of these, the Indian Christian Marriage Act 1872 is in need of urgent improvement on several points of substance. To mention the most important changes at this state (i) the conditions of marriage are nowhere set out conveniently in the Act in a manner that will give at a glance the position in that respect as regards all Christian. This has been taken care of; (ii) secondly, there is a bewildering variety of forms of marriage as envisaged by the 1872 Act. It is felt that while the parties should be allowed to enjoy, at their option, the facility of a religious or a secular marriage (as at present) there is scope for simplifying the law in this regard. Besides this, from the linguistic point of view, the provisions of the 1872 Act on marriage are very badly in need of revision. All these changes have been conveniently carried out, keeping in mind the objectives mentioned above. (iii) There are provisions for marriage for minors, which have been excluded. (iv) Marriages annulled by any Church has been declared null and void under this Act in order to avoid a double process of obtaining annulment under the existing State laws.

(b) Divorce. 1. The topic of divorce amongst Christians was in even greater need of law reform. Both from the constitutional point of view which demands that discrimination between men and women should go, and from the social point of view, substantial expansion of the grounds of divorce was needed. This did not, of course, mean that divorce at the sweet will of one party should be granted for the mere asking. However, reasonably acceptable grounds of divorce, particularly where one party has been guilty of cruelty should at least receive serious consideration. In addition, (with certain safe-guards) divorce by mutual consent of the couple should be available to Christians, as it is now available to Hindus and to persons married under the Special Marriage Act, 1994. There is a similar scope for making the law as to nullity and legitimacy more rational.

2. Several procedural aspects of the present divorce law have

also proved to be inconvenient irritants in practice, and the time has come to revise the law on those points also.

3. Apart from proposing improvements in point of substance and language, the Bill seeks to collect at one place provisions at present scattered in two enactments-and that too in a very haphazard fashion.

4. For the purpose of this Bill 'divorce' means the dissolution of the civil effects of marriage.

SPECIAL MARRIAGE ACT

The Christian Marriage Bill 1994 has been drafted to be as close to the Special Marriage Act 1954 as possible.

CHRISTIAN ADOPTION AND MAINTENANCE BILL, 1994

For the first time in the history of Indian Christians, there is a provision for adoption of children by Christians. The major points of the Bill are as follows:

1. Christian women and men should have the right to adopt children of either sex.
2. The adoption should be capable of being effected without court permission.
3. The child to be adopted should not have completed 15 years of age.
4. Sufficient protection be guaranteed for adopted child.

INDIAN SUCCESSION AMENDMENT BILL, 1994

The following changes have been made, keeping in mind also Christians belonging to the matriarchal tribal communities.

1. There should be one law of succession for all Christians, irrespective of the regions they belong to, giving equal rights to women and men in property.

2. The Succession Act should be changed, so that the wife has full right to the property of her husband, if the husband died without making a will and without leaving issue and parents. His assets should not be shared with remote kindred of the deceased and vice-versa. (See also point 5 below)

3. In case the father is dead, the mother should have the right to approve the minor's pre-marital settlement under section 22 and vice-versa.

4. The provision in section 32, depriving a widow of a share in her husband's estate if she has made pre-marriage contract to that effect should be deleted.

5. The present position (in sections 24, 33, 41, 48) under which if there are 'kindred' surviving, the widow gets only one half, should be modified and the widow should get full property.

6. The benefit of minimum guaranteed payment to the widow (section 33A) should be extended to Christians (to whom it does not, at present, apply). The amount (of Rs. 5,000) should be suitably raised and this benefit made available even if the husband has made a will.

7. Illegitimate children (section 37) should have the same rights (on intestacy), as legitimate children.

8. Where the father is alive (and there are no lineal descendants), the mother gets no share at present (section 42-46) - a position that needs to be reformed. The father and the mother should share equally.

9. Where the father is of unsound mind, the mother should have the rights to appoint a testamentary guardian and vice-versa (section 60).

10. The prohibition against death-bed bequests for religious or charitable purposes by persons having near relatives (section 118) should be deleted or substantially modified, as it is out of tune with current notions (The sections applies *inter alia* to Indian Christians).

11. The bar against a person establishing right as executor or legate without probate (section 213) should not apply to Indian Christians. Already section 370CI, allows Indian Christian to recover debts, etc. Some liberal approach should be adopted in regard to need for probate, etc.

5

Women, Children and Human Rights

THE DOWRY PROHIBITION ACT, 1961

An Act to prohibit the giving or taking of dowry

Be it enacted by Parliament in the Twelfth Year of the Republic of India as follows:

1. Short Title, Extent and Commencement. 1. This Act may be called the Dowry Prohibition Act 1961.

2. It extends to the whole of India except the State of Jammu and Kashmir.

3. It shall come into force on such date, as the Central Government may, by notification in the Official Gazette, appoint.

2. *Definition of 'Dowry'.* In this Act, 'dowry' means any property or valuable security given or agreed to be given either directly or indirectly—

(a) by one party to a marriage to the other party to the marriage or

(b) by the parents of either party to a marriage or by any other person, to either party to the marriage or to any other person, at or before [or any time after the marriage] in connection with the marriage of the said parties it does not include] dower or *mahr* in the case of person to whom the Muslim Personal Law *(Shariat)* applies.

State Amendments

Haryana: (Vide Haryana Act No. 38 of 1,376 the following sections shall be substituted for Sectarian 2).

2. *Definitions* : In this Act, unless the context otherwise requires,

(i) 'dowry' means any property or valuable security given or agreed to be given either directly or indirectly—

(a) by one party to a marriage to the other party to the marriage;
(b) by the parents of either party to a marriage or by any other person, to either party to the marriage or to another person;

at or before or after the marriage as consideration to the marriage of the said parties, but does not include dower or *mahr* in the case of person to whom the Muslim Personal law *(Shariat)* applies.

Explanation I. For the removal of doubts it is hereby declared that any presents made at the time of a marriage to either party to the marriage in the form of cash, ornaments, clothes, or other articles shall not be deemed to be dowry within the meaning of this section unless they are made as consideration for the marriage of the said parties.

Explanation II. The expression 'valuable securities' has the same meaning as in Section 30 of the Indian Penal Code (45 of 1860)

(ii) 'marriage expenses' shall include expenses incurred directly or indirectly at or before the marriage on—

(a) *thakka sagai, tikka shagum* and *milni* ceremonies;
(b) the gifts made by one party to a marriage to the other party to the marriage or by the parents, grandparents and brothers of either party a marriage, to either party to the marriage or their blood relations thereof.
(c) illuminations, food and the arrangements for serving food to the members of the marriage party and other expenses incidental thereto.

Explanation III. For the removal of doubts, it is hereby declared that any gifts made by a person other than those specified in sub-clause (b), at the time of the marriage either party to the marriage shall not be deemed to be marriage expenses

3. ***Penalty for Giving or Taking Dowry.*** [1. If any person, after the commencement of this Act, gives or take or abets the giving or taking of dowry, he shall be punishable with imprisonment for a term which shall not be less than five years, and with fine which shall not be less than fifteen thousand rupees or the amount of the value of such dowry, whichever is more.

Provided that the Court may, for adequate and special reasons to be recorded in the judgment, impose a sentence of imprisonment for a term of less than [five years].

2. Nothing in sub-section (1) shall apply to, or in relation to—

(a) presents which are given at the time of a marriage to the bride (without any demand having in that behalf)
Provided that such presents are entered in a list maintained in accordance with the rules made under this Act;

(b) presents which are given at the time of a marriage to the bridegroom (without any demand having been made in that behalf):
Provided that such presents are entered in a list maintained in accordance with the rules made under this Act :
Provided further that where such presents are made by or on behalf of the bride or any person related to the bride, such presents are of a customary nature and the value thereof is not excessive having regard to the financial status of the person by whom, or on whose behalf, such presents are given.

State Amendments

Bihar: (Vide Bihar Act No. 4 1976 for section 3 the following shall be substituted),

"Penalty for Giving or Taking Dowry. If any person after the commencement of this Act, gives or takes or abets the giving or taking of dowry, he shall be punishable with imprisonment which may extend to six months and with fine which may extend to five thousand rupees.

Haryana. (Vide Haryana Act No. 38 of 1976, for Section 3 the following, shall be substituted).

3. *Bar of Certain Acts.* No person shall

(a) give or take or abet the giving or taking of dowry
(b) demand, directly or indirectly, from the parents or guardian of a bride or bridegroom, as the case may be, any dowry:
(c) incur marriage expenses the aggregate value share of exceeds five thousand rupees:
(d) display any gifts made at or before the marriage in the form of cash, ornaments, clothes or other articles
(e) take or carry in excess of

(i) twenty-five members of the marriage party : and
(ii) eleven members of the band;

(f) deny conjugal rights to his wife on the ground that dowry has not been given or the dowry given is insufficient'.

Himachal Pradesh. (Vide H.P. Act No. 25 of 1976, the following shall be substituted for Section 3).

3. ***Penalty for Giving or Taking Dowry.*** If any person gives or takes or abets the giving or taking of dowry, he shall be punishable with imprisonment which may extend to one year and with fine which, may extend to five thousand rupees.

Punjab. Vide Punjab Act No. 26 of 1976 Section 3. For the words "six months or with fine which may extend to five thousand rupees:, the words "one year, and fine which may extend to five thousand" shall be substituted.

West Bengal. Vide W. B. Act of 35 of 1975 in Section 3. For the words "which may extend to five thousand rupees", the words "shall not be less than two thousand rupees, but which may extend to ten thousand rupees" shall be substituted.

4. ***Penalty for Demanding Dowry.*** If any person demands, directly or indirectly, from the parents or other relatives or guardian of a bride or bridegroom, as the case may be, any dowry shall be punishable with imprisonment for a term which shall not be less than six months, but which may extend to two years and with fine which may extend to ten thousand rupees;

Provided that the Court may, for adequate and special reasons to be mentioned in the judgment, impose a sentence imprisonment for a term of less than six months.

4 -A. ***Ban on Advertisement.*** If any person,

(a) offers, through any advertisement in any newspaper, periodical, journal or through any other media, any share in his property or of any money or both as a share in any business or other interest as consideration for the marriage of his son or daughter or any other relative,

(b) prints or publishes or circulates any advertisement referred to in clause (a), he shall be punishable with imprisonment for a term which shall not be less than six months, but which may extend to five years, or with fine which may extend to fifteen thousand rupees:

Provided that the Court may, for adequate and special reasons in the judgment, impose a sentence for imprisonment for a term of less than six months,

State Amendments

Bihar (Vide Bihar Act No. 4 of 1976 the following shall be substituted for Section 4)

4. Penalty for Demanding Dowry. If any person after the commencement of this Act, demands, directly or indirectly, from the parents or guardian of a bride or bridegroom, as the case may be, any dowry, he shall be punishable with imprisonment which extend to six months and with fine which may extend to five thousand rupees.

Provided that no court shall take cognizance of any offence under this section except with the previous sanction of the State Government or of such officer as the State Government may, by general order, specify in this behalf'

Haryana (Vide Haryana Act No. 38 of 1976 the following shall be substituted for Section 4)

4. Penalty. 1. If any person contravenes any of the provision of Section 3, he shall be punishable with imprisonment which may extend to six months and with fine which may extend to five thousand rupees.

2. The Court trying an offence under Clause (f) of Section 3 relating to conjugal right may, at any stage of the proceedings, on the execution of a bond by 'the husband undertaking not to demand dowry and to allow conjugal rights to the wife, drop the proceedings.

3. Any proceedings dropped under subsection (2) shall revive if the Court is satisfied on an application made by the wife, in this behalf, that the husband has failed to carry out the undertaking or has otherwise acted contrary to the terms of the bond and thereupon the Court shall proceed with the case from the stage at which it was dropped.

Provided that no application under this sub-section shall be entertained if it is made after the expiry of a period of three years from the date on which proceedings were dropped.

4. The Court may direct that the fine, if any, imposed for the coutravention of Clause (f) of Section 3 or such portion thereof, as the Court may deem proper, shall be paid to the wife.

4. *Penalty for Demanding Dowry.* "If any person demands dowry directly or indirectly, from the parents or guardian of a bride or bridegroom or from any other person, as the case may be, any dowry, he shall be punishable with imprisonment which may extend to one year and with fine which may extend to five thousand rupees.

4-A. Bar of Certain Acts. Any person who:

(i) displays any presents made at the time of marriage in the form of cash, ornaments, clothes or other articles, or

(ii) gives in the form of *shagun* at time of *thakka* betrothal or like anything the value of which exceeds eleven rupees, or

(iii) gives to the parents or any other relation of a party to the marriage anything on the occasion of milni or any other ceremony performed in relation to betrothal or marriage;

shall be punishable with imprisonment for a term which may extend to six months or with fine which may extend to five thousand rupees or with both.

4-B. Penalty for Depriving Any Part of any Rights and Privileges of Marriage. 1. If after the marriage, any party to the marriage or without assistance of any of other person deprives the other party of the rights, and privileges of marriage or tortures or refuses to maintain the said other party for non-payment of dowry before, during or after marriage, he shall be punishable with imprisonment which may extend to one year and with fine which may extend to five thousand rupees.

2. The provisions of this section shall be in addition to and not derogation of, any provision on the subject contained in any other law for time being in force.

Punjab. (Vide Punjab Act No. 26 of 1976 in Section 4 the following shall be substituted and Section 4-A and 4-B shall be inserted):

(a) For the words "six months or with fine which may extend to five thousand rupees" the words "one year and fine which may extend to five thousand rupees" shall be substituted; and

(b) the provison shall be omitted.

4-A. Bar of Certain Acts. Any person who:

(i) displays any presents made at the time of such marriage in the form of cash, ornaments, clothes or other articles, or

(ii) takes in a marriage party more than twenty-five persons exclusive of minors and the members of the band; or

(iii) gives in the form of *shagun* at the time of *thakka*, betrothal or marriage, anything the value of which exceeds eleven rupees, or

(iv) gives to the parents or any other relation of a party to the marriage anything on the occasion of *milni* or any other ceremony performed in relation to betrothal or marriage; or

(v) serves to the marriage party more than two principal meals,

shall be punishable with imprisonment for a term which may extend to six months or with fine which may extend to five thousand rupees or with both.

Explanation. In this section the expression "Principal meal" mean lunch or dinner.

4-B. ***Penalty for Depriving Any Party of Rights and Privileges of Marriage.*** Any party to the marriage who after the marriage, deprives the other party of the rights and privileges of marriage, or tortures or refuses to maintain the said other party, non-payment of dowry and any person who assists such party in the commission of such offence shall be punishable with imprisonment for a term which may extend to one year and fine which may extend to five thousand rupees.

West Bengal. (Vide West Bengal Act No. 36 of 1975 in Section 4 the following shall be substituted and Section 4-A shall be inserted).

(a) after the words 'bride or bridegroom' the words 'or from any other person', shall be inserted.

(b) for the words 'which may extend to six months or with fine— which may extend to five thousand rupees', the words which shall not be less than three months, but may extend to three years or with fine which shall not be less than two thousand rupees but may extend to ten thousand rupees shall be substituted.

(c) for the proviso, the following proviso shall be substituted, namely:

Provided that no Court shall take cognizance of any offence under this section except on a complaint made by any aggrieved party or his parents or by any other person with the previous sanction of the authority specified by the State Government in this behalf;

Provided further that no such previous sanction shall be necessary for taking cognizance on a complaint made by such organization for social welfare with a minimum standing of five years as may be specified by the State Government by notification in the Official Gazette or by any person duly authorised by such organisation.

4-A. *Penalty for Depriving Any Party of the Rights and Privileges of Marriage.* 1. If after marriage, any party to the marriage with or without assistance of his parents or guardian deprives the other party of the rights and privileges of marriage, or tortures or refuses to maintain the said other party for non-payment of dowry before, during or after marriage. He shall be punishable with imprisonment which shall not be less than three months, but may extend to one year or with fine which shall not be less than two thousand rupees, but may extend to five thousand rupees, or with both.

2. The provisions of this section shall be in addition to, and not in derogation of, any provisions on the subject contained in any other law for the time being in force.

5. *Agreement for Giving or Taking Dowry to be Void.* Any agreement for the giving or taking of dowry shall be void.

6. *Dowry to be for the Benefit of the Wife or her Heirs.* 1. Where any dowry is received by any person other than the woman in connection with whose marriage it is given that person shall transfer it to the woman:

(a) if the dowry was received before marriage, within three months after the date of marriage; or

(b) if the dowry was received at the time of or after the marriage within three months after the date of its receipt: or,

(c) if the dowry was received when the woman was a minor, within three months after she has attained the age of eighteen years and pending such transfer, shall hold it in trust for the benefit of the woman.

2. If any person fails to transfer any property as required by sub-section (1) within the time specified therefore or as required by sub-section (3), he shall be punishable with imprisonment for a term which shall not be less than six months, but which may extend to two years or with the fine which shall not be less than five thousand rupees, but which may extend to ten thousand rupees or with both.

3. Where the woman entitled to any property under sub-section

(1) (dies before receiving it, the heirs of the woman shall be entitled to claim it from the person holding it for the time being.

[Provided that whether such woman dies within seven years of her marriage, otherwise than due to natural causes, such property shall

(a) be transferred to her parents, if she has no children, or
(b) be transferred to such children and pending such transfer, be held in trust for such children, if she has children.

3A. Where a person, convicted under sub-section (2) for failure to transfer any property as required by sub-section (1) or sub-section (3) has not, before his conviction under that sub-section, transferred such property to the woman entitled thereto or, as the case may be, her heirs, parents or children, the court shall, in addition to awarding punishment under that sub-section, direct by order in writing, that such person shall transfer the property to such woman or, as the case may be, her heirs, parents or children] within such periods as may be specified in the order and if such a person fails to comply with the direction within the period so specified, an amount equal to the value of the property may be recovered from him as if it were a fine imposed by such court and paid to such woman, or as the case may be, her heirs, parents or children.

State Amendments

Haryana: In sub-section (2) of Section 6, for the words, or with fine, which may extend to five thousand rupees or with both', the words 'and with fine which may extend to five thousand rupees' shall be substituted.

Orissa. (Vide Orissa Act No. 1 of 1976, the following shall be inserted after Section 6).

6-A. Penalty for Denial of Conjugal R ights by the Husband. 1. If any person denies conjugal rights to his wife on the ground that dowry has not been given, or on the ground that the dowry given is insufficient, he shall be punishable with imprisonment which may extend to one year or with fine which may extend to ten thousand rupees or with both.

2. The Court trying an offence under this section may, at any stage of the proceedings, on the execution of a bond by the husband undertaking not to realise the dowry or any portion thereof, as the

case may be, and to allow conjugal rights to the wife, drop the proceedings.

3. Any proceeding dropped under sub-section (2) shall revive if the Court is satisfied, on an application made in that behalf by the wife that the, husband has failed to carry out the undertaking or has otherwise acted contrary to the terms of the bond, and thereupon the Court shall proceed with the case from the stage at which it was dropped.

6-B. Maintenance to be Paid by Husband on his Conviction. 1. On conviction of a person for an offence under Section 6-A, the Court trying the offence may, on a claim made, by his wife in that behalf within two months from the date of the order of the conviction, order such person to make a monthly allowance for the maintenance of his wife at such monthly rate riot exceeding five hundred rupees, as the Court deems proper :

Provided that no such order shall be made without giving the parties concerned a reasonable opportunity of being heard.

2. In determining the monthly allow under this section regard shall be held to

(a) the position and status of the parties;
(b) the reasonable wants of the wife;
The value of the wife's property and any income derived from such property, or from the wife's own earnings or from any other source;
(d) the amount of compensation awarded under Section 6-A.

3. The maintenance allow so ordered shall be a charge on the property, if any, of the husband whether, acquired before or after the date of the order.

4. Where a complaint has been filed by the wife for an offence under Section 6-A, the husband shall not transfer any of his assets till

(a) where no claim for maintenance has been preferred under this section, the date of expiry of the period of limitation specified in sub-section (1) for filing such claim; and
(b) where such claim is preferred, the disposal of the claim,

5. Notwithstanding anything contained in any other law, the wife may enforce any claim for maintenance against any property

transferred by the husband in contravention of the provisions of subsection (4) as if such transfer were null and void.

6. The provisions contained in subsection (3) of Section 125 of the Code of Criminal Procedure, 1973, shall so far as may be, apply to the recovery of the maintenance allowance ordered under this section.

7. Nothing contained in this section shall effect the provisions of Section 3 or Section 4.

*7. **Cognizance of offences.*** 1. Notwithstanding anything contained in the Code of Criminal Procedure, 1973 (2 of 1974)

(a) no court, inferior to that of Metropolitan Magistrate or a Judicial Magistrate of the first class shall try any offence under this Act.

(b) no court shall take cognizance of an offence under this Act except upon—

(i) its own knowledge or a police report of the facts which constitute such offence, or

(ii) a complaint by the person aggrieved by the offence or other relative of such person, or by any recognized welfare institution or organization.

(c) it shall be lawful for a Metropolitan Magistrate or a Judicial Magistrate of the first class to pass any sentence authorised by this Act or, any person convicted of any offence under this Act.

Explanation. For the purposes of this sub-section, recognized welfare institution or organisation means a social welfare institution or organisation recognized in the behalf by the Central or State Government.

2. Nothing in Chapter XXXVI of the Code of Criminal Procedure, 1973 (2 of 1974), shall apply to any offence punishable under this Act.

2[3] Notwithstanding anything contained any law for the time being in force, a statement made by the person aggrieved by the offence shall not subject such person to a prosecution under this Act.

Bihar. (Vide Bihar Act No. 4 of 1976 the following shall be substituted for Section 7)

'*7. **Trial of offences.*** Notwithstanding anything contained in the Code of Criminal Procedure 1973 (Act 2 of 1974) no Court inferior to that of a Metropolitan Magistrate or a Judicial Magistrate of the first class shall try any offence under this Act.

Haryana. (Vide Haryana Act No. 38 of 1,979 the following shall be substituted for Section 7)

7. ***Cognizance of Offences.*** Notwithstanding anything contained in the Code of Criminal Procedure, 1973 (2 of 1974),

(a) no Court inferior to that of a Judicial Magistrate of the first class try any offence under this Act:

(b) no Court shall take cognizance of any such offence except on a complaint made by any party to the marriage or her father, mother or brother or a Gazetted Officer specially authorised by the State Government in this behalf, within a period of one year from the date of the marriage;

(c) no Court shall take cognizance of any such offence except with the previous sanction of the District Magistrate or of such officer as the State Government may, by general or special order, specify in this behalf;

(d) no enquiry shall be got made through any Police Officer below the rank of a Deputy Superintendent of Police

(e) no woman shall be called to Police Station for the purpose of an enquiry regarding any offence under this Act."

Himachal Pradesh (vide H. P. Act No. 25 of 1976 the following shall be substituted for Section 7)

"7.***Trial of Offences.*** Notwithstanding anything contained] in the Code of Criminal Procedure, 1973 (No, 2 of 1974), no court inferior to that of a Judicial Magistrate of the first class shall try any offence under this Act.

2. No Court shall take cognizance of any offence under this Act, except that of offence under section 4-B, except on a police report or complaint made within one year of the marriage" (H.P. Act No. 25 of 1976, Section 5).

Punjab. (Vide Punjab Act No 26 of 1976 the following shall be substituted for Section 7)

"7. ***Cognizance of Offences.*** Notwithstanding anything contained in the Code of Criminal Procedure, 1973 (2 of 1974).

1. No Court inferior to that of a Judicial Magistrate of the first class shall try any offence under this Act;

2. No court shall take cognizance of any offence punishable under Section 3, 4 and 4-B, except upon a complaint made within

one year from the date of the offence by some person aggrieved by the offence.

Provided that

(a) where such person is under the age of eighteen years, or is an idiot or a lunatic, or is from sickness or infirmity unable to make a complaint, or is a woman who, according to the local customs and manners, ought not to be compelled to appear in public, some other person may, with the leave of the Court, make a complaint on his or her behalf;

(b) where the person aggrieved by an offence is the wife, complaint may be made on, her behalf by her father, mother, brother, sister or by her father's or mother's brother, or sister, and

3. every offence under Section 4-A shall be cognizable.

Provided that no Police Officer below the rank of a Deputy Superintendent of Police shall investigate any offence punishable under this Act or make any arrest therefore.

West Bengal: In Section 7 vide West Bengal Act No 35 of 1975:

(a) for the words and figures "Code of Criminal Procedure 1898 (6 of 1898), the words and figures "Code of Criminal Procedure 1971 (2 of 1974) shall be substituted;

(b) for the words "Presidency Magistrate, Magistrate of the first class" in the two places where they occur the words "Metropolitan Magistrate or a Judicial Magistrate of the first class" shall be substituted.

(c) In clause (b) for the words "one year from the, date of" the words "three years from the date of the offence" shall be substituted.

8. Offences to be Cognizable for Certain Purposes and to be Non-bailable and Non-compoundable. 1 The Code of Criminal Procedure, 1973 (2 of 1974) shall apply to offences under this Act as if they were cognizable offences.

(a) for the purposes of investigation of such offences and

(b) for the purposes of matters other man

.(i) matter referred to in Section 42 of that Code and

(ii) the arrest of a person without a warrant or without an order of a Magistrate.

2. Every offence under this Act shall be non-bailable and non-compoundable.

8A. ***Burden of Proof in Certain Cases.*** Where any person is prosecuted for taking or abetting the taking of any dowry under Section 3, or the demanding of dowry under Section 4, the burden of proving that he had not committed an offence under those sections shall be on him.

8-B. ***Dowry Prohibition Officers.*** 1. The State Government may appoint as many Dowry Prohibition Officers as it thinks fit and specify the areas in respect of which they shall exercise their jurisdiction and powers under this Act.

2. Every Dowry Prohibition Officer shall exercise and perform the following powers and functions, namely

(a) to see that the provisions of this Act are complied with

(b) to prevent as far as possible, the taking or abetting the taking of, or the demanding of, dowry.

(c) to collect such evidence as may be necessary for the prosecution of persons committing offences under the Act.

State Amendments

Bihar. The following shall be substituted for Section 8 vide Bihar Act No.4 of 1976.

8. ***Offences to be Cognizable, Non-bailable and Non-compoundable.*** Every offence under this Act shall be cognizable, non-bailable and non-compoundable

Himachal Pradesh. Section 8 shall be substituted as follows vide H.P. Act No. 25 of 1976 Section 8 A will be inserted.

"8. Offences to be Cognizable, Bailable and Non-compoundable. Notwithstanding anything contained in the Code of Criminal procedure, 1973 (Act No 2 of 1974), every offence under this Act shall be cognizable, bailable and non-compoundable,

8-A. ***Cognizance of Offences.*** No court shall take cognizance of any offence under this Act except on a police report under Section 173 of the Code of Criminal Procedure, 1973 (Act No. 2 of 1974) or a complaint made by a person aggrieved by the offence.

Provided that no police Officer of the rank lower than that of the Deputy Superintendent of Police shall investigate any case registered under this Act:

Provided further that no court shall take cognizance of any offence under this Act except with the previous sanction of the District Magistrate, having jurisdiction in the area.

Orissa **(Vide Orissa Act No. 1 of 1976 in Section 8).** For the words "Every offence", the words "save as otherwise provided every offence" shall be substituted.

Punjab. (Vide Punjab Act No. 26 of 1976 Section 8 shall be substituted and 8-A shall be inserted).

8. ***Offences to be Bailable and Non-compoundable.*** Every offence under this Act shall be bailable and non-compoundable.

8-A. ***Institution of Proceedings.*** No prosecution shall be instituted against any person in respect of any offence committed under this Act without the previous sanction of the District Magistrate or of such officer as the State Government may by special or general order appoint in this behalf.

9. ***Power to Make Rules.*** 1. The Central Government may by notification in the Official Gazette, make rules for carrying out the purposes of this Act.

In particular and without prejudice to the generality or the foregoing power, such rules may provide for:

(a) the form and manner in which, and the persons by whom, any list of presents referred to in sub-section (2) of Section 3 shall be maintained and all other matters connected therewith; and

(b) the better coordination of policy and action with respect to the administration of this Act.

2. Every rule made under this section shall be laid as soon as may be after it is made before each House of Parliament while it is in session for a total period of thirty days which may be comprised in one session or [in two or more successive sessions, and if, before the expiry of the session immediately following the session or the successive sessions aforesaid), both Houses agree in making any modification in the rule or both Houses agree that the rule should not be made, the rule shall thereafter have effect only in such modified form or be of no effect, as the case may be, so however that any such modification or annulment shall be without prejudice to the validity of anything previously done under that rule.

State Amendments

Himachal Pradesh: In Section 9 vide H.P. Act No. of 1976:

(a) after the words "Central Government", occurring in sub-section (1) the words "or the State Government with the prior approval of the Central Government" shall be inserted:

(b) in sub-section (2) after the words "every rule made" and before the words "under this section" the words "by the Central Government", shall be inserted;

(c) after sub-section (2), the following shall be inserted—

3. Every rule made by the State Government under this section shall be laid, as soon as may be, after it is made, before the State Legislature while it is in session for a total period of not less than seven days which may be comprised in one session or in two successive sessions and if before the expiry of the session in which it is as laid or the session immediately following, the Legislature requires any modification in the rule or desires that the rule should not be made, the rule snail thereafter have affect only in such modified form or be of no effect as the case may be, so, however that any such modification or annulment shall be without prejudice to the validity of anything previously one under that rule".

Punjab. In Section 9 vide Punjab Act No 28 of 1926 the following shall be substituted

(i) in sub-section (2), after the words "Central Government", the words "or the State Government" shall be inserted.

(ii) in sub-section (2), after the words "every rule made" the words "by the Central Government" shall be inserted, and

(iii) after sub-section (2) the following shall be inserted:

3. Every rule made under this section by the State Government shall be laid before the House of the State Legislature, it is in session for a total period of ten days which may be comprised in one session or in two or more successive sessions and if, before the expiry of the session in which it is so laid or the successive sessions aforesaid, the House agrees in making any modification in the rule or the House agrees that the rule should not be made, the rule shall thereafter have affect only in such modified form or be of no effect, as the case may be, so however, that any such modification or annulment shall be without prejudice to the validity or anything previously done under that rule.

10. Power of the State Government to Make Rules. 1. The State Government may, by notification in the Official Gazette, make rules for carrying out the purposes of this Act.

2. In particular, and without prejudice to the generality of the foregoing power, such rules may provide for all or any of the following matters namely:

(a) the additional functions to be performed by the Dowry Prohibition Officers under sub-section (2) of Section 813;
(b) limitations and conditions subject to which a Dowry Prohibition Officer may exercise his functions under sub-section (3) of Section 8-B.

3. Every rule made by the State Government under this section shall be laid as soon as may be after it is made before the State Legislature.

The Dowry Prohibition

G.S.R. 664 (E), in exercises of the powers conferred by Section 9 of the Dowry Prohibition Act, 1961 (28 of 1961) the Çentral Government hereby make the following rules, namely:

1. ***Short Title and Commencement.*** 1. These rules may be called the Dowry Prohibition (Maintenance of lists of Presents to the Bride and Bridegroom) Rules, 1985.

2. They shall come into force on the 2nd day of October, 1985 being the date appointed for the coming into force of the Dowry Prohibition (Amendment) Act, 1984 (63 of 1984)

2. ***Rules in Accordance with which Lists of Presents are to be Maintained.*** 1. The list of presents which are given at the time of the marriage to the bride shall be maintained by the bride.

2. The list of presents which are given at the time of the marriage to the bride shall be maintained by the bridegroom.

3. Every list of presents referred to in sub-rule (1) or sub-rule (2)—

(a) shall be prepared at the time of the marriage or as soon as possible after the marriage
(b) shall be in writing
(c) shall contain:

  (i) a brief description of each present;
  (ii) the approximate value of the present:
  (iii) the name of tire who has given the present; and
  (iv) where the person giving the present is related to the bride or bridegroom, a description of such relationship;

(d) shall be signed by both the bride and the bridegroom.

Explanation 1. Where the bride is unable to sign, she may affix her thumb impression in lieu of her signature after having the list read out to her and obtaining signature on the list of the person who has so read out the particulars contained in the list.

Explanation 2. Where the bridegroom is unable to sign, he may affix his thumb impression in lieu of his signature after having the list read out to him and obtaining the signature on the list, of the person who has so read out the particulars contained in the list.

4. The bride or the bridegroom may, if she or he so desires, obtained on either or both of the lists referred to in sub-rule (1) or sub-section (2) the signature or signatures of any relations of the bride or the bridegroom or of any other persons or person present at the time of the marriage.

THE COMMISSION OF SATI (PREVENTION) ACT, 1987
[ACT NO. 3 OF 1988]

3rd January, 1988

SYNOPSIS

An Act to provide for the more effective prevention of the commission of sati and its glorification and for matters connected herewith or incidental thereto.

Whereas, *sati* or the burning or burying alive of widows or women is revolting to the feelings of human nature and is nowhere enjoined by any of the religions of India as an imperative duty;

And whereas, it is necessary to take more effective measures to prevent the commission of *sati* and its glorification.

Be it enacted by Parliament in the Thirty-eighth Year of the Republic of India as follows:

PRELIMINARY

1. *Short Title, Extent and Commencement.* 1. This Act may be called the Commission of *Sati* (Prevention) Act, 1987.

2. It extends to the whole of India except the State of Jammu and Kashmir.

3. It shall come into force in a State on such date as the Central Government may, by notification in the Official Gazette, appoint, and different dates may be appointed for different States.

2. *Definitions.* 1. In this Act, unless the context otherwise requires—

(a) "Code" means the Code of Criminal Procedure, 1973 (2 of 1974);

(b) "Glorification", in relation to *sati*, whether such *sati*, was committed before or after the commencement of this Act, includes, among other things,—

   (i) The observance of any ceremony or the taking out of a procession in connection with the commission of *sati*; or

   (ii) The supporting, justifying or propagating the practice of *sati* in any manner; or

   (iii) The arranging of any function to eulogise the person, who has committed *sati*; or

   (iv) The creation of a trust, or the collection of funds, or the construction of a temple or other structure or the carrying on of any form of worship or the performance of any ceremony thereat, with a view to perpetuate the honour of, or to preserve the memory of, a person, who has committed *sati*;

(c) "*Sati*" means the burning or burying alive of—

(i) Any widow along with the body of her deceased husband or any other relative or with any article, object or thing associated with the husband or such relative; or

(ii) Any women along with the body of any of her relatives, irrespective of whether such burning or burying is claimed to be voluntary on the part of the widow or the women or otherwise;

(d) "Special Court" means a specially constituted Court under Section 9;

(e) "Temple" includes any building or other structure, whether roofed or not, constructed or made to preserve the memory of a person in respect of whom *sati* has been committed or used or intended to be used for the carrying on of any form of worship or for the observance of any ceremony in connection with such commission.

2. Words and expressions used but not defined in this Act and defined in the Indian Penal Code (45 of 1860), or in the Code shall have the same meanings as are respectively assigned to them in the Indian Penal Code or the Code.

PUNISHMENTS FOR OFFENCES RELATING TO *SATI*

3. Attempt to Commit Sati. Notwithstanding anything contained in the Indian Penal Code (45 of 1860), whoever, attempts to commit *sati* and does any act towards such commission shall be punishable with imprisonment for a term which may extend to one year or with fine or with both:

Provided that the Special Court trying an offence under this section shall, before convicting any person, take into consideration the circumstances leading to the commission of the offence, the act committed, the state of mind of the person charged of the offence at the time of the commission of the act and all other relevant factors.

4. *Abetment of Sati.* 1. Notwithstanding anything contained in the Indian Penal Code (45 of 1860), if any person commits *sati*, whoever abets the commission of such *sati*, either directly or indirectly, shall be punishable with death or imprisonment for life and shall also be liable to fine.

2. If any person attempts to commit *sati*, whoever abets such attempt, either directly or indirectly, shall be punishable with imprisonment for life and shall also be liable to fine.

Explanation. For the purposes of this section, any of the following acts, or the like shall also be deemed to be an abetment, namely—

(a) Any inducement to a widow or women to get her burnt, or buried alive along with the body of her deceased husband or with any other relative or with any article, object or thing associated with the husband or such relative irrespective of whether she is in a fit state of mind or is labouring under a state of intoxication or stupefaction or other cause impeding, the exercise of her free will;

(b) Making a widow or women believe that the commission of *sati* would result in some spiritual benefit to her or her deceased husband or relative, or the general well being of the family;

(c) Encouraging a widow or women to remain fixed in her resolve to commit *sati* and thus instigating her to commit *sati*;

(d) Participating in any procession in connection with the commission of *sati* or aiding the widow or women in her decision to commit *sati* by taking her along with the body of her deceased husband or relative to the cremation or burial ground;

(e) Being present at the place where *sati* is committed as an active participant to such commission or to any ceremony connected with it;

(f) Preventing or obstructing the widow or woman from saving herself from being burnt or buried alive;

(g) Obstructing or interfering with, the police in the discharge of its duties of taking any steps to prevent the commission of *sati*.

5. *Punishment for Glorification of Sati.* Whoever does any act for the glorification of *sati* shall be punishable with imprisonment for a term which shall not be less than one year but which may extend to seven years and with fine which shall not be less than five thousand rupees but which may extend to thirty thousand rupees.

POWERS OF COLLECTOR OR DISTRICT MAGISTRATE TO PREVENT OFFENCES RELATING TO *SATI*

6. Power to Prohibit Certain Acts. 1. Where the Collector or the District Magistrate is of the opinion that *sati* or any abetment thereof is being or is about to be committed, he may, by order, prohibit the doing of any act towards the commission of *sati* by any person in any area or areas specified in the order.

2. The Collector or the District Magistrate may also, by order, prohibit the glorification in any manner of *sati* by any person in any area or areas specified in the order.

3. Whoever contravenes any order made under sub-section (1) or sub-section (2) shall, if such contravention is not punishable under any other provision of this Act, be punishable with imprisonment for a term which shall not be less than one year but which may extend to seven years and with fine which shall not be less than five thousand rupees but, which may extend to thirty thousand rupees.

7. Power to Remove Certain Temples or Other Structures. 1. The State Government may, if it is satisfied that in any temple or other structure which has been in existence for not less than twenty years, any form or worship of the performance of any ceremony is carried on with a view to perpetuate the honour of, or to preserve the memory of, any person in respect of whom *sati* has been committed, by order, direct the removal of such temple or other structure.

2. The Collector or the District Magistrate may, if he is satisfied that in any temple or other structure, other than that referred to in sub-section (1), any form of worship or the performance of any ceremony is carried on with a view to perpetuate the honour of, or to preserve the memory of, any person in respect of whom *sati* has been committed, by order, direct the removal of such temple or other structure.

3. Where any order under sub-section (1), of sub-section (2) is not complied with, the State Government or the Collector or the District Magistrate, as the case may be, shall cause the temple or other structure to be removed through a police officer not below the rank of a Sub-Inspector at the cost of the defaulter.

8. Power to Seize Certain Properties. 1. Where the Collector or the District Magistrate has reason to believe that any funds or property have been collected or acquired for the purpose of glorification of the commission of any *sati* or which may be found under circumstances which create suspicion of the commission of any offence under this Act, he may seize such funds or property.

2. Every Collector or District Magistrate acting under sub-section (1) shall report the seizure to the Special Court, if any, constituted to try any offence in relation to which such funds or property were collected or acquired and shall await the orders of such Special Court as to the disposal of the same.

SPECIAL COURTS

9. Trial of Offences Under This Act. 1. Notwithstanding anything contained in the Code, all offences under this Act shall be triable only by a Special Court constituted under this section.

2. The State Government shall, by notification in the Official Gazette, constitute one or more Special Courts for the trial of offences under this Act and every Special Court shall exercise jurisdiction in respect of the whole or such part of the State as may be specified in the notification.

3. A Special Court shall be presided over by a Judge to be appointed by the State Government with the concurrence of the Chief Justice of the High Court.

4. A person shall not be qualified for appointment as a Judge of a Special Court unless he is, immediately before such appointment, a Sessions Judge or an Additional Sessions Judge in any State.

10. Special Public Prosecutors. 1. For every Special Court, the State Government shall appoint a person to be a Special Public Prosecutor.

2. A person shall be eligible to be appointed as a Special Public Prosecutor under this section only if he had been in practice as an advocate for not less than seven years or has held any post for a period of not less than seven years under the State requiring special knowledge of law.

3. Every person appointed as a Special Public Prosecutor under this section shall be deemed to be a Public Prosecutor within the meaning of clause (u) of Section 2 of the Code and the provisions of the Code shall have effect accordingly.

11. Procedure and Powers of Special Courts. 1. A Special Court may take cognizance of any offence, without the accused being committed to it for trial, upon receiving a complaint of facts which constitute such offence, or upon a police report of such facts.

2. Subject to the other provisions of this Act, a Special Court shall, for the purpose of the trial of any offence, have all the powers of a Court of Sessions and shall try such offence as if it were a Court of Session, so far as may be, in accordance with the procedure prescribed in the Code for trial before a Court of Session.

12. Power of Special Court with Respect to Other Offences. 1. When trying any offence under this Act, a Special Court may also try any other offence with which the accused may, under the Code, be charged at the same trial if the offence is connected with such other offence.

2. If, in the course of any trial of any offence under this Act, it is found that the accused person has committed any other offence under this Act or under any other law, a Special Court may convict such person also of such other offence and pass any sentence authorised by this Act or such other law for the punishment thereof.

3. In every inquiry or trial, the proceedings shall be held as expeditiously as possible, and, in particular, where the examination of witnesses has begun the same shall be continued from day to day until the witnesses in attendance have been examined, and if any Special Court finds the adjournment of the same beyond the following date to be necessary, it shall record its reasons for doing so.

13. Forfeiture of Funds or Property. Where a person has been convicted of an offence under this Act, the Special Court trying such offence may, if it is considered necessary to do so, declare that any funds or property seized under Section 8 shall stand forfeited to the State.

14. Appeal. 1. Notwithstanding anything contained in the Code, an appeal shall lie as a matter of right from any judgment, sentence or order, not being an interlocutory order, of a Special Court to the High Court both on facts and on law.

2. Every appeal under this section shall be preferred within a period of thirty days from the date of the judgment, sentence or order appealed from: Provided that the High Court may entertain an appeal after the expiry of the said period of thirty days, if it is satisfied that the appellant had sufficient cause for not preferring the appeal within the period of thirty days.

MISCELLANEOUS

15. Protection of Action Taken Under This Act. No suit, prosecution or other legal proceeding shall lie against the State Government or any officer or authority of the State Government for anything which is in good faith done or intended to be done in pursuance of this Act, or any rules or orders made under this Act.

16. Burden of Proof. Where any person is prosecuted of an offence under Section 4, the burden of proving that he had not committed the offence under the said section shall be on him.

17. Obligation of Certain Persons to Report About the Commission of Offence Under This Act. 1. All officers of Government are hereby required and empowered to assist the police in the execution of the provisions of this Act, or any rule of order made thereunder.

2. All village officers and such other officers as may be specified by the Collector or the District Magistrate in relation to any area and the inhabitants of such area shall, if they have reason to believe or have the knowledge that *sati* is about to be, or has been, committed in the area shall forthwith report such fact to the nearest police station.

3. Whoever contravenes the provisions of sub-section (1) or sub-section (2) shall be punishable with imprisonment of either description for a term which may extend to two years and shall also be liable to fine.

18. Person Convicted of an Offence Under Section 4 to be Disqualified from Inheriting Certain Properties. A person convicted of an offence under sub-section (1) of Section 4 in relation to the commission of *sati* shall be disqualified from inheriting the property of the person in respect of whom such *sati* has been committed or the property any other person which he would have been entitled to inherit on the death of the person in respect of whom such *sati* has been committed.

19. Amendment of Act 43 of 1951. In the Representation of the People Act, 1951:

(a) In Section 8, sub-section (2), after the proviso, the following proviso shall be inserted, namely:

"Provided further that a person convicted by a Special Court for the contravention of any of the provisions of the Commission of *Sati* (Prevention) Act, 1987, shall be disqualified from the date of such conviction and shall continue to be disqualified for a further period of five years since his release."

(b) In Section 123, after clause (3-A), the following clause shall be inserted, namely:

"(3-B) The propagation of the practice or the commission of *sati* or its glorification by a candidate or his agent or any other person with the consent of the candidate or his election agent for the furtherance of the prospects of the election of that candidate or for prejudicially affecting the election of any candidate."

Explanation—For the purposes of this clause, "*sati*" and "glorification" in relation to *sati* shall have the meanings respectively assigned to them in the Commission of *Sati* (Prevention) Act, 1987.

20. Act to Have Overriding Effect. The provisions of this Act or any rule or order made thereunder shall have effect notwithstanding anything inconsistent therewith contained in any enactment other than this Act or in any instrument having effect by virtue of any enactment other than this Act.

21. Power to Make Rules. 1. The Central Government may, by notification in the official Gazette, make rules for carrying out the provisions of this Act.

2. Every rule made under this section, shall be laid, as soon as may be after it is made, before each House of Parliament, while it is in session, for a total period of thirty days which may be comprised in one session or in two or more successive sessions, and if, before the expiry of the session immediately following the session or the successive sessions aforesaid, both Houses agree that the rule should not be made, the rule shall thereafter, have effect only in such modified form or be of no effect, as the case may be, so, however, that any such modification or annulment shall be without prejudice to the validity of anything previously done under that rule.

22. Repeal of Existing Laws. 1. All laws in force in any State immediately before the commencement of this Act in that State which provide for the prevention or the glorification of *sati* shall, on such commencement, stand repealed.

2. Notwithstanding such repeal, anything done or any action taken under any law repealed under sub-section (1) shall be deemed to have been done or taken under the corresponding provisions of this Act, and, in particular, any case taken cognizance of by a Special Court under the provisions of any law so repealed and pending

before it immediately before the commencement of this Act in that State shall continue to be dealt with by that Special Court after such commencement as if such Special Court had been constituted under Section 9 of this Act.

COMMISSION OF *SATI* (PREVENTION) RULES, 1988

G.S.R. 360(E), dated 21st March, 1988.—In exercise of the powers conferred by Section 21 of the Commission of *Sati* (Prevention) Act, 1987 (3 of 1988), the Central Government hereby makes the following rules, namely:

1. Short Title and Commencement. 1. These rules may be called Commission of *Sati* (Prevention) Rules, 1988.

2. They shall come into force on the date of their publication in the official Gazette.

2. Definitions. 1. In these rules, unless the context otherwise requires:

(a) "Act" means the Commission of *Sati* (Prevention) Act, 1987 (3 of 1988);

(b) "Prohibitory order" means an order issued under Section 6;

(c) "Section" means section of the Act.

2. Words and expression used but not defined in tnese rules and defined in the Act, shall have the same meanings as are respectively assigned to them in the Act.

3. Delegation of Power to Prohibit Certain Acts. 1. The State Government may, by order and subject to such conditions as it may deem fit to impose, direct that the powers of the Collector or the District Magistrate under Section 6, may also be exercised by such other officers, not below the rank of the village officers.

4. Prohibitory Orders Under Section 6, How Made. 1. Every prohibitory order under Section 6 shall be made by beat of drum or other customary mode, in the concerned village, or in case of town or city, in the locality in which the act prohibited as likely to occur or has taken place.

2. The prohibitory order shall be displayed at some conspicuous place in the area or areas to which such acts relate and a copy thereof, shall also be displayed in the office of the officer issuing the prohibitory order and such display shall be taken as a sufficient notice to all persons concerned in the area or areas to which such order relates.

5. Manner of Making Order for Removal of Temples or Structures

***under Sub-section (1) of Section** 7.* 1. Before making any order under sub-section (1) of Section 7, for removal of any temple or structure, the State Government or any other officer authorised by the State Government in this behalf, shall give at least ninety days' notice to the person or persons involved in the acts complained of, and also to the owners and occupiers of the temple or structure proposed to be removed.

2. The notice under sub-rule (1) shall specify—

(i) The temple/structure proposed to be removed, its location and other particulars,

(ii) The owners/occupiers of the temple/structure, and

(iii) The specific instance or instances of worship or ceremony contravening the provisions of Section 7.

3. The Government or the officer authorised by the State Government in this behalf shall, after giving reasonable opportunity of being heard to the persons specified in the notice, order the removal of the temple or structure through a police officer not below the rank of the Sub-Inspector.

***6. Manner of Making Order for Removal of Temples or Structures under Sub-section (2) of Section** 7.* 1. After issue of a prohibitory order under Section 7, the Collector or the District Magistrate, or such other officer as directed by the State Government by order under Rule 3 shall, before making any order of the removal of any temple or structure under sub-section (2) of Section 7, gives at least ninety days, notice to the person or persons involved in the acts complained of, and also to the owners and occupiers of the temple of structure proposed to be removed.

2. The Collector or the District Magistrate, or such other officer as directed by the State Government by order under Rule 3, shall follow the provisions of sub-rules (2) and (3) of Rule 4 in the case made under this rule.

7. Inventory and Forfeiture of the Property of Temple or Structure. As soon as the order of removal of the temple or structure is executed, the State Government or the Collector or the District Magistrate, or as the case may be, the officer as directed by the State Government by order under Rule 3, shall prepare an inventory of all the material and other property obtained after removal of such temple or structure specifying in it the place where it is lodged or kept. And shall forward the intimation thereof to the Special Court for declaration for forfeiture of the said material or property to the State under Section 13, if the Special Court considers it necessary to do so and shall also give a copy of the inventory to the owners/occupiers of the temple/structure removed.

THE NATIONAL COMMISSION FOR WOMEN ACT, 1990

[No. 20 of 1990]

[30th August, 1990]

An Act to constitute a National Commission for Women and to provide for matters connected therewith or incidental thereto.

Be it enacted by Parliament in the Forty-first Year of the Republic of India as follows:

PRELIMINARY

1. *Short Title, Extent and Commencement.* 1. This Act may be called the National Commission for Women Act, 1990.

2. It extends to the whole of India except the State of Jammu and Kashmir.

3. It shall come into force on such date as the Central Government may, by notification in the Official Gazette, appoint.

2. *Definitions.* In this Act, unless the context otherwise requires,

(a) "Commission" means the National Commission for Women constituted under Sections 3;

(b) "Member" means a Member of the Commission and includes the Member-Secretary;

(c) "Prescribed" means prescribed by rules made under this Act.

THE NATIONAL COMMISSION FOR WOMEN

3. Constitution of the National Commission for Women. 1. The Central Government shall constitute a body to be known as the National Commission for Women to exercise the powers conferred on, and to perform the functions assigned to it under this Act.

2. The Commission shall consist of—

(a) a chairperson, committed to the cause of women, to be nominated by the Central Government;

(b) five Members to be nominated by the Central Government from amongst persons of ability, integrity and standing who have had experience in law or legislation, trade unionism, management of an industry or organisation committed to increasing the employment potential of women, women's voluntary organizations (including women activists), administration, economic development, health, education or social welfare:

Provided that at least one Member each shall be from amongst persons belonging to the Scheduled Castes and Scheduled Tribes respectively;

(c) a Member-Secretary to be nominated by the Central Government, who shall be—

(i) an expert in the field of management, organizational structure or sociological movement, or

(ii) an officer who is member of a civil service of the Union or of an all-India service or holds a civil post under the Union with appropriate experience.

4. ***Term of Office and Conditions of Service of Chairperson and members.*** 1. The Chairperson and every Member shall hold office for such period, not exceeding three years, as may be specified by the Central Government in this behalf.

2. The Chairperson or a Member (other than the Member-Secretary who is a member of a civil service of the Union or of an All-India Service or holds a civil post under the Union) may be writing and addressed to the Central Government, resign from the office of Chairperson or, as the case may be of the member at any time.

3. The Central Government shall remove a person from the office of Chairperson or Member referred to in sub-section (2) if that person—

(a) becomes an undischarged insolvent;

(b) gets convicted and sentenced to imprisonment for an offence which in the opinion of the Central Government involves moral turpitude;

(c) becomes of unsound mind and stands so declared by a competent court;

(d) refuses to act or becomes incapable of acting;

(e) is, without obtaining leave of absence from the Commission, absent from three consecutive meetings of the Commission; or

(f) in the opinion of the Central Government has so abused the position of Chairperson or Member as to render that person's continuance in office detrimental to the public interest;

Provided that no person shall be removed under this clause until that person has been given a reasonable opportunity of being heard in the matter.

4. A vacancy caused under sub-section (2) or otherwise shall be filled by fresh nomination.

5. The salaries and allowances payable to and the other terms and conditions of service of the Chairperson and Members shall be such as may be prescribed.

5. Officers and Other Employees of the Commission. 1. The Central Government shall provide the Commission with such officers and employees as may be necessary for the efficient performance of the functions of the Commission under this Act.

2. The salaries and allowances payable to, and the other terms and conditions of service of the officers and other employees appointed for the purpose of the Commission shall be such as may be prescribed.

6. Salaries and Allowances to be Paid out of Grants. The salaries and allowances payable to the Chairperson and Members and the administrative expenses, including salaries, allowances and pensions payable to the officers and other employees referred to in Section 5 shall be paid out of the grants referred to in sub-section (1) of Section 11.

7. Vacancies, etc., Not to Invalidate Proceeding of the Commission. No act or proceeding of the Commission shall be questioned or shall be invalid on the ground merely of the existence of any vacancy of defect in the constitution of the Commission.

8. Committees of the Commission. 1. The Commission may appoint such committees as may be necessary for dealing with such special issues as may be taken up by the Commission from time to time.

2.The Commission shall have the power to co-opt. as members of any committee appointed under sub-section (1) such number of persons, who are not Members of the Commission, as it may think fit and the persons so co-opted shall have the right to attend the meetings of the committee and take part in its proceedings but shall not have the right to vote.

3. The person so co-opted shall be entitled to receive such allowances for attending the meetings of the Committee as may be prescribed.

9. Procedure to be Regulated by the Commission. 1. The Commission or a committee thereof shall meet as and when necessary and shall meet at such time and place as the Chairperson may think fit.

2. The Commission shall regulate its own procedure of the committees thereof.

3. All orders and decisions of the Commission shall be authenticated by the Member-Secretary or any other of the Commission duly authorized by the Member-Secretary in this behalf.

FUNCTIONS OF THE COMMISSION

10. Functions of the Commission. 1. The Commission shall perform all or any of the following functions, namely—

(a) investigate and examine all matters relating to the safeguards provided for women under the Constitution and other laws;

(b) present to the Central Government, annually and at such other time as the Commission may deem fit, reports upon the working of those safeguards;

(c) make in such reports recommendations for the effective implementation of those safeguards for improving the conditions of women by the Union or any State;

(d) review, from time to time, the existing provisions of the Constitution and other laws affecting women and recommend amendments thereto so as to suggest remedial legislative measures to meet any lacunae, inadequacies or shortcomings in such legislation;

(e) take up the cases of violation of the provisions of the Constitution and of other laws relating to women with the appropriate authorities;

(f) look into complaints and take *suo moto* notice of matters relating to—

(i) deprivation of women's rights;

(ii) non-implementation of laws enacted to provide protection to women and also to achieve the objective of equality and development;

(iii) non-compliance of policy decisions, guidelines or

instructions aimed at mitigating hardships and ensuring welfare and providing relief to women.

and take up the issues arising out of such matters with appropriate authorities;

(g) call for special studies or investigations into specific problems or situations arising out of discrimination and atrocities against women and identify the constraints so as to recommend strategies for their removal;

(h) undertake promotional and educational research so as to suggest ways of ensuring due representation of women in all spheres and identify factors responsible for impeding their advancement, such as, lack of access to housing and basic services, inadequate support services and technologies for reducing drudgery and occupational health hazards and for increasing their productivity;

(i) participate and advise on the planning process of socio-economic development of women;

(j) evaluate the progress of the development of women under the Union and any State;

(k) inspect or cause to be inspected a jail, remand home, women's institution or other place of custody where women are kept as prisoners or otherwise, and take up with the concerned authorities for remedial action, if found necessary;

(l) fund litigation involving issues affecting a large body of women;

(m) make periodical reports to the Government on any matter pertaining to women and in particular various difficulties under which women toil; and

(n) any other matter which may be referred to it by the Central Government.

2. The Central Government shall cause all the reports referred to in clause (b) of sub-section (1) to be laid before each House of Parliament along with a memorandum explaining the action taken or proposed to be taken on the recommendations relating to the Union and the reasons for the non-acceptance, if any, of any of such recommendations.

3. Where any such report or any part thereof relates to any matter with which any State Government is concerned, the Commission shall forward a copy of such report or part of such

State Government who shall cause it to be laid before the Legislature of the State along with a memorandum explaining the action taken or proposed to be taken on the recommendations relating to the State and the reasons for the non-acceptance, if any, of such recommendations.

4. The Commission shall, while investigating any matter referred to in clause (a) or sub-clause (i) of clause (f) of sub-section (1), have all the powers of a civil court trying a suit and, in particular, in respect of the following matters, namely—

(a) summoning and enforcing the attendance of any person from any part of India and examining him on oath;
(b) requiring the discovery and production of any document;
(c) receiving evidence on affidavits;
(d) requisitioning any public record or copy thereof from any Court or office;
(e) issuing commissions for the examination of witnesses and documents; and
(f) any other matter which may be prescribed.

FINANCE, ACCOUNTS AND AUDIT

11. Grants by the Central Government. 1. The Central Government shall, after due appropriation made by parliament by law in his behalf, pay to the Commission by way of grants such sums of money as the Central Government may think fit for being utilized for the purposes of this Act.

2. The Commission may spend such sums as it thinks fit for performing the functions under this Act, and such sums shall be treated as expenditure payable out of the grants referred to in sub-section (1).

12. Accounts and Audit. 1. The Commission shall maintain proper accounts and other relevant records and prepare an annual statement of accounts in such form as may be prescribed by the Central Government in consultation with the Comptroller and Auditor-General of India.

2. The accounts of the Commission shall be audited by the Comptroller and Auditor-General at such intervals as may be specified by him and any expenditure incurred in connection with such audit shall be payable by the Commission to the Comptroller and Auditor-General.

3. The Comptroller and Auditor-General and any person appointed by him in connection with the audit of the accounts of the Commission under this Act shall have the same right and privileges and the authority in connection with such audit as the Comptroller and Auditor-General generally has in connection with the audit of Government accounts and, in particular, shall have the right to demand the production of books, accounts, connected vouchers and other documents and papers and to inspect any of the offices of the Commission.

13. ***Annual Report.*** The Commission shall prepare, in such form and at such time, for each financial year, as may be prescribed, its annual report, giving a full account of its activities during the previous financial year and forward a copy thereof to the Central Government.

14. ***Annual Report and Audit Report to be Laid before Parliament.*** The Central Government shall cause the annual report together with a memorandum of action taken on the recommendations contained therein, in so far as they relate to the Central Government, and the reasons for the non-acceptance, if any, of any of such recommendations and the audit report to be laid as soon as may be after the reports are received, before each House of Parliament.

MISCELLANEOUS

15. ***Chairperson, Members and Staff of the Commission to be Public Servants.*** The Chairperson, the Members, officers and other employees of the Commission shall be deemed to be public servants within the meaning of Section 21 of Indian Penal Code (45 of 1860).

16. ***Central Government to Consult Commission.*** The Central Government shall consult the commission in all major policy matters effecting women.

17. ***Power to Make Rules.*** 1. The Central Government may, by notification in the Official Gazette, make rules for carrying out the provisions of this Act.

2. In particular, and without prejudice to the generality of the foregoing power such rules may provide for all or any of the following matters, namely:

(a) salaries and allowances payable to, and the other terms and conditions of service of the Chairperson and Members under sub-section (5) of Section 4 and of officers and other employees under sub-section (2) of Section 5;

(b) allowances for attending the meetings of the committee by the co-opted person under sub-section (3) of Section 8;

(c) other matters under clause (f) of sub-section (4) of Section 10;

(d) the form in which the annual statement of accounts shall be maintained under sub-section (1) of Section 12;

(e) the form in, and the time at, which the annual report shall be prepared under Section 13; and

(f) any other matter which is required to be, or may be, prescribed.

3. Every rule made under this Act shall be laid, as soon as may be after it is made, before each House of Parliament, while it is in session, for a total period of thirty days which may be comprised in one session or in two or more successive sessions, and of, before the expiry of the session immediately following the session or the successive sessions aforesaid, both Houses agree in making any modification in the rule or both Houses agree that the rule should not be made, the rule shall thereafter have effect only in such modified form or be of no effect, as the case may be; so, however, that any such modification of annulment shall be without prejudice to the validity of anything previously done under that rule.

THE CHILD LABOUR (PROHIBITION AND REGULATION) ACT, 1986
(Act No. 61 of 1986)
23rd December, 1986

An Act to prohibit the engagement of children in certain employments and to regulate the conditions of work or children in certain other employments.

Be it enacted by Parliament in the Thirty-seventh year of the Republic of India as follows:

Comments

Social and beneficial legislation—Social legislation is designed to protect the interest of a class of society who, because of their economic conditions, deserves such protection. With a view to pass the test of reasonable classification there must exist intelligible differentiation between persons or things grouped together from those who have been left out and there must be a reasonable nexus with the object to be achieved by the legislation.

The Court must strive to so interpret the statute as to protect and advànce the object and purpose of the enactment. Any narrow or technical interpretation of the provisions would defeat the legislative policy. The Court must, therefore, keep the legislative policy in mind in applying the provisions of the Act to the facts of the case.

PRELIMINARY

1. Short Title, Extent and Commencement. 1. This Act may be called the Child Labour (Prohibition and Regulation) Act, 1986.

2. It extends to the whole of India.

3. The provisions of this Act, other than Part III, shall come into force at once, and Part III shall come into force on such date as the Central Government may, by notification in the official Gazette, appoint, and different dates may be appointed for different States and for different classes of establishments.

Comment

May and shall—where the Legislature uses two words "may" and "shall" in two different parts of the same provision *prima facie* it would appear that the Legislature manifested its intention to make one part directory and another mandatory. But that by itself is not decisive. The power of the Court still to ascertain the real intention of the Legislature by carefully examining the scope of the statute to find out whether the provision is directory or mandatory remains unimpaired even where both the words are used in the same provision. In interpreting the provisions the exercise undertaken by the Court is to make explicit the intention of the Legislature which enacted the legislation. It is not for the Court to reframe the legislation for the very good reason that the powers to "legislate" have not been conferred on the Court.

In order to sustain the presumption of constitutionality of a legislative measure, the Court can take into consideration matters of a common knowledge, matters of common report, the history of the times and also assume every state of facts which can be conceived existing at the time of the legislation.

2. ***Definitions.*** In this Act, unless the context otherwise requires,

(i) "appropriate Government" means, in relation to an establishment under the control of the Central Government or a railway administration or a major port or a control of the Central Government or a railway administration or a major port or a mine or oilfield, the Central Government, and in all other cases, the State Government;

(ii) "child" means a person who has not completed his fourteenth year of age;

(iii) "day" means a period of twenty-four hours beginning at midnight;

(iv) "establishment" includes a shop, commercial establishment, workshop, farm, residential hotel, restaurant, eating-house, theatre or other place of public amusement or entertainment;

(v) "family", in relation to an occupier, means the individual, the wife or husbands as the ease may be, of such individual, and their children, brother or sister of such individual;

(vi) "occupier", in relation to an establishment or a workshop, means the person who has the ultimate control over the affairs of the establishment or workshop;

(vii) "prescribed" means prescribed by rules made under Sec. 18;

(viii) "week" means a period of seven days beginning at midnight on Saturday night or such other night as may be approved in writing for a particular area by the Inspector;

(ix) "workshop" means any premises (including the precincts thereof) wherein any industrial process is carried on, but does not include any premises to which the provisions of Sec. 67 of the Factories Act, 1948 (63 of 1948), for the time being, apply.

Comments

This section defines the various words and expressions occurring in the Act.

Interpretation of section—The Court can merely interpret the section: it cannot re-write, re-cast or re- design the section.

Ambiguous expression—Courts must find out the literal meaning of the expression in the task of construction. In doing so if the expressions are ambiguous then the construction that fulfills the object of the legislation must provide the key to the meaning. Courts must not make mockery of legislation and should take a constructive approach to fulfill the purpose and for that purpose, if necessary, iron out the creases.

PROHIBITION OF EMPLOYMENT OF CHILDREN IN CERTAIN OCCUPATIONS AND PROCESSES

3. *Prohibition of Employment of Children in Certain Occupations and Processes.* No child shall be employed or permitted to work in any of the occupations set forth in Part A of the Schedule or in any workshop wherein any of the processes set forth in Part B of the Schedule is carried on.

Provided that nothing in this section shall apply to any workshop wherein any process is carried on by the occupier with aid of his family or to any school established by or receiving assistance or recognition from, Government.

Comment

This section imposes prohibition on employment of children in the occupation and processes specified in the Schedule.

Proviso. A proviso is intended to limit the enacted provision so as to except something which would have otherwise been within it or in some measure to modify the enacting clause. Sometimes proviso may be embedded in the main provision and become an integral part of it so as to amount to a substantive provision itself.

4. *Power to Amend the Schedule.* The Central Government, after giving by notification in the official Gazette, not less than three months notice of its intention so to do, may, be like notification, add any occupation or process to the Schedule and thereupon the Schedule shall be deemed to have been amended accordingly.

Comment

This section empowers the Central Government to amend the Schedule so as to include therein any occupation or process considered necessary.

Construction of a section —It is an elementary rule that construction of a section is to be made of all parts together. It is not permissible to omit any part of it. For, the principle that the statute must be read as a whole is equally applicable to different parts of the same section.

5. ***Child Labour Technical Advisory Committee.*** 1. The Central Government may, by notification in the official Gazette, constitute an advisory Committee to be called the child Labour Technical. Advisory Committee (hereinafter in this section referred to as the Committee) to advise the Central Government for the purpose of addition or occupations and processes to the Schedule.

2. The Committee shall consist of a Chairman and such other members not exceeding ten, as may be appointed by the Central Government.

3. The Committee shall meet as often as it may consider necessary and shall have power to regulate its own procedure.

4. The Committee may, if it deems it necessary so to do, constitute one or more sub-committees and may appoint to any such sub-committee, whether generally or for the consideration of any particular matter, any person who is not a member of the Committee.

5. The term of office of, the manner of filling casual vacancies in the office of, and the allowances, if any, payable to, the Chairman and other members of the Committee, and the conditions and restrictions subject to which the Committee may appoint any person who is not a member of the Committee as a member of any of its sub-committees shall be such as may be prescribed.

Comment

This section empowers the Central Government to constitute the Child Labour Technical Advisory Committee for giving advice in the matter of inclusion of any occupation and process in the Schedule.

REGULATION OF CONDITIONS OF WORK OF CHILDREN

6. Application of Part. The provisions of this Part shall apply to an establishment or a class of establishments in which none of the occupations or processes referred to in Sec. 3 is carried on.

Comment

This section lays down that provisions of this Part shall apply to an establishment in which none of the prohibited occupation or processes is carried on.

7. Hours and Period of Work. 1. No child shall be required or permitted to work in any establishment in excess of such number of hours as may be prescribed for such establishment or class of establishment.

2. The period of work on each day shall be so fixed that no period shall exceed three hours and that no child shall work for more than three hours before he has had an interval for rest for at least one hour.

3. The period of work of a child shall be so arranged that inclusive of this interval for rest, under sub-section (2), it shall not be spread over more than six hours, including the time spent in waiting for work on any day.

4. No child shall be permitted or required to work between 7 p.m. and 8 a.m.

5. No child shall be permitted or required to work overtime.

6. No child shall be required or permitted to work in any establishment on any day on which he has already been working in another establishment.

Comment

This section prescribes working hours for a child labour.

Provision if mandatory or directory. The surest test for determination as to whether the provisions is mandatory or directory is to see as to whether the sanction is provided therein.

8. Weekly Holidays. Every child employed in an establishment shall be allowed in each week, a holiday of one whole day, which day shall be specified by the occupier in a notice permanently exhibited in a conspicuous place in the establishment and the day so specified shall not be altered by the occupier more than once in three months.

Comment

This section lays down that a weekly holiday should be allowed to every child labour.

9. Notice to Inspector. 1. Every occupier in relation to an establishment in which a child was employed or permitted to work immediately before the date of commencement of this Act in relation to such establishment shall, within a period of thirty days from such commencement, send to the Inspector within whose local limits the establishment is situated, a written notice containing the following particulars, namely:

(a) the name and situation of the establishment;
(b) the name of the person in actual management of the establishment;
(c) the address to which communication relating to establishment should be sent; and
(d) the nature of the occupation or process carried on it establishment.

2. Every occupier, in relation to an establishment, who employes, or permits to work, any child after the date of commencement of this Act in relation to such establishment, shall, within a period of thirty days from the date of such employment, send to the Inspector within whose local limits the establishment is situated, a written notice containing the particulars as are mentioned in sub-section (1).

Explanation. For the purpose of sub-section (1) and (2), "date of commencement of this Act, in relation to an establishment" means the date of bringing into force of this Act in relation to such establishment.

3. Nothing in sections 7, 8 and 9 shall apply to any establishment wherein any process is carried on by the occupier with the aid of his family or to any school establishment by, or receiving assistance or recognition from Government.

Comment

This section makes provision for furnishing regarding employment of a child labour to Inspector.

Explanation. It is now well settled that an explanation added to a statutory provision is not a substantive provision in any sense of the term but as the plain meaning of the word itself shows it is merely meant to explain or clarify certain ambiguities which may have crept in the provision.

10. Disputes As to Age. If any question arises between an Inspector and an occupier as to the age of any child who is employed or is permitted to work by him in an establishment, the question shall, in the absence of a certificate as to the age of such child granted by the prescribed medical authority, be referred by the Inspector for decision to the prescribed medical authority.

Comment

This section makes provision for settlement of disputes as to age of any child labour.

11. Maintenance of Register. A register shall be maintained by every occupier in respect of children employed or permitted to work in any establishment, which is to be available for inspection by an Inspector at all times during working hours or when work is being carried on in any such establishment showing—

(a) the name and date of birth of every child so employed or permitted to work;

(b) hours and periods of work of any such child and the intervals of rest to which he is entitled;

(c) the nature of work of any such child; and

(d) such other particulars as may be prescribed.

Comment

This section makes provision of maintenance of register in respect of child labour.

12. Display of Notice Containing Abstract of Sections 3 and 14. Every railway administration, every port authority and every occupier shall cause to be displayed in a conspicuous and accessible place at every station or its railway or within the limits of a post or at the place of work, as the case may be, a notice in the local language and in the English language containing an abstract of Sections 3 and 14.

Comment

This section makes provision for display of notice in a conspicuous place at every railway station or port of place of work regarding prohibition of employment of child labour, penalties, etc., in the local language and in the English language.

13. Health and Safety. 1. The Government may, by notification in the Official Gazette, make appropriate rules for the health and safety of the children employed or permitted to work in any establishment or class of establishments.

2. Without prejudice to the generality of the foregoing provisions, the said rules may provide for all or any of the following matters, namely;

(a) cleanliness in the place of work and its freedom from nuisance;
(b) disposal of wastes and effluents;
(c) ventilation and temperature;
(d) dust and fume;
(e) artificial humidification;
(f) lighting;
(g) drinking water;
(h) latrine and urinals;
(i) spittoons;
(j) fencing of machinery;
(k) work at or near machinery in motion;
(l) employment of children on dangerous machines;
(m) instructions, training and supervision in relation to employment of children on dangerous machines;
(n) device for cutting off power;
(o) self-acting machinery;
(p) easing of new machinery;
(q) floor, stairs and means of access;
(r) pits, sumps, opening in floors, etc.
(s) excessive weights;
(t) protection of eyes;
(u) explosive or inflammable dust, gas, etc.
(v) precautions in case of fire;
(w) maintenance of buildings; and
(x) safety of buildings and machinery.

Comment

This section lays down that the Government is required to make rules for the health and safety of the child labour.

14. Penalties. 1. Whoever employs any child or permits any child to work in contravention of the provisions of Section 3 shall be punishable with imprisonment for a term which shall not be less than three months but which may extend to one year or with fine which shall not be less than ten thousand rupees but which may extend to twenty thousand rupees or with both.

2. Whoever, having been convicted of an offence under Section 3 commits a like offence afterwards, he shall be punishable with imprisonment for a term which shall not be less than six months but which may extend to two years.

3. whoever

(a) fails to give notice as required by Section 9; or

(b) fails to maintain a register as required by Section 11 or makes any false entry in any such register; or

(c) fails to display a notice containing an abstract of Section 3 and this section as required by Section 12; or

(d) fails to comply with or contravenes any other provision of this Act or the rules made thereunder;

shall be punishable with simple imprisonment which may extend to one month or with fine which may extend to ten thousand rupees or with both.

Comments

This section makes provision for penalty for contravention of the provisions of the Act.

Penalty—*Mens rea*—Essential—Penalty proceedings are quasi-criminal proceedings. Before penalty can be imposed it has to be ensured that *mens rea* has been established.

Penal provision—Object of—The law in its wisdom seeks to punish the guilty who commits the sin, and not his son, who is innocent.

15. Modified Application of Certain Laws in Relation to Penalties. 1. Where any person is found guilty and convicted of contravention of any of the provisions mentioned in sub-section (2), he shall be liable to penalties as provided in sub-sections (1) and (2) of Section 14 of this Act and not under the Acts in which those provisions are contained.

2. The provision referred to in sub-section (1) are the provisions mentioned below:

(a) Section 67 of the Factories Act, 1948 (63 of 1948);

(b) Section 40 of the Mines Act, 1952 (35 of 1952); and

(c) Section 109 of the Merchant Shipping Act, 1958 (44 of 1958); and

(d) Section 21 of the Motor Transport Workers Act, 1961 (27 of 1961)

Comment

This Section makes provision of penalties under the Act even when any person is found guilty and convicted of contravention of any of the provisions of Section 67 of the Factories Act, 1948, Section 40 of the Mines Act, 1952, Sec. 109 of the Merchant Shipping Act, 1958 and Section 21 of the Motor Transport Workers Act, 1961.

16. Procedures Relating to Offences. 1. Any person, police officer or Inspector may file a complaint of the commission of an offence under this Act in any Court of competent jurisdiction.

2. Every certificate as to the age of a child which has been granted by a prescribed medical authority shall, for the purposes of this Act, be conclusive evidence as to the age of the child to whom it relates.

3. No court inferior to that of a Metropolitan Magistrate or a Magistrate of the first class shall try any offence under this Act.

Comment

This section lays down that any person, police officer or Inspector can make a complaint regarding commission of offences. It also lays down the procedure for disposal of such a complaint.

Court Duty of. The Court should meticulously consider all facts and circumstances of the case. The Court is not bound to grant specific performance merely because it is lawful to do so. The motive behind the litigation should also enter into the judicial verdict. The Court should take care to see that it is used as an instrument of oppression to have an unfair advantage to the plaintiff.

17. Appointment of Inspectors. The appropriate Government may appoint Inspectors for the purposes of securing compliance with the provisions of this Act and any Inspector so appointed shall be deemed to be a public servant within the meaning of the Indian Penal Code (45 of 1860).

Comment

This section empowers the appropriate Government to appoint Inspectors for securing compliance of the provisions of the Act. Such Inspector is deemed to be a public servant within the meaning of the Indian Penal Code (45 of 1860).

Public Servant. Every public officer is a trustee and in respect of the office he holds and the salary and other benefits which he draws, he is obliged to render appropriate service to the State. If an officer does not behave as required of him under the law he is certainly liable to be punished in accordance with law.

18. Power to Make Rules. 1. The Government may, by notification in the official Gazette and subject to the condition of previous publication, make appropriate rules for carrying into effect the provisions of this Act.

2. In particular and without prejudice to the generality of the foregoing power, such rules may provide for all or any of the following matters, namely:

(a) the term of office of, the manner of filling casual vacancies of, and the allowances payable to, the Chairman and members of the Child Labour Technical Advisory Committee and the conditions and restrictions subject to which a non-member may be appointed to a sub-committee under sub-section (5) of Section 5;

(b) number of hours for which a child may be required or permitted to work under sub-section (1) of Section 7;

(c) grant of certificates of age in respect of young persons in employment or seeking employment, the medical authorities which may issue such certificate, the form of such certificate, the charges which may be made thereunder and the manner in which such certificate may be issued;
Provided that no charge shall be made for the issue of any such certificate if the application is accompanied by evidence of age deemed satisfactory by the authority concerned;

(d) the other particulars which a register maintained under Section 11 should contain.

Comment

This section empowers the appropriate Government to make rule for carrying out the provisions of the Act.

Rules for Effectuating the Purpose of the Act. The general power of framing rules for effectuating the purposes of the Act, would plainly authorize and sanctify the framing of such a rule.

19. Rules and Notifications to be Laid before Parliament or State Legislature. 1. Every rule made under this Act by the Central Government and every notification issued under Section 4, shall be laid, as soon as may be after it is made or issued, before each House of Parliament, while it is in session for a total period of thirty days which may be comprised in one session or in two or more successive sessions, and if, before the expiry of the session immediately following the session or the successive session aforesaid, both Houses agree in making any modification in the rule or notification or both Houses agree that the rule or notification should not be made or issued, the rule or notification shall thereafter have effect only in such modified form or be of no effect, as the case may be. So, however, that any such modification or annulment shall be without prejudice to the validity of anything previously done under that rule or notification.

2. Every rule made by a State Government under this Act shall be laid as soon as may be after it is made, before the Legislature of that State.

Comment

Under this section the rules and notification are to be laid before Parliament or State Legislature for approval.

20. Certain other Provisions of Law not Barred. Subject to the provision contained in Section 15, the provision of this Act and the rules made thereunder shall be in addition to, and not in derogation of, the provisions of the Factories Act, 1948 (63 of 1948), the Plantation Labour Act, 1951 (69 of 1951) and the Mines Act 1952 (35 of 1952).

Comment

This section lays down that the provisions of this Act shall be in addition to and not in derogation of, the provisions of the Factories Act, 1948, the Plantations Labour Act, 1951 and the Mines Act, 1952.

21. Power to Remove Difficulties. 1. If any difficulty arises in giving effect of the provision of this Act, the Central Government may, by order published in the official Gazette, make such provisions not inconsistent with the provisions of this Act as appear to it to be necessary or expedient for removal of the difficulty:

Provided that no such order shall be made after the expiry of a period of three years from the date on which this Act receives the assent of the President.

2. Every order made under this section shall, as soon as may be after it is made, before the House of Parliament.

Comment

Under the provisions of this section, the Central Government is empowered to remove difficulties which arise in giving effect to the provisions of this Act.

22. *Repeal and Savings.* 1. The Employment of Children Act, 1938 (26 of 1938) is hereby repealed.

2. Notwithstanding such repeal, anything done or any action taken or purported to have been done or taken under the Act so repealed shall, in so far as it is not inconsistent with the provisions of this Act, be deemed to have been done or taken under the corresponding provisions of this Act.

Comment

The Employment of Children Act, 1938 (26 of 1938) has been repealed by this section.

Implied Repeal. It is well settled that when a competent authority makes a new law which is totally inconsistent with the earlier law and that the two cannot stand together any longer it must be construed that the earlier law had been repealed by necessary implication by the latter law.

23. *Amendment of Act 11 of 1948.* In section 2 of the Minimum Wages Act, 1948—

(1) For Clause (a), the following clauses shall be substituted, namely; "(a) 'adolescent ' means a person who has completed his fourteenth year of age but has not completed his eighteenth year;

"(aa) 'adult' means a person who has completed his eighteenth year of age;";

(ii) after Clause (b), the following clause shall be inserted, namely:

(bb) 'child' means a person who has not completed his fourteenth year of age;".

Comment

Under this section, Section 2 of the Minimum Wages Act, 1948 has been amended so as to define the term "adolescent", "adult" and "child"

24. *Amendment of Act 69 of 1951. In the Plantation Labour Act, 1951.*

(a) in Section 2, in Clauses (a) and (c), for the word "fifteenth", the word "fourteenth" shall be substituted;

(b) Section 24 shall be omitted;

(c) in Section 26, in opening portion, the words "who has completed his twelfth year" shall be committed.

Comment

Under this section, Section 2 of the Plantations Labour Act, 1951, has been amended so far as it relates to the employment of child labour.

25. Amendment of Act 44 of 1958. In the Merchant Shipping Act, 1958, in section 109, for the word "fifteen", the word "fourteen" shall be substituted.

Comment

Under this section, Section 109 of the Merchant Shipping Act. 1958, has been amended so far as it relates to the employment of child labour.

26. Amendment of Act 27 of 1961. In the Motor Transport Workers Act, 1961, in section 2, in Clause (a) and (c), for the word "fifteenth", the word " fourteenth" shall be substituted.

Comment

Under this section, Section 2 of the Motor Transport Workers Act, 1961, has been amended so far as it relates to the employment of child labour.

THE SCHEDULE

(See Section 3)

Part A

Occupations

Any occupation connected with—

1. Transport of passengers, goods or mails by railway;

2. Cinder picking, clearing of an ash pit or building operation in the railway premises;

3. Work in a catering establishment at a railway station, involving the movement of a vendor or any other employee of the establishment from one platform to another or into or out of a moving train;

4. Work relating to the construction of a railway station or with any other work where such work is done in close proximity to or between the railway lines;

5. A port authority within the limits of any port.

6. Work relating to selling of crackers and fireworks in shops with temporary licences;

7. Abattoirs/Slaughter House.

Part B

Processes

1. *Beedi*-making.
2. Carpet-weaving.
3. Cement manufacture, including bagging of cement.
4. Cloth printing, dyeing and weaving.
5. Manufacturing of matches, explosives and fire-works.
6. Mica-cutting and splitting.
7. Shellac manufacture.
8. Soap manufacture.
9. Training.
10. Wool-cleaning.
11. Building and construction industry.
12. Manufacture of slate pencils (including packing)
13. Manufacture of products from agate.
14. Manufacturing processes using toxic metals and substances such as lead, mercury, manganese, chromium, cadmium, benzene, pesticides and asbestos.
15. "Hazardous processes" as defined in Section 3 (cb) and dangerous operations' as notified in rules made under Section 87 of the Factories Act, 1948 (63 of 1948)
16. Printing as defined in section 2 (k) (iv) of the Factories Act, 1948 (63 of 1948)
17. Cashew and cashewnut descaling and processing.
18. Soldering processes in electronic industries.

SUPPLEMENT

Child Labour (Prohibition and Regulation) Act, 1986

In exercise of the powers conferred by Section 4 of the Child Labour (Prohibition and Regulation) Act, 1986, the Central Government hereby adds the following occupation and processes in the Schedule to the said Act, namely:

In the Schedule to the said Act,—

(1) In Part A, after item (5) and the entry relating thereto, the following item and entry shall be inserted, namely:

(6) "Work relating to selling of crackers and fire works in shops with temporary licences.";

(2) In Part B, after item (11) and the entry relating thereto, the following items and entries shall be inserted, namely:

(12) Manufacture of slate pencils (including packing)

(13) Manufacture of products from agate.

(14) Manufacturing processes using toxic metals and substances such as lead, mercury, managanese, chromium, cadmium, benzene, pesticides and asbestos.

THE CHILD LABOUR (PROHIBITION AND REGULATION) RULES, 1988

G.S.R.847 (e), dated 10th August, 1988—In exercise of the powers conferred by sub-section (1) of Section 18 of the said Act, the Central Government, hereby makes the following rules, namely:

Comment

Rule-making power. The general power of framing rules for effectuating the purpose of the Act, would plainly authorize and sanctify the framing of such a rule.

1. Short Title and Commencement. 1. These rules may be called the Child Labour (Prohibition and Regulation) Rules, 1988.

2. They shall come into force on the date of their publication in the official Gazette.

Comment

These rules have been framed by the Central Government in the exercise of the powers conferred by Section 18 (1) of the Child Labour (Prohibition and Regulation) Act, 1986.

Rules—*Whether Validity Framed*—The question whether rules are validly framed to carry out the purposes of the Act can be determined on the analysis of the provisions of the Act.

2. *Definitions.* In these rules, unless the context otherwise requires —

(a) "Act" means the Child Labour (Prohibition and Regulation) Act, 1986 (61 of 1986)

(b) "Committee" means the Child Labour Technical Advisory Committee constituted under sub-section (1) of Section 5 of the Act;

(c) "Chairman" means the Chairman of the Committee appointed under sub-section (2) of Section 5 of Act;

(d) "Form" means a Form appended to these rules;

(e) "Register" means the register required to be maintained under section 11 of the Act;

(f) "Schedule" means the schedule appended to the Act;

(g) "Section" means a section of the Act.

Comment

This rule defines the various expressions occurring in the Rules.

Interpretation by a Court. The Court can merely interpret the section; it cannot re-write, re-cast or re-design the section.

Otherwise—What Amounts to. The word "otherwise" is not to be construed *ejusdem generis* with the word "circulars, advertisements."

3. *Term of Office of the Members of the Committee.* 1. The term of office of the members of the Committee shall be one year from the date on which their appointment is notified in the official Gazette:

Provided that the Central Government may extend the term of office of the member of the Committee for a maximum period of two years:

Provided further that the member shall, notwithstanding the expiration of his term, continue to hold office until his successor enters upon his office.

2. The member appointed under sub-rule (1) shall be eligible for re-appointment.

Comment

"shall" cannot be interpreted as "may"

Proviso—In Abdul Jabar Butt *v.* State of Jammu and Kashmir, it was held that a proviso must be considered with relation to the principal matter to which it stands as a proviso.

4. *Secretary to the Committee.* The Central Government may appoint an officer not below the rank of an Under-Secretary to the Government of India as Secretary of the Committee.

Comment

and allowance as may be admissible to the officers of the Central Government drawing a pay of rupees four thousand and five hundred or above.

6. *Resignation.* 1. A member may resign his office by writing under his hand addressed to the Chairman.

2. The Chairman may resign his office by writing under his hand addressed to the Central Government.

3. The resignation referred to in sub-rule (1) and sub-rule (2) shall take effect from the date of its acceptance or on the expiry of thirty days from the date of its receipt of such resignation, whichever is earlier, by the Chairman or the Central Government, as the case may be.

*7. **Removal of Chairman or Member of the Committee.*** The Central Government may remove the Chairman or any member of the Committee at any time before the expiry of the term of office after giving him a reasonable opportunity of showing cause against the proposed removal.

Comment

This rule lays down procedure for removal of Chairman or member of the Committee by the Central Government.

*8. **Cessation of Membership.*** If a member:

(a) is absent without leave of the Chairman for three or more consecutive meetings of the Committee; or

(b) is declared to be of unsound mind by a competent court; or

(c) is or has been convicted of any offence which, in the opinion of the Central Government, involves moral turpitude; or

(d) is, or at any time, has been adjudicated insolvent or has suspended his debts or has compounded with his creditors, shall cease to be a member of the Committee.

*10. **Time and Place of Meetings.*** The Committee shall meet at such times and places as the Chairman may fix in this behalf.

*11. **Notice of Meetings.*** The Secretary to the Committee shall give at least seven days' notice to every member of the Committee of the time and place fixed for each meeting along with the list of business to the transacted at the said meeting.

*12. **Presiding at Meeting.*** The Chairman shall preside at every meeting of the Committee at which he is present; if however, the Chairman is unable to attend a meeting, any member elected by the members present among themselves shall preside at the meeting.

Comment

"Shall"—It is well-known principal that in the interpretation of statutes that where the situation and the context warrants it, the word "shall" used in a section or rule of a statute has to be construed as "may".

*13. **Quorum.*** No business shall be transacted at a meeting of the Committee unless at least three members of the Committee other than the Chairman and the Secretary are present:

Provided that any meeting in which less than three of the total members are present, the Chairman may adjourn the meeting to a date as he deems fit and inform the members present and notify other members that the business of the scheduled meeting shall be disposed of at the adjourned meeting irrespective of the *quorum* and it shall be lawful to dispose of the business at such adjourned meeting irrespective of the member or members attending the meeting.

Comment

Scope of proviso — The scope of a proviso is well settled. In Ram Narain Sons Ltd. *v.* Assistent. Commissioner of Sales Tax, it was held:

"It is a cardinal rule of interpretation that a proviso to a particular provision of statute only embraces the field which is covered by the main provision. It carves out an exception to the main a provision to which it has been enacted as a proviso and to no other."

14. Decision by Majority. All questions considered at a meeting of the Committee shall be decided by a majority of votes of the members present and voting and in the event of equality of votes the Chairman, or in the absence of Chairman, the member presiding at the meeting, as the case may be, shall have a second or casting vote.

Comment

This rule lays down that the matters considered by the Committee in its meeting should be decided by a majority votes of the members present. The rule further lays down that the Chairman or in his absence the member presiding at the meeting shall have a casting vote.

15. Sub-Committee. The Committee may constitute one or more Sub-Committees, whether consisting only of members of the Committee or partly of members of the Committee and partly of other persons as it thinks fit, for such purposes, as it may decide and any sub-committee so constituted shall discharge such functions as may be delegated to it by the Committee.

16. Register to be Maintained under Section 11 of the Acts. 1. Every occupier of an establishment shall maintain a register in respect of children employed or permitted to work, in Form A.

2. The register shall be maintained on a yearly basis but shall be retained by employer for a period of three years after the date of the last entry made therein.

Comment

Under this rule every occupier of an establishment is required to maintain an yearly register showing the children employed or permitted to work and to retain such registers for a period of three years.

17. Certificate of Age. 1. All young persons in employment in any of the occupations set forth in Part A of the Schedule or in any workshop wherein any of the processes set forth in Part B the Schedule is carried on, shall produce a certificate of age from the appropriate medical authority, whenever required to do so by an Inspector.

2. The certificate of age referred to in sub-rule (1) shall be issued in Form 'B'.

3. The charges payable to the medical authority for the issue of such certificate shall be the same as prescribed by the State Government or the Central Government, as the case may be, for their respective Medical Boards.

4. The charges payable to the medical authority shall be borne by the employer of the young person whose age is under question.

Explanation—For the purposes of sub-rule (1), the appropriate "Medical authority" shall be Government medical doctor not below the rank of an Assistant Surgeon of a District or a regular doctor of equivalent rank employed in Employees' State Insurance Dispensaries or hospitals.

Comment

Explanation. It is not well settled that an explanation added to a statutory provision is not a substantive provision in any sense of the term but as the plain meaning of the word itself shows it is merely meant to explain and clarify certain ambiguities which may have crept in the statutory provision.

SUPPLEMENT

THE CHILD LABOUR (PROHIBITION AND REGULATION) ACT, 1986

S.O. 333 (E), dated 26th May, 1993 — In exercise of the powers conferred by sub-section (3) of Section 1 of the Child Labour (Prohibition and Regulation) Act, 1986 (61 of 1986) the Central

Government hereby appoints the 26th day of May, 1993 as the date of which the provisions of Part III of the said Act shall come into force in respect of all classes of establishments, throughout the territory of India, in which none of the occupations and processes referred to in section 3 of the said Act is carried on.

THE PRE-NATAL DIAGNOSTIC TECHNIQUES (REGULATION AND PREVENTION OF MISUSE) ACT, 1994

[Act No. 57 of 1994]

20th September, 1994

PRELIMINARY

1. Short Title, Extent and Commencement. 1. This Act may be called the Pre-natal Diagnostic Techniques (Regulation and Prevention of Misuse) Act, 1994.

2. It shall extend to the whole of India except the State of Jammu and Kashmir.

3. It shall come into force on such date as the Central Government, may, by notification in the Official Gazette, appoint.

2. ***Definitions.*** In this Act, unless the contrary text includes—

(a) "Appropriate Authority" means the Appropriate Authority appointed under Section 17;

(b) "Board" means the Central Supervisory Board, constituted under Section 7;

(c) "Genetic Counselling Centre" means an Institute, Hospital, Nursing Home or any place, by whatever name called, which provides for genetic counselling to patients;

(d) "Genetic Clinic" means a clinic, Institute, Hospital, Nursing Home or any place.

(f) "Gynaecologist" means a person who possesses a post graduate qualification in gynaecology and obstetrics;

(g) "Medical geneticist" means a person who possesses a degree or diploma or certificate in medical genetics in the field of pre-natal diagnostic techniques or has experience of not less than two years in such field after obtaining:

   (i) Any one of the medical qualifications recognised under Indian Medical Council Act, 1956 (102 of 1956); or

   (ii) a post-graduate degree in biological sciences;

   (h) "Paediatrician" means a person who possesses a post-graduate qualification in paediatrics

(i) "Pre-natal diagnostic procedures" means all gyncological or obsterical or medical procedures such as ultra-sonographys, foetoscopy, taking or removing samples of amniotic fluid, chorionic villi, blood or any tissue of a pregnant woman for being sent to a Genetic Laboratory or Genetic Clinic for conducting pre-natal diagnostic tests;

(j) "Pre-natal diagnostic techniques" include all pre-natal diagnostic procedures and pre-natal diagnostic tests;

(k) "Pre-natal diagnostic test" means ultrasonography or chrionic villi, blood or any tissue of a pregnant womsan conducted to detect genetic or metabolic disorders of chromosomal abnormalities or congential anomalies or haemoglobin apathies or sex-linked diseases;

(l) "Prescribed" means prescribed by rules made under this Act;

(m) "Registered medical practitioner" means a medical practitioner who possesses any recognised medical qualification as defined in clause (h) of Section 2 of the Indian Medical Council Act, 1956 (102 of 1956), and whose name has been entered in a State Medical Register;

(n) "Regulations" means regulations framed by the Board under this Act.

REGULATION OF GENETIC COUNSELLING CENTRES, GENETIC LABORATORIES AND GENETIC CLINICS

3. ***Regulation of Genetic Counselling Centres, Genetic Laboratories and Genetic Clinics.*** On and from the commencement of this Act,—

1. No Genetic Counselling Centre, Genetic Laboratory or Genetic Clinic unless registered under this Act, shall conduct or associate with, or help in, conducting activities relating to pre-natal diagnostic techniques;

2. No Genetic Counselling Centre, Genetic Laboratory or Genetic Clinic shall employ or caused to be employed any person who does not possess the prescribed qualifications:

3. No medical genaeticist, gynecologists, paediatrician, registered medical practitioner or any other person shall conduct or cause to be conducted or aid in conducting by himself or through any other person, any pre-natal diagnostic techniques at a place other than a place registered under this Act.

REGULATION OF PRE-NATAL DIAGNOSTIC TECHNIQUES

4. ***Regulation of Pre-natal Diagnostic Techniques.*** On and from commencement of this Act,—

1. No place including a registered Genetic Counselling Centre, or Genetic Laboratory or Genetic Clinic shall be used or caused to be used by any person for conducting pre-natal diagnostic techniques except for the purposes specified in clause (2) and after satisfying any of the conditions specified in clause (3);

2. No pre-natal diagnostic techniques shall be conducted except for the purposes of detection of any of the following abnormalities, namely:

(i) chromosomal abnormalities
(ii) genetic metabolic diseases;
(iii) Haemoglobinopathies;
(iv) Sex-linked genetic diseases;
(v) congenital anomalies;
(vi) cogenital anomalies;
(vii) any other abnormalities or disease as may be specified by the Central Supervisory Board.

3. No pre-natal diagnostic techniques shall be used or conducted unless the person qualified to do so is satisfied that any of the following conditions are fulfilled, namely:

(i) age of the pregnant woman is above thirty-five years;
(ii) the pregnant woman has undergone two or more spontaneous abortions or foetal loss;
(iii) the pregnant woman had been exposed to potentialy teratogenic agents such as drugs, radiation, infection or chemicals;
(iv) the pregnant woman has a family history of mental retardation or physical deformities such as spasticity or any other genetic disease;
(v) any other conditions as may be specified by the Central Supervisory Board.

4. No person, being a relative or the husband of the pregnant woman shall seek or encourage the conduct of any pre-natal diagnostic techniques on her except for the purpose specified in clause (2).

5. ***Written Consent of Pregnant Woman and Prohibition of Communicating the Sex of Foetus.*** 1. No person referred to in clause (2) of Section 3 shall conduct the pre-natal diagnostic procedures unless (a) he has explained all known side and after effects of such

procedures to the pregnant woman concerned; (b) he has obtained in the prescribed form her written consent to undergo such procedures in the language which she understands; and (c) a copy of her written consent obtained under such clause (b) is given to the pregnant woman.

2. No person conducting pre-natal diagnostic procedures shall communicate to the pregnant woman concerned or her relatives the sex of the foetus by words, signs or in any other manner.

6. Determination of Sex Prohibited. On and from commencement of this Act,—

(a) no Genetic Counselling Centre or Genetic Laboratory or Genetic Clinic shall conduct or cause to be conducted in its Centres, Laboratory or Clinic, pre-natal diagnostic techniques including ultrasonography, for the purpose of determining the sex of a foetus;
(b) no person shall conduct or cause to be conducted any pre-natal diagnostic techniques including ultrasonography for the purpose of determining the sex of a foetus.

CENTRAL SUPERVISORY BOARD

7. Constitution of Central Supervisory Board. 1. The Central Government shall constitute a Board to be known as the Central Supervisory Board to exercise the powers and perform the functions conferred on the Board under this Act.

2. The Board shall consist of—

(a) The Minister-in-charge of the Ministry or Department of Family Welfare, who shall be the Chairman, *ex-officio;*
(b) The Secretary to the Government of India incharge of the Department of Family Welfare, who shall be the Vice-Chairman, *ex officio;*
(c) Two members to be appointed by the Central Government to represent the ministries of Central Government in charge of Woman and Child Development and of Law and Justice, *ex-officio;*
(d) Director-General of Health Services of the Central Government;
(e) Ten members to be appointed by the Central Government; two each from amongst—

(i) Eminent medical geneticist;
(ii) Eminent gynaecologists and obsterians;
(iii) Eminent paediatricians;
(iv) Eminent social scientists;
(v) representatives of Women Welfare Organisations;

(f) Three women Members of Parliament of whom two shall be elected by the House of the People and one by the Council of States;

(g) Four members to be appointed by Central Government by rotation to represent the State and the Union territories, two in the alphabetical order and two in the reverse alphabetical order; Provided that no appointment under this clause shall be made except on the recommendation of the State Government or, as the case may be, the Union Territory;

(h) An officer, not below the post of Joint Secretary or equivalent of the Central Government, Officer-in-Charge of Family Welfare, who shall be Member-Secretary *ex-officio.*

8. ***Term of Office of Members.*** 1. The term of office of a member, other than an *ex-officio* member, shall be—

(a) In case of appointment under clause (e) or clause (f) of sub-section 2, of Section 7,—Three years; and

(b) in case of appointment under clause (g) of the said sub-section—one year.

2. If a casual vacancy occurs in the office of any other members, whether by reason of his death, resignation or inability to discharge his functions owing to illness or other incapacity, such vacancy shall be filled by the Central Government by making a fresh appointment and the members so appointed shall hold office for the remainder of the term of office of the person in whose place he is so appointed.

3. The Vice-Chairman shall perform such functions, as may be assigned to him by the Chairman from time to time.

4. The procedure to be followed by the members in the discharge of their functions shall be such as may be prescribed.

9. ***Meetings of the Board.*** 1. The Board shall meet at such time and place, and shall observe such rules of procedure in regard to the transaction of business at its meetings (including the quorum at such meetings) as may be provided by the regulations;

Provided that the Board shall meet at least once in six months.

2. The Chairman and in his absence the Vice-Chairman shall preside at the meetings of the Board.

3. If for any reason the Chairman or the Vice-Chairman is unable to attend any meeting of the Board, any other member chosen by the members present at the meeting shall preside at the meeting.

4. All questions which come up before any meeting of the Board shall be decided by a majority of the votes of the members present and voting, and in the event of an equality of votes, the Chairman, or in his absence, the person presiding shall have and exercise a second or casting vote.

5. Members other than *ex-officio* members, shall receive such allowance, if any, from the Board as may be prescribed.

10. Vacancies, etc. not to Invalidate Proceedings of the Board. No act of proceeding of the Board shall be invalid merely by reason of—

(a) any vacancy in, or any defect in the constitution of the Board; or

(b) any defect in the appointment of a person acting as a member of the Board; or

(c) any irregularity in the procedure of the Board not affecting the merits of the case.

11. Temporary Association of Persons with the Board for Particular Purposes. 1. The Board may associate with itself, in such manner and for such purposes as may be determined by the regulations, any person whose assistance or advice it may desire in carrying out any of the provisions of this Act.

2. A person associated with it by the Board under sub-section (1) for any purpose shall have a right to take part in the discussions relevant to that purpose, but shall not have a right to vote at a meeting of the Board and shall not be a member for any other purpose.

12. Appointment of Officers and Other Employees of the Board. 1. For the purpose of enabling it efficiently to discharge its functions under this Act, the Board, may subject to such regulations as may be made in this behalf, appoint (whether on deputation or otherwise) such number of officers and other employees as it may consider necessary:

Provided that the appointment of such category of officers, as may be specified in such regulations, shall be subject to the approval of the Central Government.

2. Every officer or other employee appointed by the Board shall be subject to such conditions of service and shall be entitled to such remuneration as may be specified in the regulations.

13. Authentication of Orders and other Instruments of the Board. All orders and decisions of the Board shall be authenticated by the signature of the Chairman or any other member authorised by the Board in this behalf, and all other instrument issued by the Board shall be authenticated by the signature of the Member-Secretary or any other Officer of the Board authorised in like manner in this behalf.

14. Disqualifications for Appointment as a Member. A person shall be disqualified for being appointed as a member if, he—

(a) has been convicted and sentenced to imprisonment for an offence which, in the opinion of the Central Government, involves moral turpitude; or

(b) is an undischarged insolvent; or

(c) is of unsound mind, and stands so declared by a competent Court; or

(d) has been removed or dismissed from the service of the Government or a Corporation owned or controlled by the Government; or

(e) has, in the opinion of the Central Government, such financial or other interest in the Board as is likely to affect pre-judicially the discharge by him of his functions as a member; or

(f) has, in the opinion of the Central Government, been associated with the use of or promotion of pre-natal technique for determination of sex.

15. Eligibility of Member for Re-appointment. Subject to the other terms and conditions of service, as may be prescribed, any person ceasing to be a member shall be eligible for reappointment as such member.

16. Functions of the Board. The Board shall have the following functions, namely:

(i) to advise the Government on policy matters relating to use of pre-natal diagnostic techniques;

(ii) to review implementation of the Act and the rules made thereunder and recommend changes in the said Act and rules to the Central Government;

(iii) to create public awareness against the practice of pre-natal determination of sex and female foeticide;

(iv) to lay down Code of Conduct to be observed by person working at genetic counselling centres, genetic laboratories and genetic clinics.

(v) any other functions as may be specified under the Act.

APPROPRIATE AUTHORITY AND ADVISORY COMMITTEE

17. Appropriate Authority and Advisory Committee. 1. The Central Government shall appoint by notification in the Official Gazette, one or more officers as appropriate authorities for each of the Union territories for the purposes of this Act.

2. The State Government shall appoint, by notification in the Official Gazette, one or more appropriate authorities for the whole or part of the State for the purposes of this Act having regard to the intensity of the problem of pre-natal sex determination leading to female foeticide.

3. The officers appointed as appropriate authorities under sub-section (1) or sub-section (2), shall be, (a) when appointed for the whole of the State or the Union Territory, of or (b) when appointed for any part of the State or the Union Territory, of such other rank as the State Government or the Central Government, as the case may be, may deem fit, to aid and advise the appropriate authority in the discharge of its functions, and shall appoint one of the members of the Advisory Committee to be its Chairman, above the rank of the Joint Director of Health and Family Welfare; and

4. The appropriate authority shall have the following functions, namely:

(a) to grant, suspend or cancel registration of a Genetic, Genetic Laboratory or Genetic Clinic;

(b) to enforce standards prescribed for the Genetic Counselling Centre, Genetic Laboratories and Genetic Clinics; or

(c) to investigate complaints of the breach of provisions of this Act or the rules made thereunder and take immediate action.

(d) to seek and consider the advice of the Advisory Committee, constituted under sub-section (5), on application for registration and on complaints for suspension or cancellation of registration.

5. (i) The Central Government or the State Government, as the case may be, shall constitute an Advisory Committee for each appropriate authority.

6. The Advisory Committee shall consist of—

(a) three medical experts from amongst gynaecologists, obstetricians, paediatricians and medical geneticists;
(b) one legal expert;
(c) one officer to represent the department dealing with information and publicity of the State Government or the Union Territory, as the case may be;
(d) three eminent social workers of whom not less than one shall be from amongst representatives of woman's organisations.

7. No person, who, in the opinion of the Central Government or the State Government, as the case may be, has been associated with the use or promotion of pre-natal diagnostic technique for determination of sex shall be appointed as a member of the Advisory Committee.

8. The Advisory Committee may meet as and when it thinks fit or on the request of the appropriate authority for consideration of any application for registration or any complaint for suspension or cancellation of registration and to give advice thereon;

Provided that the period of intervening between any two meetings shall not exceed the prescribed period.

9. The terms and conditions subject to which a person may be appointed to the Advisory Committee and the procedure to be followed by such committee in the discharge of its functions shall be such as may be prescribed.

REGISTRATION OF GENETIC COUNSELLING CENTRES, GENETIC LABORATORIES OR GENETIC CLINICS

18. Registration of Genetic Counselling Centres, Genetic Laboratories or Genetic Clinics. 1. No person shall open any Genetic Counselling Centre, Genetic Laboratory or Genetic Clinic after the commencement of this Act, unless such Centre, Laboratory or Clinic is duly registered separately or jointly under this Act.

2. Every application for registration under sub-section (1), shall

be made to the appropriate authority in such form and in such manner and shall be accompanied by such fees as may be prescribed.

3. Every Genetic Counselling Centre, Genetic Laboratory or a Genetic Clinic engaged, either partly or exclusively, in counselling or conducting pre-natal diagnostic techniques for any of the purposes mentioned in Section 4, immediately before the commencement of this Act, shall apply for registration within sixty days from the date of such commencement.

4. Subject to the provisions of Section 6, every Genetic Counselling Centre, Genetic Laboratory or Genetic Clinic engaged in counselling or conducting pre-natal diagnostic techniques shall cease to conduct any such counselling or technique on the expiry of six months from the date of commencement of this Act unless such Centre, Laboratory or Clinic has applied for registration and is so registered separately or jointly or till such application is disposed of, whichever is earlier.

5. No Genetic Counselling Centre, Genetic Laboratory or Genetic Clinic shall be registered under this Act unless the appropriate authority is satisfied that such Centre, Laboratory or Clinic is in a position to provide such facilities, maintain such equipments and standards as may be prescribed.

19. Certificate of registration. 1. The appropriate authority shall, after holding an inquiry and after satisfying itself that the applicant has complied with all the requirements of this Act and the rules made thereunder and having regard to the advice of the advisory committee in this behalf, grant a certificate of registration in the prescribed form jointly or separately to the Genetic Counselling Centre, Genetic Laboratory or Genetic Clinic, as the case may be.

2. If, after the inquiry and after giving an opportunity of being heard, to the applicant and having regard to the advice the Advisory Committee, the Appropriate Authority is satisfied that the applicant has not complied with the requirement of this Act or the rules, it shall, for reasons to be recorded in writing, reject the application for registration.

3. Every certificate of registration shall be renewed in such manner and after such period and on payment of such fees, as may be prescribed.

4. The certificate of registration shall be displayed by the registered Genetic Counselling Centre, Genetic Laboratory or Genetic Clinic in a conspicuous place at its place of business.

20. Cancellation or Suspension of Registration. 1. The appropriate authority may *suo moto,* or on complaint, issue a notice to the Genetic Counselling Centre, Genetic Laboratory or Genetic Clinic to show cause why its registration should not be suspended or cancelled for the reasons mentioned in the notice.

2. If, after giving a reasonable opportunity of being heard to the Genetic Counselling Centre, Genetic Laboratory or Genetic Clinic, and having regard to the advice of the Advisory Committee, the appropriate authority is satisfied that there has been a breach of the provisions of this Act or the rules, it may, without prejudice to any criminal action that it may take against such Centre, or Clinic, suspend its registration for such period as it may think fit or cancel its registration, as the case may be.

3. Notwithstanding anything contained in sub-sections (1) and (2), if the appropriate authority is of the opinion that it is necessary or expedient so to do in the public interest, it may for reasons to be recorded in writing, suspend the registration of any Genetic Counselling Centre, Genetic Laboratory or Genetic Clinic without issuing any such notice referred to in sub-section (1).

21. Appeal. The Genetic Counselling Centre, Genetic Laboratory or Genetic Clinic, may, within thirty days from the date of receipt of the order of the suspension or cancellation of registration passed by the appropriate authority under section 20, prefer an appeal against such order to—

(i) the Central Government, where the appeal is against the order of the Central appropriate authority; and
(ii) the State Government, where the appeal is against the order of the State appropriate authority, in the prescribed manner.

OFFENCES AND PENALTIES

22. Prohibition of Advertisement Relating to Pre-natal Determination of Sex and Punishment for Contravention. 1. No person, organisation, Genetic Counselling Centre, Genetic Laboratory or Genetic Clinic shall issue or cause to be issued any advertisement in any manner regarding facilities of pre-natal determination of sex available at such Centre, Laboratory, Clinic or any other place.

2. No person or organisation shall publish or distribute or

caused to be published or distributed any advertisement in any manner regarding facilities of pre-natal determination of sex available at any Genetic Counselling Centre, Genetic Laboratory, Genetic Clinic or any other place.

3. Any person, who contravenes the provisions of sub-section (1), or sub-section (2) shall be punishable with imprisonment for a term which may extend to three years and with a fine which may extend to ten thousand rupees:

Explanation. For the purpose of this section, "advertisement" includes any notice, circular, label, wrapper or other document and also includes any visible representation made by means of any light, sound, smoke or gas.

23. *Offences and Penalties*. 1. Any medical geneticist, gynaecologist, registered medical practitioner or any person who owns a Genetic Counselling Centre, a Genetic Laboratory or a Genetic Clinic or is employed in such Centre, Laboratory or Clinic and renders his professional or technical services to or at such a Centre, Laboratory or Clinic, whether on an honorary basis or otherwise, and who contravenes any of the provisions of this Act or rules made thereunder shall be punishable with imprisonment for a term which may extend to three years and with fine which may extend to ten thousand rupees and on any subsequent conviction, with imprisonment which may extend to five years and with fine which may extend to fifty thousand rupees.

2. The name of the registered medical practitioner who has been convicted by the Court under sub-section (1), shall be reported by the appropriate authority to the respective State Medical Council for taking necessary action including the removal of his name from the register of the Council for a period of two years for the first offence and permanently for the subsequent offence.

3. Any person who seeks the aid of a Genetic Counselling Centre, Genetic Laboratory or Genetic clinic or of a medical geneticist, gynaecologist or registered medical practitioner for conducting pre-natal diagnostic techniques on any pregnant woman (including such woman unless she was compelled to undergo such diagnostic techniques) for purposes other than those specified in Clause (2) of section 4, shall be punishable with imprisonment for a term which may extend to three years and with fine which may extend to ten thousand rupees and on any subsequent conviction with

imprisonment which may extend to five years and with fine which may extend to fifty thousand rupees.

24. *Presumption in the Case of Conduct on Pre-natal Diagnostic Techniques.* Notwithstanding anything in the Indian Evidence Act, 1872 (Act No.1 of 1872), the Court shall presume unless the contrary is proved that the pregnant woman has been compelled by her husband or the relative to undergo pre-natal diagnostic technique and such person shall be liable for abetment of offence under sub-section (3) of section 23 and shall be punishable for the offence specified under that section.

25. *Penalty for Contravention of the Provisions of the Act or Rules for Which no Specific Punishment is Provided.* Whoever contravenes any of the provisions of this Act or any rules made thereunder, for which no penalty has been elsewhere provided in this Act, shall be punishable to the imprisonment for a term which may extend to three months or with fine, which may extend to one thousand rupees or with both and in the case of continuing contravention with an additional fine which may extend to five hundred rupees for every day during which such contravention continues after conviction for the first such contravention.

26. *Offences by Companies.* 1. Where any offence, punishable under this Act, has been committed by a company, every person who, at the time the offence was committed, was in charge of , and was responsible to, the company for the conduct of the business of the company, as well as the company, shall be deemed to be guilty of the offence and shall be liable to be proceeded against and punished accordingly:

Provided that nothing contained in this sub-section shall render any such person liable to any punishment, if he proves that the offence was committed without his knowledge or that he has exercised all due diligence to prevent the commission of such offence.

2. Notwithstanding anything contained in sub-section (1), where any offence punishable under this Act has been committed by a company and it is proved that the offence has been committed with the consent or connivance of, or is attributable to any neglect on the part of, any Director, Manager, Secretary or other officer of the company such Director, Manager Secretary or other Officer shall also be deemed to be guilty of that offence and shall be liable to be proceeded against and punished accordingly.

Explanation. For the purposes of this section.

(a) "company" means any body corporate and includes a firm or other association of individuals; and

(b) "director" in relation to a firm, means a partner in the firm.

27. Offence to be Cognizable, Non-bailable and Non-compoundable. Every offence under this Act shall be cognizable, non-bailable and non-compoundable.

28. Cognizance of Offence. 1. No Court shall take cognizance of an offence under this Act except on a complaint made by—

(a) the appropriate authority concerned, or any officer authorised in this behalf by the Central Government or the State Government, as the case may be, or the appropriate authority; or

(b) a person who has given notice of not less than thirty days, in the manner prescribed, to the appropriate authority, of the alleged offence and of his intention to make a complaint to the Court.

Explanation. For the purpose of this clause "person", includes a social organisation.

2. No Court other than that of a Metropolitan Magistrate or a Judicial Magistrate of the First Class shall try any offence punishable under this Act.

3. Where a complaint has been made under clause (b) of sub-section (1), the Court may, on demand by such person, direct the appropriate authority to make available copies of the relevant records in its possession to such person.

MISCELLANEOUS

29. Maintenance of Records. 1. All records, charts, forms, reports, consent letters and all other documents required to be maintained under this Act and the rules shall be preserved for a period of two years or for such period as may be prescribed:

Provided that, if any criminal or other proceedings are instituted against any Genetic Counselling Centre, Genetic Laboratory or Genetic Clinic, the records and all other documents of such Centre, Laboratory or Clinic shall be preserved till the final disposal of such proceedings.

2. All such records shall, at all reasonable times, be made available for inspection to the appropriate authority or to any

other person authorised by the appropriate authority in this behalf.

30. Power to Search and Seize Records, etc. 1. If the appropriate authority has reason to believe that an offence under this Act has been or is being committed at any Genetic Counselling Centre, Genetic Laboratory or Genetic Clinic, such authority or any officer authorised, in this behalf thereof may, subject to such rules as may be prescribed enter and search at all reasonable times with such assistance, if any, as such authority or officer considers necessary, such Genetic Counselling Centre, Genetic Laboratory or Genetic Clinic and examine any record, register, document, book, pamphlet, advertisement or any other object found therein and seize the same if such authority or officer has reason to believe that it may furnish evidence of the commission of an offence punishable under this Act.

2. The provisions of the Code of Criminal Procedure, 1973 (2 of 1974) relating to searches and seizures, shall, so far as may be, apply to every search or seizure made under this Act.

31. Protection of Action Taken in Good Faith. No suit, prosecution or other legal proceeding shall lie against the Central or the State Government or the appropriate authority or any officer authorised by the Central or State Government, or by the Authority for anything which is in good faith done or intended to be done in pursuance of the provisions of this Act.

32. Power to Make Rules. 1. The Central Government may make rules for carrying out the provisions of this Act.

2. In particular and without prejudice to the generality of the foregoing power such rules may provide for—

(i) the minimum qualifications for persons employed at a registered Genetic Counselling Centre, Genetic Laboratory or Genetic Clinic under clause (1) of Section 3;

(ii) the form in which consent of a pregnant woman has to be obtained under section 5;

(iii) the procedure to be followed by the members of the Central Supervisory Board in the discharge of their functions under sub- section (4) of section 8;

(iv) allowances for members other than *ex officio* members admissible under sub-section (5) of Section 9;

(v) the period intervening between any two meetings of the

Advisory Committee under the proviso to sub-section (8) of Section 17;

(vi) the terms and conditions subject to which a person may be appointed to the Advisory Committee and the procedure to be followed by such committee under sub-section (9) of Section 17.

(vii) the form and manner in which an application shall be made for registration and the fee payable thereof under sub-section (2) of Section 18;

(viii) the facilities to be provided, equipment and other standards to be maintained by the Genetic Counselling Centre, Genetic Laboratory or Genetic Clinic under sub- section (5) of section 18;

(ix) the form in which a certificate of registration shall be issued under sub-section (1) of Section 19;

(x) the manner in which and the period after which a certificate of registration shall be renewed and the fee payable for such renewal under sub-section (3) of Section 19;

(xi) the manner in which an appeal may be preferred under Section 21;

(xii) the period up to which records, charts, etc., shall be preserved under sub- section (1) of Section 29;

(xiii) the manner in which the seizure of documents, records, objects etc. shall be made and the manner in which seizure list shall be prepared and delivered to the person from whose custody such documents, records or objects were seized under sub-section (1) of Section 30;

(xiv) any other matter that is required to be, or may be, prescribed.

33. Power to Make Regulations. The Board, may, with the previous sanction of the Central Government, by notification in the Official Gazette, or regulations not inconsistent with the provision of this Act and the rules made thereunder to provide for—

(a) the time and place of the meetings of the Board and the procedure to be followed for the transaction of business at such meetings and the number of members which shall form the quorum under sub-section (1) of Section 9;

(b) the manner in which a person may be temporarily associated with the Board under sub-section (1) of Section 11;

(c) the method of appointment, the conditions of service and scales of pay and allowances of the officer and other employees of the Board appointed under Section 12;

(d) generally for the efficient conduct of the affairs of the Board.

34. Rules and Regulations to be Laid before the Parliament. Every rule and regulation made under this Act shall be laid, as soon as may be after it is made, before each House of Parliament, while it is in session, for a total period of thirty days which may be comprised in one session or in two or more successive sessions, and if, before the expiry of the session immediately following the session or the successive sessions aforesaid, both Houses agree in making any modification in the rule or regulation, or both Houses agree that the rule or regulation should not be made, the rule or regulation shall thereafter have effect only in such modified form or be of no effect, as the case may be; so, however, that any such modification or annulment shall be without prejudice to the validity of anything previously done under that rule or regulation.